Praise for
THE CARNATION REVOLUTION

'A brilliantly detailed and evocative account of a revolution unlike any other: the Portuguese Revolution of 1974... A book that needs to be read.'
Helder Macedo, Emeritus Professor of Portuguese,
King's College London

'I feel like I've been waiting three decades for precisely this book... In clear language, with a brilliantly detailed narrative, Alex Fernandes leaves us in no doubt why we should celebrate the fiftieth anniversary of the Carnation Revolution and never forget why it came about.'
Lara Pawson, author of *This Is the Place to Be*

'Alex Fernandes displays an encyclopaedic knowledge of modern Portuguese political history in this admirably detailed exploration of the revolution that ushered in democracy in 1974. A thrilling and inspiring page-turner.'
Richard Zimler, author of international bestseller
The Last Kabbalist of Lisbon

'A gripping account of an episode in European history that should be better known. Alex Fernandes narrates in vivid detail how junior officers disillusioned by Portugal's colonial wars launched a daring coup to bring down a dictator, winning popular support in the face of the regime's brutal repression.'
Catherine Fletcher, author of *The Beauty and the Terror*

'This is a real page-turner of a history book, a truly riveting account of the build-up to Portugal's near-bloodless 1974 Carnation Revolution, the revolution itself, and its messy aftermath, bringing all the participants vividly to life.'
Margaret Jull Costa, translator of
The Elephant's Journey by José Saramago

'In this in-depth and passionate book about the 1974 revolution that changed Portugal's destiny, Fernandes introduces us to the places where the historic events took place, and provides vivid portraits of the protagonists.'
Nick Caistor, translator of *The Lizard* by José Saramago

'Alex Fernandes has given the Carnation Revolution what it deserves: an animating account that gives life to its course... Whether when he is writing of cafés in Lisbon where the revolutionaries gathered or the battlefields of Angola and Mozambique, where they were first radicalised, Fernandes's prose is compelling with an eye for the details that make history come alive... A book that takes you to Portugal – and makes you not want to leave.'
Arash Azizi, author of *What Iranians Want*

THE CARNATION REVOLUTION

THE DAY PORTUGAL'S DICTATORSHIP FELL

ALEX FERNANDES

ONEWORLD

Oneworld Publications
First published by Oneworld Publications, 2024
Reprinted 2024

ISBN 978-0-86154-754-8
eISBN 978-0-86154-755-5

Typeset by Geethik Technologies

Printed and bound in Great Britain by Clays Ltd, Elcograf S.p.A.

Oneworld Publications
10 Bloomsbury Street
London WC1B 3SR
England

Stay up to date with the latest books,
special offers, and exclusive content from
Oneworld with our newsletter

Sign up on our website
oneworld-publications.com

To all who carried the torch during Portugal's long night, and to all the anti-fascists out there who carry it now.

CONTENTS

PROLOGUE

On the afternoon of 25 April 1974, in his cramped apartment on the corner of Praça Paiva Couceiro in downtown Lisbon, my grandfather Rafael Vicente Lopes takes a book off his shelf. This one isn't stacked up conventionally with the others; it's been hidden away behind rows of books, purposefully out of sight. With a beaming smile, Rafael carries the book a few steps to the dining room table where he lays it down, on display. My mother Maria Alexandra and her two siblings, Dina and Luís, gather around the book with my grandmother and grandfather. They are too young to truly understand what's going on, but they know it's important. The book is *O Assalto ao 'Santa Maria'* (The Assault on the *Santa Maria*), by Henrique Galvão. It's the personal account of how, in 1961, former Army captain Henrique Galvão, in a spectacular act of rebellion against the Portuguese state, hijacked the cruise liner *Santa Maria* off the coast of Latin America and led a thrilling chase around the Atlantic in a madcap revolutionary plan that ultimately failed. For years, Galvão was considered Enemy Number One by Portugal's fascist dictator António de Oliveira Salazar. And until this afternoon, this book, along with hundreds of others, was banned by the state.

*

THE CARNATION REVOLUTION

On 25 April 1974, a group of junior officers in the Portuguese armed forces led a military coup that, in a scant few hours, achieved the total surrender of the Portuguese government. In doing so they toppled the oldest dictatorship in Europe and ended a brutal colonial war that had raged for thirteen years on three fronts in Africa. The operation had been planned in secret since late 1973. What started as a barbecue in the countryside, organised so the officers could air their frustrations about the war and the regime's incompetence among themselves, soon spiralled into a secret conspiracy that reached all across the crumbling Portuguese Empire and led to what poet Sophia de Mello Breyner called 'the first day, whole and clean' – the first day in forty-eight years that the Portuguese people could pour out onto the streets, unafraid of raising their voices in a chorus of freedom. A day that began with a Eurovision song and ended with the streets of Lisbon blanketed in the carnations that gave the revolution its name.

But the military coup of 25 April, and the complicated, turbulent revolution that followed it, didn't happen in isolation. Whether they knew it or not, the captains who led the rebellion against the Portuguese regime delivered the final blow to an edifice that had started crumbling, piece by piece, decades before. The coup of 25 April wasn't the first revolt against the regime, or even the first revolt against the regime led by the armed forces – it came at the end of a long line of failed rebellions like Henrique Galvão's, of bloodshed and torture and colonial subjugation and a thousand acts of resistance that coursed like stitching through the tapestry of Portuguese society. The Portuguese revolution didn't start in April of 1974, or in September of 1973, or in 1961 with the colonial war. It started in May of 1926, when a military dictatorship first took control of the country and with those who first stood up against it. This is the story of the Captains of April – who some of them were, what led them to take up arms against their own government, and how they did it. It's also the story of some of what came before them, and some of what came after. And it's also a story centred, primarily, on the city of Lisbon – the seat of government, the historic heart of a globe-spanning Empire, the cockpit of the revolution. As such, this story is not academic or definitive. It zooms in on one city among dozens, focuses on a few men among hundreds. This is the story of the Carnation Revolution by synecdoche. And it's one hell of a story.

Captain Salgueiro Maia is twenty-nine years old when, on the morning of 25 April 1974, he leads a convoy of armoured vehicles on the ninety-kilometre drive from Santarém to downtown Lisbon. He has already been to war more than once and has seen his men brutally maimed and killed in the African bush. Most of the two hundred-odd soldiers he's brought with him on this mission have never seen combat. Many of their weapons don't even have bullets in them. He doesn't know what's waiting for them in the capital, but he understands his mission intimately. He understands that, come dawn on 26 April, he will have liberated his fellow countrymen from the shackles of a corrosive, authoritarian fascism – or he will be dead.

GLOSSARY OF INITIALISMS

ANP People's National Action (*Acção Nacional Popular*)

AOC Worker-Peasant Alliance (*Aliança Operária-Camponesa*)

ARA Armed Revolutionary Action (*Acção Revolucionária Armada*)

BR Revolutionary Brigades (*Brigadas Revolucionárias*)

CCCO Operational Control and Coordination Centre (*Centro de Coordenação e Controle Operacional*)

CDE Democratic Electoral Commission (*Comissão Democrática Eleitoral*)

CDS Democratic and Social Centre Party (*Centro Democrático e Social*)

CEI House of the Students of the Empire (*Casa dos Estudantes do Império*)

CGT General Confederation of Labour (*Confederação Geral do Trabalho*)

CGTP General Confederation of Portuguese Workers (*Confederação Geral dos Trabalhadores Portugueses*)

CIOE Special Operations Training Centre (*Centro de Instrução de Operações Especiais*)

CIS Inter-Syndical Commission (*Comissão Inter-Sindical*)

CONCP Conference of Nationalist Organisations of the Portuguese Colonies (*Conferência das Organizações Nacionalistas das Colónias Portuguesas*)

COPCON Operational Command of the Continent (*Comando Operacional do Continente*)

CR Revolutionary Council (*Conselho da Revolução*)

DGS Directorate-General of Security (*Direcção Geral de Segurança*)

DRIL Iberian Revolutionary Liberation Directory (*Directório Revolucionário Ibérico de Libertação*)

EAL Lisbon Associated Broadcasters (*Emissores Associados de Lisboa*)

ELP Portuguese Liberation Army (*Exército de Libertação de Portugal*)

EPAM Practical Military Administration School (*Escola Prática de Administração Militar*)

EPC Army Cavalry School (*Escola Prática de Cavalaria*)

EPE Practical Engineering School (*Escola Prática de Engenharia*)

EPI Practical Infantry School (*Escola Prática de Infantaria*)

ETN National Work Statute (*Estatuto de Trabalho Nacional*)

FAO Federation of Workers' Associations (*Federação de Associações Operárias*)

FAP Popular Action Front (*Frente de Acção Popular*)

FNLA National Front for the Liberation of Angola (*Frente Nacional de Libertação de Angola*)

FP25 Popular Forces 25 April (*Forças Populares 25 de Abril*)

FRELIMO Liberation Front of Mozambique (*Frente de Libertação de Moçambique*)

FSP People's Socialist Front (*Frente Socialista Popular*)

FUR United Revolutionary Front (*Frente de Unidade Revolucionária*)

GDUP Popular Unity Promotion Groups (*Grupos Dinamizadores de Unidade Popular*)

GNR Republican National Guard (*Guarda Nacional Republicana*)

IL Liberal Initiative (*Iniciativa Liberal*)

IST Superior Technical Institute (*Instituto Superior Técnico*)

LUAR Unity and Revolutionary Action League (*Liga de União e Acção Revolucionária*)

GLOSSARY OF INITIALISMS

MDLP Democratic Movement of Portuguese Liberation (*Movimento Democrático de Libertação de Portugal*)

MDP Portuguese Democratic Movement (*Movimento Democrático Português*)

MES Movement of Left Socialists (*Movimento de Esquerda Socialista*)

MFA Armed Forces Movement (*Movimento das Forças Armadas*)

MLSTP Movement for the Liberation of São Tomé and Príncipe (*Movimento de Libertação de São Tomé e Príncipe*)

MOFA Movement of Armed Forces Officers (*Movimento de Oficiais das Forças Armadas*)

MPLA People's Movement for the Liberation of Angola (*Movimento Popular de Libertação de Angola*)

MRPP Re-organised Movement of the Party of the Proletariat (*Movimento Reorganizativo do Partido do Proletariado*)

MUD Movement of Democratic Unity (*Movimento de Unidade Democrática*)

ORA Revolutionary Organisation of the Armada (*Organização Revolucionária da Armada*)

PAIGC African Party for the Independence of Guinea and Cape Verde (*Partido Africano para a Independência da Guiné e Cabo Verde*)

PAP Plan for Political Action (*Plano de Acção Política*)

PCA Angolan Communist Party (*Partido Comunista Angolano*)

PCP Portuguese Communist Party (*Partido Comunista Português*)

PDC Christian Democratic Party (*Partido da Democracia Cristã*)

PIDE International and State Defence Police (*Polícia Internacional e de Defesa do Estado*)

PL Liberal Party (*Partido Liberal*)

PP Progress Party (*Partido do Progresso*)

PPD Popular Democratic Party (*Partido Popular Democrático*)

PREC Ongoing Revolutionary Process (*Processo Revolucionário Em Curso*)

PRP Portuguese Republican Party (*Partido Republicano Português*)

PRP-BR Revolutionary Party of the Proletariat-Revolutionary Brigades (*Partido Revolucionário do Proletariado–Brigadas Revolucionárias*)

PS Portuguese Socialist Party (*Partido Socialista Português*)

PSD Social Democratic Party (*Partido Social Democrata*)

PVDE Vigilance and State Defence Police (*Polícia de Vigilância e Defesa do Estado*)

RCP Rádio Clube Português

SNI National Secretariat for Information, Popular Culture and Tourism (*Secretariado Nacional de Informação, Cultura Popular e Turismo*)

SPN National Propaganda Secretariat (*Secretariado de Propaganda Nacional*)

SUV Soldiers United Will Win (*Soldados Unidos Vencerão*)

UN National Union (*União Nacional*)

UNITA National Union for the Total Independence of Angola (*União Nacional Para a Independência Total de Angola*)

UPA Union of Peoples of Angola (*União dos Povos de Angola*)

A common motif in Lisbon cemeteries: two flowers, the *Saudade* and the *Perpétua*, crossed in a symbol of eternal longing.

PART ONE

ONE THOUSAND ACTS OF RESISTANCE

...the European and African Portuguese fight, without spectacle and without alliances, proudly alone.
António de Oliveira Salazar, 1963

Lisbon's Monument of the Discoveries under construction on the north bank of the Tagus, 1940.

CHAPTER ONE

THE STORIES WE
TELL OURSELVES

On the north bank of the Tagus river in Belém, a few miles west
of the Lisbon docks and east of the line where river becomes sea,
stands a tall stone monument. Seen from the side, it resembles a
large sailing ship rendered in a quasi-brutalist fashion, its prow
jutting out over the water. Two square fifteenth-century
Portuguese flags appear in relief in stone above the sails. On the
deck stand thirty-three figures, depicted larger than life in limestone. They are posed in a tableau of medieval action – knights
and queens genuflecting in prayer, men in tabards lifting a heavy
stone marker, stoic figures gripping a sword or globe or compass
and staring, expectantly, out to sea. The rear of the monument
presents a massive longsword, its tip pointed at the ground. This
is the *Padrão dos Descobrimentos*, 'Monument to the Discoveries',
an homage to a time when Portugal's influence stretched to the
furthest extents of the globe. The time when Portugal first
conquered the sea.

One would be forgiven for thinking the monument dates back
centuries, perhaps a contemporary of some of the figures depicted
on it. The parish of Belém, despite being a few train stops out of
the city centre, constitutes Lisbon's museum quarter, abounding
with monuments and buildings from Portugal's maritime golden
age and earlier. The *Padrão*, however, is much newer. The

monument was initially conceived in 1939 for an exhibition commemorating the eight-hundredth anniversary of the Portuguese state, held in 1940. By that point, Portugal had been under the conservative authoritarian rule of António de Oliveira Salazar for seven years, and under a military dictatorship for fourteen – the ideological narrative of the *Estado Novo* (New State) had entrenched itself into the culture. That monument, built in 1940, was dismantled; this one on the banks of the Tagus is the permanent recreation, installed in 1960, ten years before Salazar's death and fourteen years before the revolution that changed everything. The monument to the 'discoveries' encapsulates a big part of Portugal's mythos about itself, one that was carefully developed and cultivated over centuries before being incorporated into the narrative of the *Estado Novo*. To understand the Portuguese revolution of 1974, you have to understand the *Estado Novo*, and to understand the *Estado Novo* you have to understand the building blocks that make up the Portuguese national myth.

By the middle of the thirteenth century, a young and virulently Christian Portuguese nation is at the end of the process of expelling the Moors from its territory on the edge of the Iberian Peninsula – a bloody and protracted military campaign referred to even now as the *Reconquista*. This name is already a subtle but deeply effective piece of state propaganda. *Reconquista*: re-conquest, the taking back of something wrongfully lost. It implies an ownership of the land that goes beyond the accident of living there: a historic, moral and true ownership, one that justifies whatever means are used to reclaim it. The same logic operates in the European crusades, in which Portugal is a regular enthusiastic participant – just as the Holy Land belongs, rightfully, to Christendom, so the lands of Iberia belong rightfully to the Portuguese and Spanish. The narrative of the *Reconquista* is heavily popularised in education under the regime of General

Francisco Franco in Spain, and adopted with similar enthusiasm by Salazar and Portugal's *Estado Novo*. And at the start of the fifteenth century, Portugal sets its sights beyond its established borders with the conquest of the North African city of Ceuta, the principles of the *Reconquista* extended beyond 'historic' borders. In 1420 and 1427, the uninhabited islands of Madeira and the Azores archipelago are discovered and swiftly populated. The next century is one of extensive naval exploration and conquest, the start of Portugal's establishment as a dominant global super-power as its sailing ships trace the perimeter of Africa, setting records for European exploration and establishing trading posts and permanent settlements strategically, which facilitate the ulti-mate goal – a consistent route to India and its bountiful wealth, around the African continent. This is first accomplished by the pioneering navigator Vasco da Gama in 1498. Through a combi-nation of political savvy and overwhelming technological might, a significant foothold is established in India. Crucial to this is the fated Battle of Cochin in 1504, in which a minuscule Portuguese detachment holds off a vast attacking force from the Zamorin of Calicut, a prolonged battle where superior firepower and clever tactical placement leads to a decisive Portuguese victory. The Battle of Cochin joins other key battles in Portuguese history, like the Battle of Ourique against the Moors in 1139 and Aljubarrota against Castile in 1385, where an underdog Portuguese Army dominates what seems like an impossible situa-tion, always spun as the work of divine providence. Each victory is another brushstroke in the image of a people graced by God. By the end of King João III's reign in 1557, Portugal has substan-tial colonies in Cape Verde, Brazil, Angola, Mozambique, Goa, Damão and Diu, and has ventured as far east as Japan. Those colonial holdings are maintained and expanded through violence and subjugation, and though Portugal generates a successful trade in spices and precious metals, the Portuguese also establish a

thriving slave trade, predominantly from West Africa but captur-
ing and selling slaves as far as India, China and Japan. The slave
traders justify their actions through the claim that the slaves are
being 'saved' through baptism – a concern for their souls that is
not extended to their flesh, which is branded with irons, burned
with wax, whipped and chained on the horrifically long passages
across the ocean.

It's during the country's 'golden age' of exploration that
Portugal crafts its national myth. You can map the history of a
nation through the stories it tells itself. Most European peoples
whose past involves Roman conquest hold tightly to the history
of their own rebellious tribes, the plucky underdogs that opposed
Roman invasion. We see it in the French self-labelling as Gauls
from *Gallia*, their own national mythology kept alive through,
among more sober ways, *Asterix and Obelix*. The English and
Welsh have *Britannia*, the Scots *Caledonia*, the Swiss see themselves heirs to *Helvetia* and the Germans to *Germania* and
Allemania. For Portugal it's *Lusitania*, a tribe first encountered by
the Romans after the Second Punic War, and eventually subju-
gated after decades of valiant resistance, epitomised by the
talented Lusitanian warrior and tactician Viriathus. Reaching
back through its history, there is a concerted effort by historians
and the clergy to make a direct link between the Lusitanian
people of pre-Roman Iberia and the modern-day Portuguese,
skipping over centuries of Moorish occupation to reinforce this
idea of unbroken, untainted Lusitanian heritage, with Viriathus
as the first 'national' hero. In aid of that idea, no work has done
more to promote this myth than *Os Lusíadas* (The Lusiads) by
Luís de Camões, published in 1572. Camões, Portugal's most
influential poet, often held alongside Renaissance contemporar-
ies such as Shakespeare and Milton, unashamedly mixes classical
mythology with the story of Vasco da Gama's journey to India.
The heroes of the epic are the Lusiads, sons of Lusus, a cipher for

the whole of the Portuguese people, destined to accomplish great deeds. The fantastical retelling of da Gama's voyage is peppered through with accounts of the battles of Ourique, Aljubarrota and Cochin, while the characters face off against various dangers ranging from vicious storms and giants to the wrath of Roman gods. *Os Lusíadas* finds immediate success in a nation drunk on its own expansionist power, entrenching Camões' version as the true national myth.

It's ironic, then, that *Os Lusíadas* contains within it numerous homages and words of advice to the young King Sebastian I. The 21-year-old king launches an ill-fated crusade into Morocco in 1578, and has his army immediately routed. He instantly disappears in the desert and kicks off a crisis of succession. This crisis leads to sixty years of Spanish rule, a moment that marks the start of Portugal's decline as a global superpower. Sebastian's (almost certain) death in the battle of Alcácer Quibir is perhaps the last piece of the Portuguese national myth – the vanishing king comes to represent a heroic ideal, a version of the 'King Beyond the Mountain', a messianic figure destined to one day return and restore Portugal to its rightful place as a global hegemon. Sebastianism, beginning as a literal belief that the king would return, over time becomes a religious movement with the missing king appearing as a saint or spiritual figure. Sebastianism as a movement makes a regular resurgence throughout periods of strife in Portuguese history such as the Napoleonic occupation, reflecting moods of Portuguese nationalism, anti-Spanish reaction and a nostalgia for the ideals of the *Reconquista* and imperial expansion.

A revolution in 1640 followed by a long restoration war returns Portugal's independence, and in the following centuries Portugal maintains and expands its colonial holdings slowly, its history punctuated by a devastating earthquake in 1755, the French peninsular invasions of 1807 and the transition to constitutional monarchy in 1822, leading to Brazilian independence. During the 'Scramble for Africa' and the Berlin Conference of 1890, the Portuguese government falls into a diplomatic conflict with the United Kingdom over the respective nations' ambitions towards the land between Angola and Mozambique. The aftermath of the Scramble establishes the borders of Portuguese Guinea, Angola and Mozambique permanently, and Portugal's status alongside its European neighbours as a serious colonial power. The king kowtowing to the British, however, becomes one of numerous gripes against the monarchy in a country shaking with nascent Republican ambitions. In 1908 King Carlos I and his heir-apparent Prince Luís Filipe are assassinated in Terreiro do Paço in Lisbon by Republican activists, and in 1910 the Portuguese Republican Party (*Partido Republicano Português*, PRP) leads a revolution that establishes the First Republic, exiling Portugal's last king.

The First Republic is sixteen years of unrelenting chaos, one that sets the scene for the fascist state that follows it. Between 1910 and 1926 Portugal goes through eight presidents and forty-five governments, all the while experiencing an economic crisis, crushing debt and the Europe-spanning threats of the First World War. Mirroring similar movements in France and Mexico, early Portuguese republicanism's defining feature is its fierce anti-clericalism, imposing a crackdown on churches, convents and monasteries and persecuting religious leaders. The turbulent political landscape is marked by escalating acts of violence, militant strike action, periodic military uprisings and borderline civil war, the government fluctuating wildly between different republican factions. There is a brief attempted monarchist resurgence and – anticipating a European trend – a year-long protofascist dictatorship under Sidónio Pais, starting in December 1917. Pais' New Republic, with its banning of political parties, realignment with the Church and return to 'traditional' values, with reliance on the absolute authority of one charismatic figure, is a blueprint for what the Portuguese government will come to look like. His assassination in 1918 restores an increasingly unstable situation, each subsequent government seemingly another piece of evidence damning republicanism and parliamentary democracy as failed experiments. Portugal's intervention in the First World War, on the Allied side, is justified partly as a way of maintaining control of the colonies, but the costly intervention in the conflict also has the effect of politicising and radicalising the armed forces against the Republic. On 28 May 1926, backed by the majority of political parties and a significant proportion of the population, a military coup mobilises across the country and overthrows the sitting government. Parading down Lisbon's Avenida da Liberdade, General Manuel Gomes da Costa, resplendent in his military regalia and prodigious white moustache, is hailed by a crowd anxious to see the end of decades of street violence and political strife. Gomes da Costa's reign is brief, however, as the dictatorship is immediately beset by internal political manoeuvring that puts General Óscar Carmona in charge, less than a month after the coup.

The new Military Dictatorship is quick to tear apart the progressive reforms of the First Republic, following in the footsteps of Sidónio Pais to establish an authoritarian state with control over every aspect of society, guaranteed by the military. What Carmona can't do on his own, however, is resolve the economic crisis he inherits. For this, in 1928, the dictator turns to the keen mind of a professor of law from the University of Coimbra, Doctor António de Oliveira Salazar. Salazar, a respected thinker and orator among the religious and political right, and a strong Catholic voice with a reputation for economic brilliance, had spent the First Republic as a fierce opponent of the government's anti-clerical attacks. His condition for taking over the post of finance minister is full control of all ministerial spending, giving him unprecedented power over the government. The result is an 'economic miracle' – a regime of austerity and tax hikes that balances the books – hailed by the international press as unparalleled. The professor's economic and political acumen, combined with a cunning propaganda campaign designed to increase his standing, grants him, on the sixth anniversary of the coup, the Ancient and Most Noble Military Order of Tower and Sword – the oldest and highest honour awarded by the state. But Salazar has higher ambitions still, and a clear political framework in mind. Seeking to give direction to the Military Dictatorship, Salazar creates the National Union (*União Nacional*, UN), a political organisation (crucially never given the title of 'party') aiming to take forward his vision for the country. In 1932 Salazar is officially offered the title of Head of the Council of Ministers – head of the government. He still clings to his role as finance minister, but now holds an overall incontestable amount of power. From this new role Salazar births the *Estado Novo*.

The *Estado Novo* is a conservative, Catholic, authoritarian dictatorship, one that finds itself reflected in the ascendant politics of neighbouring European nations such as Franco's Spain, Mussolini's Italy and Hitler's Germany. Unlike these figures, however, Salazar is far from a 'strong man' figure and does not bring with him the thuggish street movement typical of the other regimes. Salazar is thin, sombre, serious, his voice carrying a weedy sibilance more suited to a schoolteacher or clergyman than a fascist leader. His power stems from his status, political skill and the support of the nation's upper class and elites, whom he puts into the driver's seat of the new fascist state. The *Estado Novo* doesn't derive its political legitimacy from the masses, or through anything as messy as representative democracy – it is a purely patriarchal system, a government of elite technocrats guiding the nation along an innately correct path, outside of which there is only ruin. Salazar presents himself as a man above political intrigue and parties, brought out under duress from his academic 'splendid isolation' in the nation's time of need.[1] King Sebastian, finally returned from Morocco to steer the nation away from crisis. The fundamental tenets of his *Estado Novo*, or rather the areas which are considered beyond the realm of debate, are outlined in an infamous speech of Salazar's from 1936:

> To souls torn by the doubts and negativity of the century, we seek to restore the comfort of the great certainties. We do not discuss God and virtue; we do not discuss Homeland* and its History; we do not discuss authority and its prestige; we do not discuss family and its morals; we do not discuss the glory of work and its duty.

This speech is subsequently summarised neatly into a slogan, used by the regime and its detractors alike: *Deus, Pátria, Familia*, God, Homeland, Family, the pillars upon which the *New State* stands unwavering. It is within this refusal to question the Homeland's history that the Portuguese myth lies, and forms the backbone of both the *Estado Novo*'s colonial policy and its internal educational drive. The First Republic had never seriously challenged the status of the *Ultramar* (the collective name Portugal's colonial holdings are known by). Now the new regime places Portugal's colonial holdings as an integral part of its programme – and identity.

The *Estado Novo*'s Colonial Act of 1930 asserts Portugal's 'essential historic function of possessing, civilising and colonising overseas territories', stripping the colonies of their limited

---

* I am here choosing to translate the word 'Pátria', used ubiquitously in Portuguese as Homeland, though the ambiguous nature of the word means that at times 'Fatherland' or simply 'Nation' are more appropriate alternatives which may be used instead.

financial and administrative independence and concentrating power in Lisbon in the hands of the colonies ministers – usually proponents of reactionary race theory. This is driven by two core beliefs. Firstly, Portugal's latter-day colonialists see the overseas territories as an extension of the *Reconquista* and themselves as a civilising force among the savages, with a God-given and historical duty to rule the land and convert its inhabitants to Christianity. Foreign critics of the colonial project are accordingly dismissed as simply jealous – and part of a vast conspiracy of international powers intent on stripping Portugal of its hard-won land. Henrique Galvão, Commissioner-General of the 1934 Colonial Exhibition in Porto, states in a speech that Portugal's Empire is part of a historic mission, forgotten after the liberal 1820s and revived under the *Estado Novo*. The colonies are themselves the very *raison d'être* of the nation, without which Portugal would lose its soul.[2] This peculiar idea, the result of modern Portuguese exceptionalism colliding with the historic colonial holdings, is fully on display in a speech by General João de Almeida at that same conference. Almeida suggests Lusitanian heritage has its own character, bordering on an entirely different species, *Homo Atlanticus*, whose occupation of the Iberian coastline is an expression of nationality even before the existence of a state. With regards to the colonies, Almeida goes on to declare Portugal as integrating 'the world into Western civilisation, of which Portugal became the apostolic, disseminating and defending People, like no other'.[3]

Back to the Monument to the Discoveries. On the occasion of Portugal's eight-hundredth anniversary, the *Estado Novo* razes the parts of Belém in front of and surrounding the majestic Jerónimos monastery. Prior to 1940, the monastery sat at the centre of a thriving working-class neighbourhood, its front facing a river beach frequented by fishermen who would dry their catches under the building's arches. Now, under the regime's direction, it becomes *Praça do Império* – Imperial Square – thoroughly sanitised for official events and military pageantry.[4] At its centre, the caravel with its body of stone and steel and figures of plaster towers above the eight-hundredth anniversary expo as a statement of intent. The figures are a rogues' gallery of navigators and the royalty who sponsored their journeys; the men who carved out the Empire, their swords and crosses alluding to how it was done. As even the ardent followers of the *Estado Novo* understood it in 1934: 'The Portuguese navigated to arrive at colonisation. Navigation was always a means [to an end].'[5] The one-eyed Luís de Camões stands there as well, the great storyteller given a place among those whose stories he helped fix into the national psyche. The only woman on the vast structure is Philippa of Lancaster, mother of the so-called 'Illustrious Generation' that launched the golden age of exploration, forever knelt in prayer. The pious mother the *Estado Novo* wishes all women to be. This monument is God, Homeland and Family writ large.

Between the monument's original unveiling in 1940 and its permanent placement on the bank of the Tagus in 1960, the *Estado Novo* is forced to reframe its colonial policies. In the half century since the Berlin Conference, and especially after the Second World War, colonies and colonial powers are less broadly accepted by the international community, as the politics of national self-determination have come to dominate. In order to remain in good standing with its budding Western allies and hold on to its colonies, the Portuguese state has to change. In the 1950s Salazar and the regime become more amenable to the theories of the Brazilian sociologist Gilberto Freyre, whose work *Casa-Grande e Senzala* (The Masters and the Slaves) begins to put forward a unique perspective on Portuguese colonialism. Freyre suggests that the Portuguese are more suited to colonialism, as they are more adaptable, in terms of climate and society, and more open to miscegenation. This results in a comparatively kinder and more civilised colonialism. Colonialism isn't colonialism any more – it's national integration. These broad strokes are eventually developed into the theory of Lusotropicalism, after Freyre visits Portugal and its African colonies on Salazar's invitation. Using Lusotropicalism as a theoretical basis, the *Estado Novo* carries out a wholesale rebrand – the colonies are no longer colonies but 'Overseas Provinces', Portugal is no longer a colonial superpower but rather a multicultural, multiracial and, crucially, multi-continental singular nation – united and indivisible, 'from Minho to Timor', to quote an oft-used catchphrase. Under these new terms, to suggest giving up any of these provinces would be a gross violation of national integrity. In the background, the 1950s and '60s see a spate of independent nations flourish across the African continent as France, Britain, Spain and Belgium relinquish their colonial holdings – including nations on the borders of Portuguese territories, such as Senegal and the Democratic Republic of the Congo. Portugal's stubborn insistence on clinging on becomes an outlier.

It's in the middle of Portugal's colonial rebrand that the Monument to the Discoveries makes its way permanently onto the southern bank of the Tagus. The ground behind the structure is a vast colourful compass rose made of cobbles with a map of the world at its centre, a gift from Apartheid South Africa. And despite Portugal's attempt to frame its expansionism as benevolent, civilised and historically necessary, despite the further reforms intended to integrate the various colonised peoples into the *Estado Novo*'s culture, the experiment – trying to keep a colonial empire alive into the twentieth century – fails. One consequence of that failed attempt is showcased only a short walk away from the Monument to the Discoveries, in an old military fort: the Monument to the Overseas Combatants, a split stone and steel triangle jutting out of a pool of blue water, memorialising the countless dead in the service of preserving the Empire.

In early 1961 a series of labour disputes and raids by armed insurgents in Angola leads to a Portuguese military response, starting a war. In December of that year, after several years of diplomatic embargo and pushes for decolonisation, India invades the Portuguese territories on the subcontinent, leaving the paltry Portuguese defenders with no choice but to surrender. African independence movements start armed conflicts in Portuguese Guinea in 1962 and in Mozambique in 1964, the regime flatout refusing to cede to any external or internal demands for anything other than all-out war. The colonial war consumes the regime and its resources, the *Estado Novo* sending thousands of men to lose life and limb in Africa with singular, borderline fanatical purpose. The regime's fundamental tenets force it into a corner – it cannot escape without also destroying itself.

In 1968, António Salazar suffers a brain haemorrhage and falls into a coma, leading President Américo Tomás to hand power to Salazar's long-time ally Marcelo Caetano. And while Caetano arrives on the scene as an alleged reformist, ushering in a so-called 'Marceline Spring', the entrenchment of the reactionary right within the government and the top levels of the armed forces continues the policies of all-out war in the colonies, even as it becomes less and less tenable. The conquest of Africa, the plundering of its people and resources and its strategic use in the service of a sea route to India were the foundations of the Portuguese Empire. Over half a millennium later, clutching on to the legacy of that maritime golden age is what finally causes that Empire to crumble. The self-determination struggles of Angola, Mozambique, Guinea-Bissau and Cape Verde have an indelible effect on the Portuguese Army, one that ultimately causes a critical mass of its junior officers to turn their guns against their own generals and launch a military coup, with the primary goal of ending the war. These officers, most of whom are in their late twenties to early thirties, succeed where decades of dissidents and opposition movements failed.

General Humberto Delgado addresses a crowd on his campaign tour, May 1958.

CHAPTER TWO

FEARLESS

Many of the gravestones, tombs and mausoleums of Alto de São João cemetery are decorated with an odd feature – crossed stone flowers, in bas-relief. To someone unfamiliar with the flora of southern Europe and the Mediterranean, the flowers might seem strange, alien. In English they are known as the globe amaranth and the spiny thrift, but in Portuguese their names carry a much more poetic meaning – the *Perpétua*, a colourful, bulbous flower whose vibrant longevity even once plucked gives it its name – and the *Saudade*, a thistle-like thing that grows on sand dunes, its name meaning melancholic longing. It doesn't take an academic to decipher the blunt symbolism of the flowers depicted together, and the prevalence of this detail is the exclusive preserve of Lisbon cemeteries, especially this one. Once you notice it, the flowers seem to peek out from everywhere, haunting this space where many of the regime's greatest detractors were cremated years after the revolution.

But Alto de São João's most striking monument doesn't rely on subtle details. At the edge of one of the cemetery's many pedestrian intersections stands a slab of black marble, framed by a curving ramp of concrete that surrounds it like a brutalist cloak. In white block lettering, the slab reads:

TO THOSE WHO
IN THE LONG NIGHT OF FASCISM

THE CARNATION REVOLUTION

CARRIED THE FLAME OF LIBERTY
AND FOR LIBERTY
DIED
IN THE CONCENTRATION CAMP
OF TARRAFAL

The mausoleum marks the location of the remains of thirty-two men who died on the island of Santiago, Cape Verde, where the *Estado Novo* established a penal colony specifically for the anti-fascists who dared oppose it: Tarrafal. The history of Tarrafal is a history of the priorities of the *Estado Novo*. Between 1936 and 1954 it holds Portuguese dissidents whose 'crimes' need to be made an example of; and after a brief spell of disuse, between 1961 and 1974 its focus shifts to holding African freedom fighters, captured in the colonial war. The camp's official name is the Cape Verde Penal Colony, but the people sent there who make it out alive call it the Slow Death, or the Village of Death, the Swamp of Death or the Yellow Hell, or simply – Tarrafal. Its location is chosen by Salazar and the regime's secret police, PIDE, for its geographic isolation and harsh environment: the natural severe heat, lack of water and mosquitoes exploited by the guards as instruments of torture. The men who come here are told on arrival that 'those who come to Tarrafal come to die.' For a civilian dissident in the *Estado Novo*, Tarrafal is the threat that hovers perpetually overhead. Yet dissidence persists, even here, where members of the Portuguese Communist Party (*Partido Comunista Português*, PCP) strive to remain in contact with their comrades on the mainland and continue their struggle against the state. The forty-eight years of Portuguese dictatorship are marked by thousands of acts of rebellion, a tapestry of resistance that is all too often soaked in blood. Piece by piece, those acts build up a history that leads, inexorably, to the revolution.

18

It takes ten years for the autocrats at the top of the regime to decide Tarrafal is necessary. Resistance against the dictatorship starts long before Salazar is a household name, certainly among the general population. It doesn't take long after the 1926 military coup for rebellion to begin brewing among the republican, democratic and liberal wings of society. The longevity of the National Dictatorship of Óscar Carmona is not a given – the constant turmoil of the First Republic suggests this might be another in a long line of failed governments, another beat in what has become a rhythm of constant change. The new regime is aware of the threat of rebellion the way a bus driver is aware of traffic – not a question of if, but when. Its attempts to crack down on democratic and republican organisations across the country are as yet a fruitless game of whack-a-mole; the republican parties, democratic organisations and trade unions are still too embedded in society and the military, the new regime is still consolidating its power and constructing its apparatus of repression. In the weeks leading up to February 1927, anti-regime forces attempt to congregate around a shared programme: defending the constitutional republic. Adherence to this notion isn't universal – there is a feeling among many in the upper ranks of the military that, while their sympathies may lie with the republican cause, there is a danger of returning to the pre-coup chaos of the First Republic, to which the current military dictatorship is preferable.

It's under these conditions that, on 3 February 1927, a ragtag assembly of intellectuals, anarchists, syndicalists and communists form the armed civilian wing of a first attempt at a coup.[1] The military side is led by republican general Adalberto de Sousa Dias and a scattering of sympathetic officers, garrisons and police units. The rebellion begins in Porto, with the expectation that forces in Lisbon would start their own revolutionary front twelve hours later. The Porto units are outmatched and outnumbered by government forces, and they lack the element of surprise. Despite this they engage in pitched battles, barricade streets, entrench themselves and prepare for the inevitable siege. They wait for Lisbon to rise as well, to take control of train lines and prevent the government from sending reinforcements north, trying to force the government to fight a battle on two fronts. Lisbon's military garrisons, however, are silent. For two days the Porto rebellion holds out, sending frantic messages to the capital for support.

When support finally comes in Lisbon, it is not out of the garrisons but from the labour movement. Across the city, workers begin to mobilise – spontaneous strikes and demonstrations materialise in solidarity with the actions in Porto and the police and the Republican National Guard (*Guarda Nacional Republicana*, GNR – the Portuguese gendarmerie) are engaging in violent clashes with the population. The coffee house A Brasileira, a Lisbon landmark regularly frequented by the poet Fernando Pessoa and the city's intelligentsia, is shut down by the police for being an alleged site of republican agitation, one of several public establishments to receive this treatment. Syndicalist blocs south of the Tagus call a general strike and attempt to occupy the railways, but they are beaten to the punch by loyalist police and GNR battalions, who forcibly wrest control back from the workers. The relatively late action on the part of the Lisbon rebels means the government has already managed to send reinforcements north. As the rebellion in Porto begins to run out of ammunition, the support from Lisbon is too little, and too late.

It is only on the morning of 7 February that Lisbon military units finally break cover and get involved. A hundred and fifty sailors from the Marine Arsenal, a shipyard on the northern edge of the Tagus, sweep through GNR headquarters and police stations and pull together a force of over six hundred armed men and a dozen civilians. They raid the weapons factory at Santa Clara, inside an ancient red building that began as a thirteenth-century convent. In the north-western Lisbon outskirts of Pontinha, soldiers from the Sappers Regiment (*Sapadores Mineiros*) place government-loyal officers under arrest, and bring a sizeable squadron of men into the centre of the city. This is not the last time this particular regiment will face off against the government. They set up barricades in Largo do Rato and its arterial streets,* the revolutionary forces occupying a healthy swathe of central Lisbon north of the Tagus. They are joined now by Colonel Mendes dos Reis – now up to a force of eight hundred, the paltry rebellion chooses the Hotel Bristol, an unassuming thirty-six-room building at the top of Rua São Pedro de Alcântara, as the base of its operations. These men know their actions on this day are likely to amount to nothing – the rebellion in Porto has already been crushed, and the news of the northern surrender is already percolating through Lisbon. This is the 'Revolution of Remorse', the officers leading the rebellion racked with guilt at having left their northern comrades out to dry, in a feeble thrust of defiance at a regime that, they suspect, has already won.

Their suspicions are right. The next day Lisbon falls into a state of emergency, and the government gives any civilians carrying weapons four hours to surrender. The penalty for not doing so is execution without trial. For two days the Hotel Bristol and the rebel barricades are bombarded by government artillery, cannons from the top of São Jorge Castle raining fire on central Lisbon and the Marine Arsenal. The only armaments the rebels have that come close to matching the government forces are on

---

* Rato refers to aristocrat Luís Gomes de Sá e Menezes, who adopted the nickname 'the Rat' and was patron of a local convent. In 1910 the budding Portuguese Republic attempts to rename this square Praça Brasil (Brazil Square) – the name it holds when the republican forces mount their rebellion – but the name doesn't stick, and in 1948 it goes back to being called Largo do Rato.

the Navy cruiser *Carvalho Araújo*, captured by rebel sailors, which floats impotently on the Tagus in the face of the regime's might. On the morning of 9 February, Colonel Mendes dos Reis makes a phone call from inside the Hotel Bristol, negotiating the surrender of the rebel forces. The Marine Arsenal holds out a little longer, until a brutal Air Force bombardment accelerates the inevitable surrender.[2]

On the south-west corner of Rato Square stands an ornate limestone fountain. The ivory stone is weathered grey with soot and age, blending in anonymously with the surrounding buildings, its two levels a relic from a time when pack animals were brought to drink here by the denizens of Lisbon. It is against the smooth surface of this fountain that the regime lines up captured rebels and opens fire, the bodies adding to the death count – ninety in Lisbon, a hundred in Porto, mostly civilians. Those numbers would be higher if Lieutenant Assis Gonçalves, given the order to execute all 'nocturnal and recalcitrant' elements, had not responded that he 'only know[s] how to shoot enemies with guns in their hands'. Instead, the regime proceeds in a wholesale purging of republican and revolutionary elements, up and down the country. Those intellectuals associated with the rebellion who have senior positions in government departments, such as the directorates of the Lisbon Library, are removed from their posts. For the soldiers, officers and police who participated in the rebellion, their fate is a brief stint in Lisbon penitentiary followed by deportation without trial – to the distant Portuguese colonies of Guinea, Timor and Cape Verde, and to the Azores, a scattering of almost seven hundred conspirators now banned from returning to their homes in mainland Portugal. Some of the figures who escape the initial government sweep choose to exile themselves to Spain and France, where they found the Madrid and Paris Republican Leagues – groups made up of exiles and émigrés geared around drumming up support against the dictatorship.

The failure of the 1927 rebellion provides an unfortunate blueprint for not just the next decade of activity against the regime, but also the vast majority of later attempts to oust the government from power. Assessing the reasons for its failure after the fact, General Sousa Dias attributes it to tactical shortcomings: the rebel forces were outmatched in artillery and cavalry, and had insufficient military reserves for the job at hand. A more important factor, however, was the improvised and chaotic nature of the rebel plans, the lack of coordination and the fact that the Lisbon garrisons didn't rise in sync with the forces in Porto. That society, and by extension the armed forces, was split on whether or not to back the rebellion meant the defeat was ordained before the first boots were ever on the ground. It will take nearly fifty years for the lessons of 1927, consciously or unconsciously, to be learned and put into practice.

The government crackdown in the aftermath of February 1927 is severe. Carmona's dictatorship moves from, according to historian Irene Flunser Pimentel, 'military and transitional to civilian and definite',[3] and with that shift comes the banning of republican movements, labour organisations and political parties. Among those affected is the anarcho-syndicalist General Confederation of Labour (*Confederação Geral do Trabalho*, CGT), whose militants were actively involved in the attempted rebellion and particularly the strike action that surrounded it. On 6 May 1927, a police force raids the old palace building at 38 Calçada do Combro, the CGT's headquarters and the site of the printing press for their organ *A Batalha*. At the height of the CGT's activity during the First Republic, *A Batalha* was a daily that had the third highest circulation of any newspaper in Lisbon – rising to the highest whenever the typographers were on strike. On 26 May, in another raid, the police completely destroy the Confederation's offices – from that point *A Batalha* only re-emerges sporadically and illegally. Press censorship comes fully into force,

and in the shadows of Portuguese society a clandestine movement begins to form and strengthen, the backbone of a republican movement that refuses, still, to be killed off. On the front
pages of one of these clandestine republican papers, *A Victoria*,
from 19 November 1927, the editors lay out a position that will
come to define the next few years. Under the headline 'Let us
fight to the death', the paper reads:

> *We need to react. We need to insist. Open war on the dicta-*
> *torship, war without pause, everywhere and at all hours: in*
> *workshops and schools; in the cities, towns and villages; in*
> *the barracks and within the structures of the State; every-*
> *where there is a will to push, a good man to convince. The*
> *dictatorship is the death of the Nation and the Nation*
> *cannot die.*[4]

The 1927 rebellion marks the beginning of a prolonged period of
struggle against the dictatorship, bordering on civil war – a chain
of successive failed putsches known as the *Reviralho*, a term that
translates as an act or movement of overturning. *Reviralhismo* is
not a coherent political movement – it's a strategy predominantly
led by underground republican and democratic organisations
with little ideological coherence beyond the reintroduction of a
constitutional republic. Between 1927 and 1931 the regime faces
off against multiple attempted rebellions and coups, none with
nearly as much clout as February 1927, and with each one the
surviving manpower of the resistance is further whittled away.

At the same time as the country is being successively rocked
by the death spasms of Portuguese republicanism, the Communist Party is trying to find its place in the struggle. Unlike other
European communist parties, the PCP doesn't emerge from a
split in an existing socialist party, but is formed from a tendency
within the syndicalist movements and the CGT in the aftermath

of the Bolshevik revolution, turning away from syndicalism to a Leninist conception of communism and of the Party. The communists intend themselves as the vanguard party of the working class, looking to steer the masses of the First Republic towards a system that deposes capitalism altogether. The founding congress of the Party takes place in Lisbon, in the headquarters of the Association of Office Workers on Rua da Madalena in 1921, and the Party affiliates to the Communist International not long after. The PCP's modest growth during the First Republic is abruptly cut short by the military coup, which unfolds a day before the Party's second congress and catches the communists by surprise. Disorganised and unable to put up an independent response to the coup, the PCP's presence in Lisbon takes its first major hit when its headquarters on Rua do Arco do Marquês do Alegrete is raided and shut down by the police in August 1926. The crackdown in the aftermath of February 1927 drives the Party further underground, and begins years of internal soul-searching on the tactics and strategy to take against the authoritarian regime.

In July 1928 the 7th Chasseurs Regiment based in São Jorge Castle, the barracks that just over a year before was the source of sustained artillery fire onto the rebellious forces in the city centre, attempt their own coup. Once again syndicalists south of the river stage spontaneous strikes in solidarity with the soldiers, but this time the rebellion is crushed almost immediately, government batteries stationed in Parque Eduardo VII hammering the castle followed by an assault with armoured vehicles. The casualties are fewer, but nearly one hundred senior officers are arrested along with almost a thousand soldiers and junior officers, four hundred of whom are deported to the colonies.

The various police forces of the regime begin to gain a foothold in the revolutionary movements, infiltrating dissident groups and preventing rebellions before they can even get off the ground. A dozen conspiracies are dismantled *in utero*, each incident followed by arrests and deportations. This is the background hum to António Salazar's rise to power. In the wake of another failed military rebellion on the island of Madeira in 1931, and of violent 1 May protests staged around the country by militant students and young communists, Salazar takes a big step outside of his role as finance minister to publicly condemn the 'disorder'.

In August 1931, the importation of a substantial stockpile of weapons from newly formed republican Spain is the catalyst for another crack against the government. This time it is concentrated on the northern outskirts of the capital, in the neighbourhoods of Liberdade and the area surrounding Parque Eduardo VII, as well as further afield in Alverca, Sacavém, Pontinha and Alcântara. Once again, the rebellion is poorly coordinated; its instigators are unprepared and too quick off the mark, mistakenly relying on various military units that turn out to be loyal to the regime. Once again the Sappers Regiment in Pontinha joins the revolutionaries, but its decision to march towards central Lisbon on foot proves disastrous, as this gives the regime time to mobilise forces against it and violently decimate the Sappers in the alleys surrounding Lisbon Zoo. The parallels with 1927 are stark – once again rebels barricade themselves in Rato, once again they are bombarded from the castle on high. This time, after the government forces are victorious through sheer numbers and military might, the captured civilians are lined up and shot against the wall of the zoo; forty dead, thirty injured, over seven hundred deported to the colonies, including to newly built prisons in Timor that are precursors to the horrors of Tarrafal. In the midst of all this, popular opinion rallies around a calm, collected, stoic Salazar, one captured by the photographer Ferreira da Cunha. In the widely circulated photo, the soon-to-be dictator leans forward in the back of a car, his face furrowed in concentration as he listens to moustachioed Captain David Neto in full military regalia give a report on the developing situation. Salazar looks every inch the dignified leader ready to take Portugal into a new period of stability.

August 1931 marks the beginning of the end for republican-led insurrections against the regime. While the country sees a few more attempted uprisings, many coordinated by exiles in republican Spain, the inability to coalesce the republican forces around a positive political programme means the wind is decisively taken out of their sails. There is also a sense that the mood of the general public towards the republicans has hardened, that the constant violence is starting to take its toll on the population. In May 1932 Salazar gives a speech in which he appeals to the depoliticisation of the Church and the few remaining monarchists, and turns his attention to what are to become the primary enemies of his nascent *Estado Novo* – anarchists, socialists and communists – whom he derides for defending a society 'without nationality, without family, without property and without morals'.[5] In June, Carmona formally invites Salazar to form a government, and the conquest of power is complete. Salazar's first moves are restating the ban on political parties and extending the apparatus of state censorship, as well as bringing in laws that punish 'crimes of rebellion', which include 'offences against the prestige of the Republic' as well as various forms of industrial action. In 1933 the main apparatus for enforcing these laws is brought into being: the Vigilance and State Defence Police (*Polícia de Vigilância e Defesa do Estado*, PVDE) which, alongside the newly formed National Propaganda Secretariat (*Secretariado de Propaganda Nacional*, SPN), forms the backbone of the *Estado Novo*'s quest to repress any ideological framework at odds with Salazar's. Thus the stage is set for a direct confrontation between the *Estado Novo* and the labour movement.

Among Salazar's multiple internal reforms is a new National Work Statute (*Estatuto de Trabalho Nacional*, ETN), which besides banning strikes and lock-outs essentially makes any trade union that doesn't meet with government approval illegal. The government takes effective legislative control of all collective bargaining, bringing wages and working conditions into the sphere of the state. At this time the bulk of the organised labour movement is made up of three main organisations: the CGT led by anarcho-syndicalists, the Inter-Syndical Commission (*Comissão Inter-Sindical*, CIS) led by the communists, and the Federation of Workers' Associations (*Federação de Associações Operárias*, FAO), led by the small Portuguese Socialist Party (*Partido Socialista Português*, PS). In the wake of the regime's crackdown on the trade unions, the various groups attempt to coordinate a response, plagued by internal programmatic and strategic differences. The CGT and FAO form a joint plan for an 'insurrectionist general strike', where a national wave of strike action paves the way for yet another military uprising, and begin conspiring with the few remaining republican elements within the armed forces. This insistence on tying strike action to another republican uprising is opposed by the communists, who accuse the CGT of subordinating the workers' movement to the bourgeois opposition. Despite this anti-putschist turn within the PCP leadership, some Party members in the CIS publish a call for a general strike and throw their lot in with the syndicalists. But in the meantime, the PVDE successfully sweeps through the country, first arresting the republican officers conspiring with the CGT and then hundreds of militant CGT and FAO members, leaving the organisations considerably weakened. Despite it being clear that the regime is aware of the plan, the call for strike action goes ahead, tabled for 18 January 1934.

The resulting workers' mobilisation turns out to be explosive, literally. On the morning of the 18th, a PCP activist lobs a bomb onto a railway line on the eastern outskirts of Lisbon, causing a train to derail and immediately alerting the government's military forces that the action is under way.[6] The capital is rocked by more explosions, on Travessa do Cabral in central Lisbon and underneath a tram on Avenida da Liberdade. These actions, however, are not the triumphant herald to anything that could be described as a general strike. There are hubs of action in some Lisbon neighbourhoods, as well as in various towns and cities up and down the country – but the total participation doesn't rise above a few thousand. In the town of Marinha Grande, workers manage to occupy the town hall and the GNR barracks, but a lack of organised leadership and a real plan for what to do next means the police take control of the situation in a few hours, scattering the armed strikers into the surrounding pine forests. Syndicalists in Almada and Barreiro, south of the Tagus, bring the railways to a halt, and in the town of Silves the cork manufacturers hoist a red flag above the workshops. Ultimately, however, this first salvo from the workers' movement meets the same end that befell the various republican uprisings: failure, arrests, increased government repression, death. This is the first real test of Salazar's mettle as de facto head of state, the first glimpse into how the *Estado Novo* deals with dissent. His answer to 18 January is the creation of the Tarrafal penal colony, its construction proposed in 1934 and the first prisoners shipped out in 1936. Of the 152 men imprisoned when the Swamp of Death is inaugurated, over a third are there due to their actions in January 1934.

The particular brand of fascist authoritarianism implemented by Salazar notably differs from the regimes in Italy and Germany in a few key ways. The violent goons that put Mussolini and Hitler in power are not required for the creation of the *Estado Novo*, and Salazar remains opposed to an independent paramilitary force – or street thugs outside of his control. Yet the Portuguese far right are itching to imitate the Brownshirts. Salazar sees an opportunity to kill two birds with one stone, directing the ebullience of the would-be street fascists against

29

what he sees as the real enemies of the state. In the mid-1930s the Portuguese press is awash with articles decrying the dangers posed by next-door republican Spain, as well as the increasing influence of the Soviet Union. The year 1936 sees the creation of two organisations designed to combat that influence: the Portuguese Legion, a formal militia integrated into the state through the Ministry of the Interior, and the Portuguese Youth (*Mocidade Portuguesa*), in essence a youth extension of the former, modelled partly on the Hitler Youth. With these two organisations the *Estado Novo* can keep a close eye on the more extreme fascist elements in the country, and has another tool of repression against what Salazar calls 'the great heresy of our time': communism. From late 1936 public servants are required to make a statement under oath that they repudiate 'communism and all subversive ideas'.

The communists, for their part, manage to come out of the events of 1934 relatively intact, and gain a certain amount of underground political clout as the chief target of Salazar's ire. With a ringing endorsement as the main 'enemy within', the Party grows, and begins to expand its front organisations and youth wings, setting up printing presses for its various illegal newspapers within Lisbon apartments. The PCP's membership is still modest, but its influence in various workplaces, as well as civil and military institutions, becomes hard to ignore. In late 1936, sailors on board the Portuguese warship *Afonso de Albuquerque* are seen to express support for the Spanish Republic as the ship makes stops along Levante, on the Mediterranean coast. On their return to Portugal, the seventeen corporals and cabin boys responsible are dismissed – leading to a wave of unrest and protest within that section of the Armada. In response to the dismissals, a group of around fifty sailors in the Revolutionary Organisation of the Armada (*Organização Revolucionária da Armada*, ORA) hold a meeting in Parque Eduardo VII. The regime's repressive surveillance means parks and other open spaces, like secluded beaches, have become a standard meeting point for large groups such as this. ORA is one of the groups heavily influenced by the PCP, and the Lisbon Armada in particular has enough of a membership that they merit their own propaganda bulletin, the *Red Sailor* (*Marinheiro Vermelho*).

On the morning of 8 September, several dozen ORA men steal small rowing boats from the Cais do Sodré and paddle along the Tagus, making their way onto the *Afonso de Albuquerque* and another two warships, the *Dão* and the *Bartolomeu Dias*. The sailors subdue the ships' commanding officers and hijack the vessels. It's unclear what the final goal of the hijacking is – accounts range from an attempt to topple the government there and then, to delivering the ships to republican forces in Spain, or sailing the vessels to the Azores to free political prisoners and establish a base against the regime. Ultimately, whatever the plan is, it is unsuccessful – the regime mounts a speedy and decisive response, and the ships receive vicious sustained fire from shore as well as from the Air Force. It's a bloodbath on the Tagus – ten sailors dead, over forty injured, and ultimately eighty arrests[7] – thirty-four of whom have the dubious honour of being among the first shipped to Tarrafal. This rebellion is crushed – but a radical, communist wing of the Navy will persist for decades.

With its links to the Communist International, the PCP is able to smuggle its militants abroad to receive training in Moscow's International Lenin School – a relationship that persists until 1939 when, suspecting the PCP has been infiltrated by the PVDE, the Comintern severs ties with its Portuguese section. Among those who make the journey to Russia is a young Álvaro Cunhal, cadre name 'David'. A law student at the University of Lisbon, Cunhal has a fiery energy that belies his years, joining the Party at eighteen and becoming a member of the Central Committee only four years later. Like many of his fellow militants, Cunhal's activity is interrupted periodically with stints in political prisons. During a rare period of 'legal' life in 1940, where he isn't being actively pursued by the secret police, Cunhal teaches geography at the Colégio Moderno, a school in Lisbon's Campo Grande. It's at this school that Cunhal forges a relationship with Mário Soares, the bright young son of the Colégio's founder. Soares' childhood is marked by his father's peripheral involvement in the anti-regime movements of the 1930s – even as a student he shows an enthusiasm for new ideas, and Cunhal is happy to oblige by bringing him into the communist fold. Soares becomes an active member of the PCP's youth wing, and as the Party undergoes a period of internal restructuring, both Cunhal and Soares take on more significant roles in the left opposition to Salazar's regime. Over three decades later, Mário Soares and Álvaro Cunhal will be on opposite ends of a political firestorm that will threaten to plunge the country into civil war.

As the regime becomes more practised in its repression, its politics grow decidedly out of fashion on the global stage. The victory of the Allied forces in the Second World War is awkward for the *Estado Novo*. Having started from a position of complete neutrality, towards the end of 1943 Portugal veers towards a tacit support for the Allied powers, granting the US use of the Azores as a strategic stop for its aircraft and ships. With the Allied victory the global mood towards fascism and authoritarian dictatorships, as well as colonialism, is soured. Salazar tries to keep the new global hegemons onside by renaming the more obviously fascistic state institutions – the National Propaganda Secretariat, for instance, becomes the National Secretariat for Information, Popular Culture and Tourism (*Secretariado Nacional de Informação, Cultura Popular e Turismo*, SNI). With these shifts the *Estado Novo* pays lip service to a more pluralist, free society – Salazar declares in a 1945 speech that 'it is undeniable that totalitarianism has died as a result of this victory', but that democracy in its various forms 'is still subject to discussion'. The democratic opposition jumps on this moment of weakness. In late 1945 a new organisation, the Movement of Democratic Unity (*Movimento de Unidade Democrática*, MUD) is founded by a group of democrats in the Café Portugal, in the heart of Lisbon. The MUD writes a letter to the government requesting the right to hold an open meeting, which is granted. In a meeting room at the Almirante Reis Republican Centre, ensconced in a narrow alley down Rua do Benformoso, the chair Mário Lima Alves brings the gathered crowd to rapturous applause through a speech calling for the immediate closure of the Tarrafal concentration camp, and the installation of a new democratic system of government.

The end of the war, and the formation of the MUD, marks a decisive shift in the tactics of the opposition – away from *Reviralhismo* and failed putsches and towards an attempt to remove Salazar through electoral means. This approach is also favoured by sections of the PCP but opposed by, among others, Álvaro Cunhal. Despite the banning of political parties, the *Estado Novo* still holds regular presidential and legislative elections. The apparatus of state repression turns these into essentially symbolic events, marked by an extremely low turnout, a restricted franchise and an inevitable result that is in favour of the regime. In 1945, for example, only 12% of the Portuguese population has the right to vote – the franchise is restricted on the basis of education, sex and property, in such a way as to concentrate the vote into the hands of a tiny, sympathetic, conservative elite. This elite is given its ballot papers directly by the state, whereas the opposition has to print and distribute its own to its supporters, during a narrow thirty-day campaigning period. These periodic nods towards representative democracy, token though they are, are useful for the government – they allow them to make an assessment of the political state of play, to take note of their political allies and, more importantly, keep track of the opposition. As the MUD picks up steam, holding meetings across the country and preparing for the upcoming legislative election, they make the mistake of gathering lists of signatures in support of their statements. The regime captures these lists and, under the guise of determining if the signatures were given freely, proceeds to track down and interrogate each of the over fifty thousand signatories – a scare tactic that pushes the MUD to not contest the upcoming elections. The poster that appears on the dilapidated walls and street corners of Lisbon, circulated by MUD activists, depicts a line drawing of a distraught-looking woman with her hands raised, chained to others at the wrist. 'Without free elections,' it reads, 'DON'T VOTE.'

The PVDE goes through its own rebrand, becoming the PIDE (*Polícia Internacional e de Defesa do Estado*) with a permanent staff of over five hundred – a number that will only continue to rise under Salazar's tenure. While comparisons to the Gestapo and the NKVD are easy to make, PIDE actually models itself on the British secret service – the pride of Portugal's longest and most consistent ally. PIDE establishes an iron grip across the country, its infiltration and interrogation tactics a perpetual blight on any organised opposition. The MUD is hounded by the police, under the pretext that the organisation collaborates with the PCP – an allegation that leads the MUD and its youth wing to be officially declared illegal in 1946. Alongside PIDE's brutal repression, characterised by the imprisonment of hundreds of activists, some of whom are tortured and suffer 'accidental' deaths, sits the *Estado Novo*'s court system, the flagship of which is the Boa Hora plenary tribunal on Rua Nova de Almada, in Lisbon's downtown. The powers granted by the state to PIDE and the plenary courts mean the trials are, like the state's elections, purely for show, another nod towards due process that is insidiously manipulated from within by the police. In 1948 a trial of 108 defendants, all accused of associating with the PCP and the MUD, leads the state to implement further legislation allowing PIDE to imprison defendants for up to three years on grounds of security concerns, regardless of the outcome of the trial.

In March 1949, in a sting operation conducted at their branch headquarters in the town of Luso, Álvaro Cunhal is arrested alongside another member of the Communist Party's Central Committee, Militão Ribeiro, and an activist, Sofia Ferreira. The capture of two leading lights of the PCP is a coup for the regime, hailed in the press and in the chamber of the National Assembly. Cunhal and Ribeiro are taken to Lisbon and placed in isolation within Lisbon penitentiary. They are held there for months in a regime of solitary confinement that leads Ribeiro to go on hunger strike and die in January 1950. When Cunhal is finally brought to trial in the Boa Hora court it is May 1950, over a year after his arrest. It's only there that he discovers his comrade is dead. The man the police bring in front of the state judge is thin, his pale cheekbones rendered sharp by hunger. Despite the torture he has endured, his eyes shine bright as he takes the stand. Cunhal has a degree in law and a gift for words – he has used his time in isolation to prepare for this moment. When the judge asks him if he has anything to say in his defence, Cunhal embarks on a tirade against the regime, a long, bombastic speech in which he decries the torture he and his comrades have experienced at the hands of PIDE. Comprehensively, systematically, Cunhal takes the opportunity to go through in immense detail the politics of the PCP, to dismantle the lies, propaganda and hypocrisy of the regime, and to accuse Salazar and his henchmen of being the true 'political terrorists'. If the trial is to be a show trial, Cunhal puts on a show that will become the blueprint for all communist defences going forward. He concludes his speech:

We will be judged and certainly found guilty. [...] Our people* think that if someone should be tried and condemned for acting against the interests of the people and the nation, for wanting to drag Portugal into a criminal war, for using unconstitutional and illegal methods, for employing terrorism, that someone is not us, the communists. Our people think that, if someone should be tried for such crimes, let it be the fascists that sit in the dock, let the current governors of the nation and their chief, Salazar, sit in the dock.

Álvaro Cunhal will spend the next decade behind bars, much of that time in complete isolation – a sentence only cut short by a fortuitous escape from the political prison in Peniche. In his absence, and in light of the PIDE crackdown that decimated the organisation, the PCP winds down its activity and proceeds to another period of soul-searching and sometimes violent internal reorganisation. The Party drives away members whom it considers politically deviant, with social democratic politics, among them Mário Soares. The decline in the Party's activity falls in line with a broader period of oppositional hibernation characteristic of the early 1950s. The brief honeymoon period experienced by the democratic opposition, where Portugal's status as an authoritarian regime sits at odds with the global shift towards liberal democracy, comes to an abrupt end with the arrival of the Cold War. The US is briefly willing to accept Portugal's surviving colonial empire and fascistic tendencies as long as the regime remains staunchly anti-communist, and the *Estado Novo* is happy to oblige.

---

* When Cunhal refers here to 'people' he's not just talking about members of the PCP – he sees himself as a spokesperson for the Portuguese working class as a whole, who, he proclaims earlier in his speech, support the aims of the party.

*

In 1956, Nikita Khruschev's speech at the 10th General Congress of the USSR, denouncing the crimes of Stalin, takes the Party in a new, reformist direction. This tips the scales in favour of the reformist faction within the PCP, led by Júlio Fogaça – one in favour of electoral strategies, and collaboration with the broader elements organising against the regime. The democratic opposition has had a few cracks at supporting electoral candidates, with MUD president General Norton de Matos running a brief and popular campaign in 1949 that he cuts short due to the brazen disdain the regime has for democracy. There is a clear, growing appetite for a candidate who can challenge Salazar, and the opposition finds that candidate in Air Force general Humberto Delgado. It will turn out to be the first, and only, real chance to challenge the regime at the ballot box.

On the face of it, Humberto Delgado's political past makes him an odd choice to challenge the primacy of the *Estado Novo*. As a young officer Delgado participated in the military coup of 1926 and would become a loyal supporter of the regime, including its anti-communism, going so far as to write in praise of Adolf Hitler and condemn both monarchists and republicans. The war softens Delgado, however, and in 1952 he is sent as a military attaché to the Portuguese embassy in Washington, where he spends five years. His time in the US reinforces his favourable opinions of representative democracy[8] – and witnessing the election of Dwight D. Eisenhower introduces him to the pomp and spectacle of an American election.[9] Delgado returns to Portugal in 1957 as a newly promoted general – at that time the youngest in Portuguese history. His re-emergence onto the Portuguese political stage sets the gears turning for a few people in the opposition. In late 1957, Delgado visits his old friend, Captain Henrique Galvão, in the prison wing of Santa Maria hospital. Galvão had been arrested in 1952 for attempting to organise a military coup against the government, and his subsequent tour of the *Estado Novo*'s prison system leaves him emaciated and seriously ill. In the hospital, Galvão lets Delgado in on his master plan: Delgado will run for president. His status as a young, loyal general will leave the regime unable to undermine his campaign in the usual ways – he is the perfect candidate, poised to sweep Salazar away via legal means. Delgado is initially shocked by the proposal, but his reticence is short-lived, and a few days later he sends a coded message back to Galvão: in a letter filled with banal chit-chat, Delgado's signature is underlined, meaning he agrees to be put forward as a candidate. Galvão begins work behind the scenes.

When the democratic opposition's first choice, Francisco Cunha Leal, withdraws due to illness, Delgado is approached to stand as the opposition candidate, and accepts. The PCP, at this point, is sceptical – Humberto is still seen as a loyal lapdog of the regime, even a puppet of US imperialism – and their plan is still to put their efforts behind Arlindo Vicente, a fellow traveller of the Party and an ardent anti-fascist with a proven track record of opposing Salazar. The PCP's trepidation over Delgado is short-lived. 10 May 1958 is the date of Delgado's press conference announcing his candidacy. The top floor of the Chave d'Ouro café in Rossio is packed with journalists from the foreign press, jostling in the small space to get a look at the general. There are not enough chairs for the gathered guests. Delgado is a confident public speaker, unafraid to pull punches. In this room, with its gentle morning light dappled by cigarette smoke, it's as if the oppressive veil of the state has been briefly lifted. In his deep, gruff voice, Delgado calls out the regime's lack of democracy – 'The Portuguese government lies whenever it says, abroad, that there are free elections in Portugal!' His words are met with periodic applause, cheers – the mood in the room is light. The first question for the opposition candidate falls to journalist Lindorfe Pinto Basto, writing for France Presse. Basto leans forward, posing the question that seems to be on everyone's mind: 'General, if you're elected president, what will you do with the president of the Council?'[10] The gentle hubbub dies at once. Delgado lets the pause linger. Then, in a display of almost flippant boldness, the man who will soon receive the moniker 'the Fearless General' replies: 'I'll dismiss him, obviously.'

This short phrase sends a shock wave through the regime and Portuguese society. At this point Salazar has been at the head of the government for over twenty-five years, his power firmly consolidated. His longevity, combined with the *Estado Novo* propaganda machine, makes him out to be part of the woodwork – it is by design that removing him should seem as absurd as removing one's own head. Yet, the 1933 constitution, flawed and fascistic as it is, makes Delgado's promise imminently possible: the president has the power to dismiss the prime minister. The journalists who are present are astonished by the frankness of Delgado's press conference. This is not a man cut from the same cloth as the typical *Estado Novo* politicians – his answers are clear, frank, to the point, absent of the usual cynical political calculus. And the general comes equipped with something new and exotic – the knowledge of how to run a dazzling election campaign *à Americana*, with an energy that will cut through the usual deliberate tedium of Portuguese politics. It's only four days later that the effect of Delgado's declaration is really felt – at Santa Apolónia train station, where Delgado catches a train towards Porto for a campaign tour, a crowd of several hundred gathers around the general, cheering him in a spontaneous public demonstration. People board the train in order to shake the general's hand; a group of women on the platform break into a speedy rendition of the national anthem, as the train is about to leave. As the train pulls away, one of Delgado's election commit-tee throws copies of the regime-loyalist paper *Diário da Manhã* out of the window, shouting 'Tear that crap up! Down with the dictatorship!' The crowd on his arrival in Porto, however, is extraordinary: over two hundred thousand people cheering for liberty, forcing his campaign car to a slow crawl through the city, accompanied by a guard of honour of thousands that fills even the widest city streets. The size of the gatherings in Porto begins to ring serious alarm bells for the regime – civilian crowds the size of which this government has never seen and is ill-prepared to contain. Delgado's visit to Porto is already looking like a victory lap.

When Delgado returns to Lisbon two days later, the platform at Santa Apolónia and the adjacent streets are thronged with supporters. The idea of Delgado carrying out a repeat of his Porto performance is too much for the regime to bear, and the streets are also packed with police and GNR officers on horseback, literally rattling their sabres to get the gathered crowd to disperse. It doesn't work – around the station Delgado's supporters begin a strange back-and-forth dance with the police, refusing to be chased away. As the units on horseback push the crowd back, they leave a gap for the station to fill with members of the Portuguese Legion, in civilian clothes. The legionnaires are there for a vocal counter-protest; while the crowd outside the station jostles with the police, the legionnaires inside chant 'Salazar! Salazar! Salazar!' and scuffle with Delgado's supporters. When Delgado's train finally pulls into the station at 18:48, the chanting gives the impression that he might be about to wander into a counter-demonstration. That impression is dispelled as soon as he steps through the station's main doors – the general feels hands grip him by his ankles as the crowd hoists him up into the air, the streets filled with chants of 'Humberto! Humberto! Humberto!' As his campaign car tries to make an exit away from Santa

Apolónia, however, a GNR officer on a white horse waves his sabre at the driver and orders him to turn left, away from the city centre and on a detour that will take the general far from the gathered crowds. Delgado is angry, his wife flustered – he considers refusing the order until the decision is taken out of his hands: another GNR officer levels a pistol at Delgado's driver and threatens to shoot. The general's triumphant return to the capital is sabotaged, the crowd attempting to follow his car through the city beaten back by the police. In the city centre, the crowds expecting the general's car are chased through the streets with baton charges and gunfire, the air filled with screams and the sound of breaking glass as shop fronts are kicked in by fleeing civilians hoping to find shelter from the police. Taxis ferry the injured to hospitals. As night falls, civilians peek from the windows around the general's campaign headquarters on Avenida da Liberdade, waiting for him to arrive. Delgado, however, has been taken home, where he sits with his shell-shocked wife and daughters. The tumult in central Lisbon carries on well into the night.

Not everyone around Delgado's candidacy has their hopes set on a victorious election. Within the armed forces, other senior officers have grown tired of the trappings of the regime, having gone on a similar political journey to Delgado and his turn towards democracy. Those stirrings within the armed forces have already led to the failed revolutionary conspiracy by Captain Henrique Galvão in 1951. Now, some of the officers tied to Galvão see Delgado's campaign as the civilian backdrop to a military revolution – one that, for the first time in a while, it seems the population has an appetite for. Delgado is involved in the early conspiratorial meetings, agreeing to participate in a coup a week before polling day. But as the campaign carries on, as his popularity becomes more and more apparent, Delgado begins to believe he can really become president without military intervention. It is undeniable that there is unprecedented popular momentum behind the campaign – which makes the potential government response all the more dangerous. When he is cautioned by his closest military advisors about relying on the regime playing fair, Delgado replies that 'no government can steal this election from me. I have the people, and Europe.'[11] After only a few weeks of campaigning, even the Communist Party concedes that Delgado has the best chance of success, having 'taken the masses with him', and withdraws Arlindo Vicente from the race. The plans for a military rebellion are, quietly, shelved – Humberto Delgado intends to see this election through to the end.

As the general's national campaign tour gains momentum, so too does the regime's response on the ground. The government makes a public declaration that any demonstrations will be 'repressed with the greatest severity' – and this is soon shown to be true. On 18 May, Delgado makes an address at the Liceu Camões school in central Lisbon. The main hall is filled to the brim, the José Fontana square outside overflows with the mass of supporters. He is joined on stage by Major David Neto – the same man who was photographed as a young lieutenant informing Salazar of the failed 1931 rebellion. Delgado's speech rises to a fever pitch to cheers from the gathered thousands as he reiterates his plans for Salazar – 'I'll throw him out!' he cries. The repression he's experienced throughout the campaign so far lends a rage to his words – he gesticulates wildly as he repeats the slogan he coined in Porto – 'You have tired us! You have tired us! Reform yourselves! Reform yourselves! Leave! Leave!' When the speech ends, however, in a different register such that it's only heard by the confidants gathered around him, the Fearless General mutters: 'I scent fear, I have the physical feeling that danger surrounds me. But I don't know where from. It's terrible!'[12] Outside, six hundred GNR and police shock troops descend upon the crowd with truncheons, horseback charges and gunfire, met by a modest hail of cobblestones thrown by the young crowd. Nearby on Avenida Fontes Pereira de Melo, the Café Monte Carlo* hosts vocal Delgado supporters and is raided by police carrying automatic weapons, leaving a trail of smashed chairs and broken glass. The glass facade of the Monumental Cinema next door is shattered by gunfire, the police aiming high to scatter the crowd. The riots last until the early hours of the morning, dozens injured in the aftermath. Lisbon is plunged into a state of emergency with the military on high alert, and Delgado is bundled into a PIDE car on his exit from the school and told it's for his own safety.

Humberto Delgado's address at Liceu Camões marks the end of his independence from the spectre of the secret police. From this point on he is under the constant eye of PIDE agents, their cars trailing his campaign stops around the country, dragging a coordinated wave of police repression in their wake. Behind the scenes, PIDE is also busy making the electoral process as difficult as possible for Delgado's campaign. When the Portuguese people finally go to the polls on 8 June 1958, the scale of the regime's electoral manipulation becomes fully apparent. The polling stations are filled with PIDE agents and uniformed members of the Portuguese Legion, anyone arriving with an opposition ballot paper being subjected to violent intimidation and removal on spurious grounds. There is little attempt to mask the fraud – PIDE agents and police officers and even the military governor of Lisbon[13] are seen pouring buckets of ballot papers into the collection boxes, as if daring their opponents to confront them. These are the obvious cases, highlights of a thorough campaign that also involves last-minute registration of members of the

---

* In 1958 the Monte Carlo was a well-loved Lisbon institution, considered a 'cathedral' of coffee shops and frequented by all manner of celebrities, intellectuals and artists. It is now a Zara.

clergy and numerous reported cases of repeat voting. When the results are revealed on 28 June, they are hardly surprising: Américo Tomás, the government's loyal candidate who had barely deigned to even campaign, receives 75.8% of the vote, from a total of just under one million votes.

Salazar's humiliation of Humberto Delgado doesn't stop with smashing him at the ballot box. The general makes a few feeble protestations to the sitting president, but his letters are ignored completely. While PIDE carries out a systematic hounding of opposition organisers, in early 1959 Humberto Delgado has his military status degraded to 'separated from the service', just short of full dismissal from the Air Force. Delgado sees in his future the same fate that befell his friend Henrique Galvão – real danger surrounds the general. PIDE is a terrifying force of oppression, but the political police's jurisdiction only really covers the civilian population – the military is governed by a whole separate structure of internal discipline and punishment. For a PIDE agent to do something as simple as following a military officer requires layers of tedious bureaucracy. Bringing Delgado's status down to that of a civilian would thus open up the threat of plenary tribunals and imprisonment, which is what PIDE is clearly angling for. To that end, the secret police organise a 'popular demonstration' outside Delgado's house as a pretext for his arrest – but Delgado has already been tipped off, allegedly by a CIA operative in Portugal, and on the afternoon of 12 January requests asylum in the Brazilian embassy. Delgado will carry on from there to Rio de Janeiro, beginning a period of international exile where he is relentlessly pursued by agents of PIDE, but forever plotting his return. In the upper echelons of Portuguese politics, the newly elected government learns a lesson from Delgado's campaign and brings in legislation that changes the Electoral Act – as of August 1959, the president is no longer elected by direct popular vote, but by an internal electoral college made up of government departments and members of the National Assembly. The case of Humberto Delgado is the final nail in the coffin for any notion the opposition has of removing the regime through 'legal' means. It is clear that something much more drastic is required if the dictatorship is to be brought down.

Mugshots of Henrique Galvão kept on file by PIDE, 1952.

CHAPTER THREE

DISSIDENT CONFETTI

Nestled among the winding streets of Alfama, on Rua Augusto Rosa opposite Lisbon's cathedral, is a white building whose windows and doors are blocked by a criss-cross of thick, black iron bars. This is the Aljube Museum of Resistance and Liberty – one of the few Lisbon institutions that openly confronts the horrors of the dictatorship. Underneath the museum's logo, a simple geometric arch that evokes the bars on the windows is a stone plaque from 1984, before the building was converted into a museum. The plaque reads:

> Here
> From the silence of the 'drawers'
> From a gagged nation
> From breasts shredded by the tortures of PIDE
> rose the clamour of freedom
> [and] April flowered

This museum was once the complex of the Aljube, one of the main prisons used by the *Estado Novo* for its political dissidents and particularly communists. The 'drawers' refer to the Aljube cells – notoriously small and built to an exacting standard, which means guards can peer into every corner through a specially designed hatch, known as the Eye of Judas. During the *Estado Novo*, Aljube is particularly used as a hub for prisoner interrogation. PCP militant Jaime Serra described Aljube as 'an extension of PIDE headquarters', where the processes of incarceration and torture can be conveniently carried out within the same building. In Álvaro Cunhal's infamous trial at the Boa Hora Tribunal, he begins by describing the PIDE agents' response to his silence under interrogation:

> The first time I was arrested, as I refused to make a statement, they handcuffed me, placed me in a circle of agents and beat me with fists, kicks, whips and with thick cabled wooden boards. After they beat me like this for a long time, they let me fall, held me down on the floor, took my shoes and socks off and beat me violently on the soles of my feet. When they were tired, they lifted me up, making me walk on painful and swollen feet, at the same time that they would beat me again. This repeated itself numerous times, for a long stretch of time, until I lost my senses...

When a new communist militant is put into Aljube, they are told by their fellow inmates 'be strong, comrade – this will be tough'. In Aljube the beatings are only one of a horrifying array of torture methods employed against prisoners – often the preferable one. Others include periods of complete isolation in darkness, the food reduced to simply water and bread, or sleep torture where prisoners are kept awake for days – all drawn from the CIA playbook. The torture that features the most in the recollections and diaries of the prisoners who make their way through these cells, however, is the 'statue'. Prisoners are forced to stand on their feet in complete stillness for hours on end, under the watchful eye of a PIDE interrogator. The punishment for touching the wall, collapsing or otherwise taking the weight off their feet is another vicious beating. Some prisoners simply choose to lie on the floor of the interrogation room, preferring the immediate violence over the combined psychological and physical torture the 'statue' presents. The effects of PIDE's torture methods drive prisoners to the very edge of what a human being can tolerate, some succumbing to strokes or cardiac arrest – part of the reason why Aljube has an on-site doctor, who often has to intervene in the PIDE interrogations so as to avoid premature deaths. The gaps between the police interrogations are often as bad as the interrogations themselves – people left alone with their thoughts in the dark for days, weeks, months on end, listening out for the jangle of keys or the ringing telephone that could mean more pain. PIDE are careful to maintain deniability in their torture methods, their paperwork full of euphemisms – a severe beating is attributed to a 'clumsy stumble down stairs', for instance, and advice from one agent to another on which methods to use might say 'this man does not sleep' to indicate that sleep deprivation isn't working. This kind of phraseology constitutes the *Estado Novo*'s very own Newspeak. In police reports about suppressing crowds at protests, all gunshots are reported as being fired 'into the air'. In clandestine circles the running joke is that the opposition must have some of the tallest protestors in the world, given how many end up with bullet wounds in their legs.

The Aljube's location at the heart of Lisbon is no accident. Since its establishment as the primary arm of state repression, PIDE has spent a great deal of time cultivating its public image as an institution to be feared, one that it's important to stay on the right side of. The rapprochement between Portugal and the US with the prolongation of the Cold War gives PIDE contacts within the CIA and training in a whole host of surveillance techniques. PIDE puts these into effect as part of their dual strategy of 'preventive violence' and 'punitive violence'. Those practical skills in gumshoe-level surveillance are supported by a network of collaborators from civilian society so extensive it creates an atmosphere of intense paranoia, where the fear of any stray conversation getting fed back to PIDE is pervasive. According to historian João Madeira, the post-war *Estado Novo* operates in a 'culture of denouncement'. Lisbon's PIDE branch receives detailed reports and tips on a daily basis. The tip-offs to the state police do not emerge exclusively from so-called 'good nationalists' (though many of the anonymous letters received by the interior minister are signed thus) but from all manner of civilians and for reasons beyond the political. A report to PIDE might be used to settle quarrels, as revenge for an argument, or even for pure financial gain, as collaborators are often paid for their tips. Tips which lead, on thousands of occasions, to a compulsory visit to the PIDE headquarters on Rua António Maria Cardoso – and in the more extreme cases to the prisons in Aljube, Caxias and Peniche.

The regime's political prison system is intended to deter dissent and conspiracy, through violence. Places like Aljube are designed to mould their residents into citizens more fitting of the *Estado Novo* and its morals, whose harrowing experiences can serve as an example to others that might cross the line. However, within the prison walls an unintended dynamic begins to thrive. In a similar way to the continued activity of the Communist Party's members in Tarrafal, Aljube's bundling together of dissidents and rebels breeds a culture of solidarity and political organisation. In the brief moments when prisoners are allowed to socialise, despite being under constant watch and barely allowed to interact, they exchange information, educate and disseminate propaganda. The ones who are kept under closer watch, or subjected to prolonged periods of complete isolation in their cells, send and receive messages in the dead of night by tapping out codes on their cell walls – each letter assigned a number of taps according to the alphabet, such that even communication becomes a lengthy and tedious ordeal. It is in these hushed conversations that prisoners are further radicalised, convinced to carry on the struggle. Many who come into these prisons as unaffiliated rebels come out as members of the Communist Party or other clandestine resistance networks. And once they become dissidents, returning to a 'normal' life in society, as much as that might be the goal of the state's prison system, becomes all the more difficult.

In the rare cases where writing materials make their way in, the communist and anarchist militants revert to a time-honoured tradition: newspapers. Handwritten and intricately detailed, often by the scarce light that filters in through barred windows, each of the regime's political prisons hosts a thriving underground 'printing press'. The papers that circulate in the prisons are remarkable pastiches of the illegal press many of the prisoners created when they were free – often beautifully illustrated, covering anything from current affairs (gleaned in dribs and drabs from the outside world) to political debate. Over two hundred issues of these prison newspapers are made between 1934 and 1945, some written by specific prisoner groups such as railway workers (*Carril Vermelho*) and sailors (*Potenkin**). In Aljube the Communist Party's semi-regular paper is the *Boletim Inter-Prisional* (Inter-Prison Bulletin), each issue illustrated in the top left corner with a hammer and sickle laid over the unmistakable square bars of the Aljube's windows. These newspapers and bulletins are the most precious contraband in a system that relies on starving the minds of its prisoners, the often single issues passed around in secret, then hidden and perused in the scant light of the 'drawers'.

It's the continuity of struggle outside and inside the prisons, the refusal to give up fighting despite the constant repression, that means the political prisons of the *Estado Novo* are the hosts of some truly extraordinary escapes. In 1956, 23-year-old PCP activist Carlos Brito[1] is arrested for Party activity and taken to Aljube to

---

* Either a misremembering or deliberate pastiche of the name of the battleship *Potemkin*, which underwent a mutiny in 1905.

51

await trial. This is his second arrest – his first, a three-month stint for his links with the youth wing of the MUD, is what first brought him into the PCP fold. Like the vast majority of the prisoners there, Brito's wait is long – PIDE has a host of legal methods to keep citizens detained almost indefinitely without facing a judge, to the point where only around 15% of those arrested for political crimes ever see the inside of a courtroom. Early 1957 sees Aljube uncharacteristically full, in part due to sections of the prison in Caxias undergoing renovations, as well as a particularly exuberant burst of student and labour movement activity in January. The prison is packed, and the more militant prisoners see an opportunity to try and agitate for better prison conditions, including better food, hygiene and visitation rights. PIDE are quick to nip this in the bud – they round up the eight ringleaders, Carlos Brito among them, and separate them from the rest of the prison population by temporarily locking them in the disused infirmary on the top floor of the prison. Designed for inmates who are too injured or otherwise ill, this part of Aljube is less secure – absent are the sadistically designed cells and the 'Eyes of Judas'. By separating those they deem more dangerous from the rest of the prison, PIDE has made a crucial error that the regime has not yet learned to avoid: putting all their enemies in one place. A place where, unlike in the restrictive cells of the lower floors, they can speak freely. It's here that Brito and his conspirators begin to plan an escape.

The first thing they notice is that the level where they find themselves is slightly recessed relative to the other floors, and ringed by a drain designed to divert rainwater. This means that should they manage to make their way out of the window, they would at least have a narrow ledge to stand on, and be able to shuffle along the outside of the building towards the neighbouring flats. But what of the bars on the windows? A few of the PCP militants in the group have experience in breaking and entering – they know that with a saw the bars can be cut, and removing just four of the bars in a cross-shape would allow an exit. The conspirators take meticulous notes on the guards' routines. A stroke of luck here – unlike in other prisons run by the regime, these guards don't hit the windows with their batons to check their integrity, but merely give the bars a passing glance under a flashlight. Using all the methods at their disposal, developed through years of experience of incarceration, the now ten cell-mates begin sending messages back and forth to PCP comrades on the outside to coordinate the exit.

Outside the prison, the PCP's clandestine network prepares the groundwork for their comrades in Aljube. Some time after contact is made, a package arrives for one of the prisoners, containing a present – a pair of shoes. Inside the sole are the pieces of a disassembled hacksaw. Wary of the high-pitched whine that the saw makes against the bars, the prisoners time the cutting to when they know for sure the guards are otherwise occupied. The cutting sessions are brief, and tense. As the bars of the window begin to fall apart, the prisoners disguise the emerging gaps with mashed breadcrumbs painted grey. The guards, on their cursory investigation, miss the cuts. In the long breaks between sawing sessions, the prisoners iron out the plans in hushed tones, share bread, discuss politics. Blanqui Teixeira, a leading PCP activist, backs out of the proposed escape – his intense vertigo leaves him unable to face walking along the outside edge of the building. Others think the escape is too dangerous, and decide to risk their remaining time in the prison system. By the time the plan is near-ing its apex, only three of the ten men are willing to face the precipitous drop out of the fifth floor of the prison: Carlos Brito, Américo Gonçalves de Sousa and Rolando Verdial. Meanwhile, the PCP comrades on the outside notice that on the top floor of the block of flats adjacent to the prison an apartment lies empty. Deolinda Franco, Carlos Brito's wife and fellow PCP militant, makes an appointment to visit the flat under the guise of a potential tenant. On her tour around the dilapidated property, she steals a moment to open the window facing out towards the Aljube. The prison towers above the rooftops, her husband trapped in a room that she can just glimpse from here.

It's in the early hours of 26 May that Brito and his two daring comrades finally, gently pop the cross of iron from the barred window. The men tie their shoes and jackets around their waists, hoping that the ratty socks on their feet will deaden their steps on the tiled roof-tops. Gonçalves is the first out, followed by Brito, who pulls himself through the bars until his whole body is out and he's gripping the cold metal from the other side. He lowers himself onto the ledge and begins to inch across, meeting Gonçalves by the next window along. They attach their makeshift rope to these bars here, leaving a line of knotted-together grey bedsheets to drift several metres below. Gonçalves makes his way down first, his legs braced against the side of the stone prison, sliding down the cotton sheets inch by inch. Brito can see the GNR guard standing at his post on the ground below, mercifully oblivious to what's happening several metres above and behind him. Gonçalves reaches the end of the rope, where he encounters his first problem: even dangling off the very end, the rope is too short. Their rough calculation of a six-metre drop turns out to be off by quite a bit. Gonçalves lets go of the rope and drops the remaining distance, his feet landing on the tiled rooftop with an audible crash. Without waiting to see if the sound has triggered any sort of alarm, Verdial climbs down, Gonçalves stepping in below to soften his landing. Brito is the last to make it down. They stand on the rooftop for a brief moment, checking their surroundings. In the pitch darkness, it feels like they're floating above the city.

In the apartment below the three men, a small child is roused from sleep by the noise of footsteps on the roof above him.

'Dad, dad!' he cries, 'it's thieves!'

'What thieves?' replies his bleary-eyed father. 'Can't you tell it's cats? Go back to sleep.' The child lies back down – the sounds above him recede, and as he drifts away he begins to believe it really was cats after all.

Above him, the three conspirators tiptoe their way across the rooftops. When they reach the vacant apartment, they find that no one has undone Deolinda's good work. The apartment window is ajar, and the men climb through and into the empty flat. To a casual passerby, the three men who exit the ground floor of the apartment on Rua Augusto Rosa – a mere fifty metres from the guard stationed by the Aljube's front door – are indistinguishable from any three citizens returning home from a night out. Veering away from the shadow of the prison, Brito and his companions make their way to the street where a vehicle is meant to whisk them away to freedom. Here, it seems they have been let down – there is no car in sight. Unwilling to risk the walk, the men jog to Graça square and hail a taxi, hoping the issue of money can be resolved when they arrive at their destination. They drive to the streets around Rato, to the home of fellow PCP member Arnaldo Aboim. When Brito knocks on the door, it's Aboim's sister-in-law who answers.

'Who's there?' she asks.

Biting back laughter, Brito replies, 'It's Carlos Brito!'

'It can't be,' replies the woman. 'Carlos Brito is in prison!'

In the morning, hearing the Aljube's alarm blaring out and the streets being swept by searchlights, the child whose sleep was disturbed by Américo Gonçalves' footsteps asks his father: 'So dad, was it really cats?'

The father replies: 'Those who escaped are good people. Friends of the people. They'll keep fighting to better the lives of poor people like us. If we get asked any questions, we didn't hear anything, we didn't notice anything.' These glimmers of solidarity are what keep the resistance alive, even under Portugal's culture of denouncement.

For prisoners placed in cells facing south, the main sight glimpsed through the iron bars is Lisbon's Holy See, an enormous stone cathedral that blocks out much of the light to the inside of the prison. The cathedral is the oldest church in Lisbon, its foundations laid in 1147, and it is the seat of Lisbon's archdiocese. The inside of the building is vast, its cloisters dimly lit, a place where every footstep reverberates loudly against the stone walls; yet hushed words can be exchanged in relative privacy. It is the perfect place for conspiracy. In 1959, the opposition in Portugal is still reeling from Humberto Delgado's brutal election loss and his exile. Within the armed forces, the flames of a military revolution that were put aside for Delgado are now revived, emboldened by the expression of popular support Delgado received as well as a bitter rage at the government's response to the election. On 11 February 1959, an organising committee of senior military officers holds a meeting in Lisbon, in which they make a solemn oath, handwritten onto a sheet of blue paper and signed by all present. The paper declares the creation of an Independent Military Movement, the goals of which the signatories will fight for 'until the sacrifice of life or liberty'. In this document, this Independent Military Movement sketches out its goals in a rough political manifesto: freeing the nation from the dictatorship, establishing a temporary military junta that grants political freedoms to the population, abolishing the political police and freeing political prisoners, with the ultimate goal of granting power to whatever political force is ultimately chosen, freely, by the Portuguese people.[2] It is a bare-bones manifesto, but one that demonstrates the presence of democratic ideas within the armed forces over a decade before the revolution. There are ten signatories to the document – four majors, three captains, one ensign and two civilians, Manuel Serra and Francisco Sousa Tavares. Together these men represent a military force consisting of detachments from infantry, cavalry and artillery regiments in Lisbon, as well as roughly three hundred armed civilians, among them many communist militants.

The plan is detailed, if ambitious. Those in charge of military units have orders to capture military bases and strategic points throughout Lisbon, as well as arm the civilians. Set for the evening of 11 March, the numerous civilian units are given detailed instructions and placed around the city, in late-night cafés, bars and street corners. The heads of the civilian units congregate inside Lisbon cathedral, granted access by the Catholic priest Perestrelo de Vasconcelos, while the military command is based elsewhere in a magazine office. The organisers are rattled – in the days running up to the coup attempt, the Communist Party decided to withdraw its support, leaving the remaining conspirators concerned about the viability of the operation. And just before the moment of execution, it becomes clear that the alarm has been sounded in the upper levels of government. News trickles in to the rebels that various military regiments around Lisbon have been locked down, and Salazar himself has been whisked away to safety in the GNR barracks at Carmo where, ironically, a detachment of rebellious forces is stationed. The sudden lockdown causes a panic – the element of surprise has been lost, and the military officers lose their nerve. Manuel Serra, head of the civilian wing of the operation, is forced to drive around the city in a last-minute dash to prevent several of the civilian units from attempting anything, lest they get arrested or shot. The 'See Coup' might well have been successful had it not been for the actions of an officious member of the Portuguese Legion who, based on some surveillance data, had an inkling that a conspiracy was under way and managed to convince the Army minister to put Lisbon's units on emergency standby. Having pulled their forces back from the brink, the conspirators agree to a meeting the following day, but by this point it's too late – Manuel Serra is arrested along with roughly forty of the participants, mostly from the civilian wing of the operation.[3]

The 'See Coup' is a harbinger of the increasing troubles the *Estado Novo* will face over the coming decade and beyond. At the end of

1959, Álvaro Cunhal is one of several PCP organisers to mount an escape from the political prison in Peniche, aided by a sympathetic GNR corporal. Cunhal's escape, and return to action on the clandestine front line, means internal change for the PCP – the Party moves away from the reformist, electoral strategies of the last five years to a more hardline position of building a mass popular revolt against the regime. Cunhal is at this point a legendary figure within the movement – his reputation and compelling political nous raises him to the position of general secretary of the PCP, a position he will hold for many years. Yet the PCP organisers' grand escape from Peniche is not even the most threatening prison break for the regime.

In early 1959, 64-year-old Captain Henrique Galvão, former regime loyalist turned dangerous conspirator, the man who convinced Humberto Delgado to run for office, finds himself trapped in a room at Santa Maria hospital in northern Lisbon, kept under close watch by two PIDE agents. Galvão is serving an eighteen-year sentence, the consequence of having produced inflammatory pamphlets against Salazar from his cell at Lisbon penitentiary. Unlike much of the opposition, Galvão is not a communist – his hatred of the regime stems from his experiences as a military man in Angola, witnessing the horrors of the regime's colonial politics. His hospital stay due to ill health is a small reprieve from what, given his advanced age, is expected to be a life sentence. To the nurses and doctors who treat him, Galvão is the hospital's favourite eccentric – deeply eloquent and charming, the old rebel treats his hospital prison like his personal drawing room, where he regales the staff with wild stories of his time in the military, full of fascinating figures and thrilling African adventures. It is certainly through his charm that he is allowed to keep a pet sparrow, Pascoal, who perches on his shoulder while he plays Solitaire and chirps at his guests. Galvão gathers around him a circle of nurses who vie for his company, eager to spend time with the charismatic gentleman. Among them is 22-year-old Maria do

Carmo Veiga, who becomes so fond of the captain that she begins to treat him like an adoptive father. It is with Maria do Carmo's help that Galvão arranges his escape from Santa Maria hospital.

It begins gradually: in front of his guards Galvão begins to act as though his health has taken a turn for the worse, while in the evening behind closed doors he begins an exercise regimen aided by multivitamins brought in by the nursing staff. His possessions are slowly smuggled out of the hospital by Maria do Carmo and his family, including Pascoal, who is removed in a thin cage hidden under an overcoat. On the evening of 15 January, Galvão is handed a sketch of the hospital floor plan, and shortly afterwards one of the PIDE agents outside his door falls into a gentle sleep, aided by something mixed into his coffee. The other agent has disappeared, perhaps distracted by Maria do Carmo's beguiling looks. Either way, the path is clear for Galvão to make his way out of the door and to the clean room down the hall. Here, in a series of actions that belie his age, the captain climbs out of the twelfth-storey window onto the narrow parapet and edges his way around the building until he reaches an open window. It's in that room that he finds and dons an overcoat, hat, doctor's briefcase and, crucially, a fake moustache. His disguise complete, he follows the map drawn for him through the hospital's corridors and down several flights of stairs, until he reaches the exit. The night porter bids him goodnight. Galvão replies 'and a very good night to you, my friend', and disappears into the city.[4]

Galvão's escape becomes PIDE's number one priority for several weeks. The nurses at Santa Maria hospital are brutally interrogated, the captain's family is tailed and even his former lovers are pursued through Lisbon on the chance Galvão might try to reignite an old flame. The fugitive, however, moves quietly between flats in Lisbon, ferried around in secret by a network of loyal friends. A few weeks after his escape, Galvão makes his way into the Argentinian embassy disguised as a delivery man, and formally requests asylum. This causes a diplomatic furore, but one that the Argentinian government is willing to bear. Galvão stays in the small embassy for several weeks; granted access to a type-writer, the old captain spends his hours writing letters and pamphlets that he is convinced will do serious damage to the regime if they are given a proper airing, and distributes them to fellow conspirators throughout Lisbon. As much as Galvão is eloquent and charismatic, he is also somewhat of a fantasist – as well as circulating his pamphlets, Galvão insists that his associates should distribute a collection of his poems (which he claims will galvanise the youth), as well as photos of himself standing at the window of the Argentinian embassy, looking sombre in a suit and tie, accompanied with snippets of text against Salazar. Galvão would happily spend his days fomenting a rebellion against the regime from this small room in the centre of Lisbon, but this is clearly untenable for the Argentinian diplomatic staff. After days of furtive negotiation, the regime allows Galvão to travel to Buenos Aires under Argentinian protection, on the condition that he be prevented from continuing his political work in Argentina. This decision, one arrived at from diplomatic necessity, plagues Salazar – in a conversation with his foreign minister, the now elderly dictator fumes: 'We're going to regret this a thousand times. He is much more dangerous than Delgado.' On 11 May 1959, Henrique Galvão is put on an Argentinian Airlines flight, beginning his 29-hour journey to Buenos Aires. Left behind are his wife, his adopted daughter Beatriz, his pet sparrow and a trail of broken-hearted mistresses. He will never see Portugal again.

From his exile, Henrique Galvão will mount bombastic attacks on Salazar. The first two are among the most exciting incidents of resistance in Salazar's long reign. After a few months in Argentina, Galvão begins to despair at his distance from Portuguese society. He tries to arrange travel to Brazil to liaise with his old friend Humberto Delgado, but his visa is rejected. Deciding to settle for the next best option, Galvão manages to travel to Caracas, Venezuela, where he knows there is a considerable Portuguese community. In his classic roguish style, the captain brings with him 33-year-old Rosa Soskin, an Argentinian woman who, having fallen into the captain's orbit in Buenos Aires, had left her husband to follow the old revolutionary on his adventures. In Caracas, Galvão meets José Velo Mosquera ('Pepe Velo'), a Galician refugee from Franco's Spain. Despite significant political differences, Velo and Galvão are united in one goal – the defeat of their respective national dictatorships. Together with Humberto Delgado they form the Iberian Revolutionary Liberation Directory (*Directório Revolucionário Ibérico de Libertação*, DRIL), a democratic, anti-fascist organisation with the goal of defeating Franco and Salazar, by violent means if necessary. Due to the reputation of its organisers, DRIL has an international network of supporters, and its first big action is to set off bombs in Madrid, coinciding with the Portuguese foreign minister's visit to the Spanish capital. In the press afterwards, DRIL openly takes responsibility for the action, announcing similar future attacks in Portuguese cities. Galvão adds: 'Salazar will be toppled in the near future, and the fall of one of the tyrants will drag the other to Hell, where they both should have been for a long time.'[5]

Setting their ambitions even higher, the DRIL committee in Venezuela concoct what becomes known as Operation Dulcinea. The name is Galvão's idea – a reference to a 1943 play *Dulcinea, or D. Quixote's Last Adventure*. The plan is based around the fact that the Portuguese cruise liner *Santa Maria* is soon to make port in nearby La Guaira. The ship, a large luxury vessel making a leisurely journey to Miami, carries over 350 crew and 1,000 passengers. In January of 1961, in the ports of La Guaira and Curaçao, DRIL arranges for twenty-five Portuguese and Spanish rebels to secretly board the *Santa Maria*, including Pepe Velo, Henrique Galvão and his second in command Camilo Mortágua. They also manage to smuggle aboard fourteen weapons. The plan is to commandeer the

Santa Maria and sail the ship to the island of Fernando Po, from where the rebels can coordinate an invasion of Angola and establish a government dedicated to overthrowing the Iberian fascisms. The hijacking doesn't go to plan – the rebels are twitchy, operating in the dark, and in the commotion four people are shot, including the ship's third pilot Nascimento Costa, who ultimately succumbs to his wounds. The remaining crew are gathered together and told the ship is under the command of a revolutionary force led by General Humberto Delgado, and cautioned not to resist. The *Santa Maria* is renamed *Santa Liberdade* by the rebels, but its lofty goals are swiftly put aside. In order to save one of the wounded crew, the revolutionaries are forced to change course for the island of Saint Lucia. This isn't done for entirely humanitarian reasons – Galvão's time on the ship leads him to conclude that it is inadequate for launching a military attack, and the mission is better off reverting to a propaganda campaign. In any case, landing at Saint Lucia removes the element of surprise. Within hours of the landing, the world knows of the hijacking. On board the ship, the rebels' radios are tuned to the world's news stations as the navigator plots an unpredictable trajectory, making their journey more difficult to track by anyone giving chase. For the passengers, apart from the initial shock of the piracy, life on the ship goes on very much as before – only a few days after the hijacking, the orchestra is back to doing its evening performance, and the pool is once again full.

Back in Lisbon, the news of the *Santa Maria*'s capture hits the regime like a blow to the face. The news is delivered gently to Salazar, as the old dictator is recovering from a bout of flu. His reservations about releasing his most vocal opponent into the world are suddenly proving prophetic. The regime goes into overdrive, denouncing the operation as an unacceptable act of vulgar piracy. Meanwhile, on the other side of the Atlantic, General Humberto Delgado reads of the hijacking in the newspaper and sends an immediate message to his diplomatic connections that the operation is political in nature, and goes beyond mere piracy. Galvão, on board the cruise liner, is busy fielding a bombardment of international press requests, which he handles enthusiastically. Whether through Delgado's intervention or the various interviews given by Galvão to the international press from the ship, both the American and British governments pull away their respective rescue missions and sit back, opting not to interfere in what they now choose to see as an internal political matter. After twelve days at the centre of the world's attention, the *Santa Maria* docks in the Brazilian city of Recife, its passengers released and the rebels ushered away to political asylum, hailed by many as anti-fascist heroes. Brazil's housing of the rebels, on top of their already generous accommodation of Humberto Delgado, serves to further sour Portuguese–Brazilian relations. In Brazil, and in relative freedom despite the circumstances, Galvão and Humberto Delgado have a mission debrief over dinner where their respective egos get the better of them. Galvão demands military control of the resistance movement, suggesting that Delgado should focus on coordinating the political side of the struggle. Delgado is outraged – the suggestion that he, nominally a general, should take orders from a man who never went past the rank of captain, is too much. Going forward, the relationship between the two officers is fraught.

Despite the growing tensions of their nominal leaders, Galvão and Delgado's network of conspirators, buoyed by the events surrounding the *Santa Maria*, begin actioning the next steps of an anti-Salazar revolution. The *Santa Maria* operation brings a new figure into their orbit – Hermínio da Palma Inácio, a Portuguese exile whose reputation precedes him. Palma Inácio, as a young Air Force quartermaster, had been arrested in 1948 for sabotaging aircraft at Granja airbase near Sintra, the only successful mission in another early failed coup attempt.[6] His time in Aljube was cut short dramatically when he took advantage of a guard's inattentiveness to fling himself out of an open window, falling fifteen metres and disappearing into a crowd, uninjured due to the prison blankets he'd managed to wrap around his legs. He spends the next decade on the move, working as an aircraft mechanic in the United States until his presence becomes awkward for the American government and he's forced to leave. His exile lands him, eventually, in Rio de Janeiro, where Camilo Mortágua convinces him to come back into the resistance fold. Palma Inácio agrees to join the rebels on their next mission, leaving Brazil in late September 1961.

Galvão and Delgado agree that the next phase of their plan should be an operation in Portugal, a military uprising, but they disagree on what form that should take. They convene, accompanied by their small army of rebels, in Morocco. Galvão and Delgado's perpetual bickering and strategic differences mean they arrive in Tangiers with two separate plans, but also trailing a group of commandos loyal to both. Behind the backs of the two officers, the remaining conspirators agree to try and combine, as much as possible, the two operations – Delgado's Operation Icarus and Galvão's Operation Vagô. Both plans involve the hijacking of a plane in Morocco and dropping leaflets over Portugal that urge the population into action. The officers are convinced that for the seeds of a budding revolution to take hold, they need to bring 'the masses' with them, which is why a delegation is smuggled into Portugal with the goal of building a civilian and military force that can coordinate with the exile forces and launch a full-scale rebellion. The Portugal delegation, however, falls short – after a few days of failed meetings with Delgado's contacts on the ground, they determine that the conditions aren't right, and any attempted military operation is doomed to failure.

Back in Tangiers, the various commandos awaiting orders are running out of money and patience. The Tangiers branch of PIDE is very aware of the presence of the Portuguese revolutionaries in the city, but unable to make any arrests on foreign soil the PIDE agents resort to openly tailing the men, and exchanging occasional bouts of verbal abuse. Receiving the news that undertaking the main mission is out of the question, the rebels, unwilling to face returning to Brazil empty-handed, decide to go ahead with part of the intended operation: the hijacking. As with the *Santa Maria* episode, Galvão once again turns a military operation into an opportunity to propagandise against the regime. Whereas the pamphlets originally intended for the operation were blueprints for guerrilla warfare, urging civilians to make Molotov cocktails and strategically fell trees to disrupt transport infrastructure, Galvão drafts a new document for this mission. It opens:

MEN AND WOMEN OF PORTUGAL!
STUDENTS, AIMLESS YOUTH!
SOLDIERS REMOVED FROM THE PEOPLE,
THAT BELONG TO THE PEOPLE!
WORKERS WITH NEITHER FREEDOM NOR
BREAD!

Galvão's pamphlet is focused on the upcoming legislative elections, urging the Portuguese people to make their displeasure with the dictatorship known by tearing up their voting slips and taking to the streets en masse against the regime. He writes 'PIDE can arrest and exert violence against 100 or 1,000 men, but it will be impotent against 10,000 that demonstrate.' Further along, he makes a prophetic statement about what a future under Salazar will look like: 'Another year of Salazar will be chaos: irrecoverable misery [...], the sacrifice of our youth in a war without end.' Galvão concludes with a short appeal, and a clear statement with regards to his own politics: 'Help us go further – to your liberation. Otherwise, it will be a fall into total misery, or into the communism that waits to install itself.' Reaching out to an exiled Spanish republican based in Tangiers, Galvão prints 100,000 copies of his latest missive, and the members of the operation set off for Casablanca.

10 November 1961, 08:00 Casablanca airport.[7] The foyer bustles with young children carrying shoeshine kits, hoping to make some money from the passengers. One of the children latches onto Palma Inácio's leg, where he keeps a small pistol tucked into his sock, and is quickly brushed off. The group's other weapons are strapped to a belt around Maria Helena Vidal's waist, hidden underneath her pregnant belly. The leaflets are stowed in two large suitcases. The group sit in the waiting room separate from one another, pretending to read newspapers and gaze out of the window, the picture of bored Portuguese tourists on their way home to Lisbon. When the TAP flight finally pulls up, Camilo Mortágua notices with some alarm that it's a Lockheed Super Constellation, not the Douglas DC-6 they had planned for, that Palma had spent hours studying.

Camilo whispers to Palma, 'It's not the plane we were expecting!'

Palma replies with a wink, 'Who cares? It's a plane!'

On board, Palma Inácio and Camilo Mortágua take the seats closest to the cabin. Maria Helena Vidal surreptitiously distributes the pistols, the crew and twelve other passengers none the wiser. The plane takes off at 09:15, and breakfast is served without incident. It's only when Palma determines that they are above Portuguese airspace that he makes his way with Mortágua to meet the pilots. Entering the cabin, Palma announces: 'We are a group of Portuguese exiles, against the dictatorship. This is a hijacking. You either follow my orders or I'll arrest you and fly the plane myself.'

The captain, shocked, asks what they intend to do. Palma Inácio explains the plan – to fly low over several Portuguese cities, dropping leaflets against the dictatorship, and then return for a landing in Tangiers. The pilot tries to suggest that the plane doesn't have the fuel for the journey, or that there's no way to open a window once it's in the air, but the former Air Force mechanic calmly and cheerfully rebuffs the claims. Sensing the operation has been well thought through, the pilot resignedly informs the rest of the crew of the situation, and asks the two French passengers sitting by the emergency window in first class to move forward so the hijackers can work. As they reach Lisbon, the pilot brings the plane in low and slow. It seems as though they could reach out with their hands and brush the rooftops underneath. Palma Inácio begins to worry that the pilot is trying for a last-minute landing, until he hears the message to Lisbon Tower.

'I'm going for a sweep over the city.'

'Okay,' comes the reply. In these relatively early days of commercial aviation, it is not uncommon for pilots to give their passengers an extended moment of sightseeing before landing – Lisbon Tower is, as yet, not aware that anything is amiss.

As the plane loops lazily in the sky, the main cabin is depressurised and the flight mechanic pops the window open. Out drop the leaflets, shimmering white in the mid-morning sun. They float out over the city centre – Marquês de Pombal, Avenida da Liberdade, Rossio, Terreiro do Paço. TAP 114 trails a wake of dissident confetti, thrown by the fistful by Maria Helena Vidal and Amândio Silva. The flight mechanic, António Corágem, holding the window open for the rebels, gets so swept up in the excitement that he joins in, helping the others toss leaflets into the open air. It's only after this first sweep over Lisbon that the pilot announces to air traffic control that he's been hijacked, and is being forced to return to Morocco. The flight carries on at low altitude, dropping more leaflets south of the Tagus in Barreiro, then over Setúbal, Beja and Faro. They land in Tangiers at 12:12 – one of the first hijackings of a commercial aircraft in history, completed in just under three hours. Henrique Galvão is waiting for them, having already informed the local authorities of what's happened. After being held briefly by the local authorities the hijackers are deported from Morocco to Senegal, and then onwards back to Brazil, carrying on their respective exiles, for a time safe from the claws of the *Estado Novo*.

Henrique Galvão and Palma Inácio's daring propaganda missions on the *Santa Maria* and TAP 114 respectively are bombastic, headline-grabbing acts that direct greater global attention on to the nature of the Portuguese state. Their impact on the ground, on the day-to-day lives of citizens, is relatively minimal, but along with Humberto Delgado's election campaign, the lasting effect is a sustained embarrassment for Salazar and the political legitimacy of the regime as a whole. While this is irritating, the real danger for the regime comes from the internal politicisation and radicalisation of its population. November 1961 is already nine months after the start of military action in Angola, action that will escalate dramatically over the next decade and become the main fuel for internal discontent among the Portuguese people.

At the heart of that radicalisation is the Portuguese student population. In a country where every aspect of society is closely monitored and guarded by the state, it's perhaps surprising that a degree of freedom continues to be allowed within educational institutions, these falling under the purview of the elite class Salazar is perpetually trying to mould. Under the *Estado Novo*, student societies continue to thrive, hold meetings, and organise large plenary sessions on a vast array of subjects, often focused around the national celebration of Students' Day – an annual holiday centred on celebrating the student bodies of higher academia. Through the student societies, they are supplied with 'an effective and independent instrument of representation',[8] something the rest of society has lacked for decades. This relative autonomy is not so easily maintained, and as the state begins to lose the ideological battle within the education institutions, with the open meetings taking a more oppositional bent, the regime attempts to curb student autonomy. Throughout the 1940s and '50s, the organised student movement clashes with the *Estado Novo* several times on issues of self-governance, notably in 1957 against Ordnance 40 900, which is intended to strip the student associations of their independence and power by replacing them with a state-sanctioned alternative. The demonstration against Ordnance 40 900, held outside the National Assembly and by all accounts peaceful, is nevertheless attacked by police – a rare instance of a state crackdown on the children of Portugal's 'elite'. In another rarity for the regime, the ordnance is never discussed or passed on the Assembly floor, leaving the status of student associations in a legal limbo exploited by both students and state.

In 1962 the periodic unrest in the centre of the student movement turns into a full-blown academic crisis. Between 1957 and 1962 the politics of the student associations veer away from the strict concerns of the association membership and autonomy, to broader discussions of the purpose and nature of education, access to it and its democratisation. The associations also feel the need to broaden links between universities, organising events and panels around Students' Day. In response to the student body's increasing itch for educational reform, the government tries to prohibit the first ever National Meeting of Students, set for 9 March 1962 – buses set to take students from Lisbon and Porto to the meeting in Coimbra are intercepted by the police and stopped. The meeting, now considerably smaller, still goes ahead, and the government orders a disciplinary process against the organisers, a small portent of things to come. The 1962 Students' Day events are scheduled for 24–26 March in Lisbon, and the regime once again puts in a banning order, stuffing the associated universities with uniformed police and arresting and beating students linked to its organisation. The student association response is to call a meeting, attended by thousands of students, and to declare a period of 'academic mourning' – essentially academic strike action – until the Students' Day events are resumed, and all imprisoned students are released. This is a clear shift within the organised student bodies to a more militant syndicalism. Students occupy the grounds of the University Stadium, filling the campus of Lisbon University with crowds and banners. The minister of education meets with a student delegation and agrees to reschedule the Students' Day events to 7–8 April.

This, it turns out, is just a delaying tactic. On 5 April the government declares that, not having received the proposed schedule of Students' Day events, the planned meetings cannot go ahead. Marcelo Caetano, rector of the University of Lisbon, resigns, despite a private direct appeal from Salazar himself. The regime links the student unrest with infiltration by the PCP, a pretext for a violent crackdown on the silent march the outraged students take through Lisbon streets to the Ministry of Education. The students resume their academic strike, and the following months are ones of tense escalation. Hoping to distance itself from accusations of communist influence, the Lisbon association votes to pause the academic strike around 1 May. For the government, 1 May sees the clamour of student protest replaced with workers' mobilisations, violently repressed on the streets of the major cities by police shock troops. In Lisbon, the workers gather in Terreiro do Paço and march north, hurling rocks as the police charge in with horses and batons and gunfire. The clashes carry on through the night, leading to one death and several injuries. Student militancy ramps up again on 9 May when, in solidarity with another legal crackdown in Coimbra, the Lisbon plenary announces a return to academic mourning – and a hunger strike. Hundreds of students occupy the canteen at the heart of Lisbon University campus, standing in solidarity with several dozen of their colleagues who refuse to eat. The canteen becomes the nexus of the protests, a convivial atmosphere punctuated by the singing of protest songs that carries on into the night. Outside, the police circle the building, but it isn't until the early hours of the 11th that the canteen is raided and the students are ushered away for interrogation and imprisonment. The academic crisis carries on until early June, when the student associations announce an exam strike. A demonstration aimed at freeing the student prisoners outside the Faculty of Medicine is again brutally repressed by the police, who bring out a water cannon to disperse the gathered students and sympathetic staff. Lindley Cintra, deacon of the Faculty of Letters, is one of the first to be injured in the scuffle. The increased and constant repression and the looming academic repercussions lead the student associations to abandon the exam strike. Despite sporadic additional arrests and clashes with the police over the summer months, the academic crisis appears to die out with the end of the academic year, followed by legislation aimed at further curbing the power and autonomy of student associations.[9]

The government's response to the student activism, however, has a powerful and lasting effect on those who experienced it, and is the tipping point in turning vast swathes of the student body against the regime. Over the following years, that increased radicalisation leads to more student activity and repression, in an escalating cycle that coincides with the ever-worsening colonial war. A second academic crisis emerges in 1968 and 1969, this time localised in Coimbra but with a burst of activity in Lisbon as well – echoing similar young revolutionary movements kicking off across Europe. Over time the tenor of activism begins to veer towards direct – and violent – action. Portugal's most influential Maoist groupings, the Popular Action Front (*Frente de Acção Popular*, FAP) in 1963 and the Re-organised Movement of the Party of the Proletariat (*Movimento Reorganizativo do Partido do Proletariado*, MRPP) in 1970, owe their origins to the student mobilisations (the former as an active split from the PCP). Isabel do Carmo, a PCP activist heavily involved in the student strike movement as a medical student, goes on to be a founding member of the Revolutionary Brigades (*Brigadas Revolucionárias*, BR) in 1970, a group also unafraid to make use of violent tactics.

These shifts in the nature of the regime's opposition mean that, when Salazar, the focus of the opposition's ire, suffers a brain haemorrhage in 1968, his successor Marcelo Caetano enters into an arena where the clandestine movements are more primed

71

against the regime than ever before. Caetano tries to bring the opposition onside by presenting himself as a liberal reformist, a break with Salazar that turns out to be more of a branding exercise than any meaningful change to the state's authoritarian tendencies. PIDE, for example, is renamed the Directorate-General of Security (*Direcção Geral de Segurança*, DGS), and Salazar's National Unity organisation is renamed People's National Action (*Acção Nacional Popular*, ANP), but neither organisation fundamentally changes. The few liberalisations Caetano does manage to push through his entrenched, reactionary Assembly have the opposite effect to what is intended. For example, legislation lightening the state's control over the trade unions, allowing their leaders to be elected without ministerial approval, spurs some of the most intense periods of strikes and labour mobilisation since the fall of the First Republic. Slight liberalisations of the censorship laws generate a black market of Marxist texts, which make their way into student circles and fuel their radicalisation.

The 1969 legislative election sees the democratic opposition putting Marcelo's platitudes to the test. The liberalisation of the election process leads to the emergence of the Portuguese Democratic Movement (*Movimento Democrático Português*, MDP), which runs a joint campaign with the Democratic Electoral Commission (*Comissão Democrática Eleitoral*, CDE), backed by large swathes of the vibrant student movement. The promised liberalisations are revealed to be a fiction in the unfolding of the campaign – MDP/CDE members are hounded and at times physically attacked by PIDE/DGS and the Portuguese Legion, and the stifling restrictions on the electoral roll mean the MDP opposition fails to make a dent in the entrenched Assembly. From within the ANP, however, a new tendency emerges, humbly, in the post-1969 Assembly: the 'Liberal Wing' of the ANP – deputies not so radical that they would be treading the lines of the traditional opposition, but who are tolerated as novelties in the Marceline Spring. The Liberal Wing will make up a modest thirty seats in the Assembly, and spend the next several years trying to push the regime into more radical reforms from within.

The high Catholic moralism of the Portuguese state had prevented anything close to a 'sexual' or 'feminist' movement from emerging openly within Portuguese society. In 1968 an outbreak of student protests at the Superior Technical Institute (*Instituto Superior Técnico*, IST) had declared, among other things, a 'sexual revolution'[10] – an indication that, perhaps late in the global context, at least among the youth the moralist grip of the state was beginning to slip. One of the more dramatic confrontations of Marcelo Caetano's tenure is the case of the Three Marias, which manages to cause waves across the international community. In 1972 Maria Isabel Barreno, Maria Teresa Horta and Maria Velho da Costa, in a window of more lax censorship, publish *Novas Cartas Portuguesas* (New Portuguese Letters, or *The Three Marias* as it appears in English translations). *Novas Cartas Portuguesas* is hard to classify – it flits between poetry, essays, letters and fragments, but these combine to paint a harsh picture of the Portuguese woman under the *Estado Novo*, reflecting on the brutality of the regime and the Church, and the female condition in Portugal. It is almost immediately banned – described as 'immoral' and 'pornographic' by the state censors – and the Three Marias are arrested, placed on trial at Boa Hora Tribunal and sentenced to prison. The resulting wave of condemnation from international feminist movements, which includes protests outside Portuguese embassies in places like New York, adds another uncomfortable layer to the international scrutiny Portugal is already under.

The main target of that scrutiny, however, is something the Portuguese state can't seem to end or escape from, something that saps more and more of the state's resources and manpower in what seems like a perpetual nightmare on three fronts: the colonial war.

General António Spínola (*second from left*) on a visit to troops in Farim, northern Guinea. Behind the general is Captain Vasco Lourenço, in dark sunglasses and light uniform, sometime between 1969 and 1971.

CHAPTER FOUR

COLONIAL WAR

On the corner of Avenida Duque de Avila and Rua de Dona Estifânia, an unassuming building in light yellow juts towards the road. It's distinguished from its surroundings only by a round marble plaque buried in the pavement, bearing a five-pointed star. Four smaller black stone stars sit alongside it, an unfamiliar constellation etched into the cobbles. Placed here in 1992, it's the worse for wear – cracks course through the marble. Along its circumference the stone reads:

1943 HOUSE OF THE STUDENTS OF THE
EMPIRE 1965
HOMAGE FROM THE CITY OF LISBON

In the 1940s, Portugal's colonial holdings lack universities. Students from Angola, Mozambique, Portuguese Guinea, Cape Verde and Timor with the will and means to pursue a higher education need to do so on the mainland. Far from home, usually only part of a modest contingent of African students in their universities, the youths who travel to Portugal for education congregate naturally along national lines. These groupings create, in Lisbon, the institutions of Angola House, Mozambique House and Cape Verde House, homes and hubs for African students to find each other.[1] The government, fearful that such groupings might foment nationalisms, moves to merge the various Houses into one that can be better managed and surveilled by the state. In 1944, Angola House is converted into the House of the Students of the Empire (*Casa dos Estudantes do Império*, CEI), a move fully sanctioned by the colonies minister. The regime hopes that the Portuguese Youth can have an ideological influence inside the CEI, intending for its members to be vessels that take the ideas of the *Estado Novo* home with them, as evangelists for colonial rule.

It's almost comical how spectacularly this plan backfires. The first elections for a management committee within the CEI replace the organisers closely tied to the regime, and the new committee institutes an open, democratic environment. The atmosphere within the CEI for these students starkly contrasts with the stifling political atmosphere in Portugal at large. Rather than imposing the values of the *Estado Novo*, the CEI gives these students a glimpse of another world, of the vibrant possibilities of free debate, democracy and autonomy. As with other student associations, the CEI's independence makes it ripe for infiltration by dissident organisations such as the youth wing of the MUD (MUD-J) and the Communist Party, with which many CEI members find common political cause. With these various elements in the mix come the usual aspects of state surveillance, repression, arrest and interrogation, which only serve to further radicalise the supposed children of the Empire against it. The CEI becomes a crucible for anti-colonial thought, debated and developed by many of the figures who go on to become leading lights in the resistance movements of the colonies – and establishing, through their friendship and collaboration, a deeper understanding of their shared struggle.[2] Among these are Amílcar Cabral, António Agostinho Neto, Samora Machel and Marcelino dos Santos. Between 1952 and 1957, the CEI is forcibly taken over by the state and put under the direct administration of the Portuguese Youth, and after a return of autonomy and radical activity after 1957 it is, eventually, closed down by the regime in 1965. By this time, however, the damage is done – the colonial war is well under way, and the regime's main opponents abroad had spent years sharpening their minds right under Salazar's nose.

The thread of communist thought is undeniable in the foundation of the major African independence movements that formally emerge in the 1950s and early 1960s. In Angola, the People's Movement for the Liberation of Angola (*Movimento Popular de Libertação de Angola*, MPLA) is founded in 1956 as a union of various existing liberation movements, as well as the Angolan Communist Party (*Partido Comunista Angolano*, PCA). The MPLA is the left, Soviet-aligned side of the independence movement, operating a politically uneasy united front with the Christian nationalist Union of Peoples of Angola (*União dos Povos de Angola*, UPA, later National Front for the Liberation of Angola, FNLA).* That same year in Portuguese Guinea, Amílcar Cabral is among those who establish the African Party for the Independence of Guinea and Cape Verde (*Partido Africano para a Independência da Guiné e Cabo Verde*, PAIGC), also with a Marxist–Leninist foundation. The PAIGC's initial strategy is one of peaceful resistance. In 1959, sailors and stevedores in the Port of Bissau begin a strike for better pay and working conditions, during which PIDE agents and other armed Portuguese units open fire on the demonstrators, killing at least forty. This event, known as the Pidjiguiti Massacre, both garners a surge of support for the independence movement in Guinea and causes the PAIGC to change tack, adopting the principles of armed resistance. Together the MPLA and PAIGC form the Conference of Nationalist Organisations of the Portuguese Colonies (*Conferência das Organizações Nacionalistas das Colónias Portuguesas*, CONCP) in

---

* These are both joined in 1966 by the National Union for the Total Independence of Angola (*União Nacional Para a Independência Total de Angola*, UNITA), which will complete the triumvirate of parties vying for power in the Angolan theatre of war.

1961, bringing in a precursor to the Liberation Front of Mozambique (*Frente de Libertação de Moçambique*, FRELIMO) and the Movement for the Liberation of São Tomé and Príncipe (*Movimento de Libertação de São Tomé e Príncipe*, MLSTP). The names and faces will change over the long colonial war, but these groups set the tone for the struggle in Portuguese Africa.

Meanwhile in Europe, throughout the 1950s, the nature of the military changes. The Second World War leaves a devastating wound across the face of the continent, one that will yet take years to heal. Before 1945, a career in the military was a sign of prestige – an acceptable and even sought-after path for a child of the aristocracy or bourgeoisie, the comparatively paltry wages of an officer seen as a small sacrifice to uphold a legacy of honour and duty. Now the upper classes have different futures in mind for their children, ones which are less likely to lead to premature death – more and more of what would have once been enthusiastic military officers are deviated to jobs managing the empires of capital, becoming heirs to shops and factories, agricultural estates and cattle farms. Portugal, despite coming out of the war unscathed relative to its European neighbours, experiences this internal shift in its Army, a shift that leaves a vacuum to be filled, for the first time, with an influx of young men from working-class families.[3] For them, a career in the military is a way up the social ladder, a route to better opportunities, and a steady wage which, while not amazing, at least allows for a few drinks at the weekend and eventually an adequate state pension on which to retire. Scores of young men are drawn to the four-year officer courses at the Army School (later renamed the Military Academy), and take pride in the uniform. With Portugal having recently become a founding member of NATO, many of the new recruits have the privilege of being stationed in multinational bases across Europe and the world, giving them a first glimpse of what life is like outside of a suffocating dictatorship.

One of this new crop of young working-class men is Otelo Saraiva de Carvalho. Otelo is born in Lourenço Marques,* capital of the Portuguese colony of Mozambique. He is the middle child of immigrants – his father from Lisbon and his mother from Goa. His mother's love of theatre is what gives him the name Otelo, after Shakespeare's Moor of Venice, and as a young man his dream is to seek a theatre career in his paternal grandfather's footsteps, setting his sights on training at The Actors Studio in New York. His father is strongly against this idea, and refuses to finance the trip, ultimately derailing the young Otelo's theatrical dreams. It's his maternal grandfather that convinces Otelo to pursue training as a military officer. He sets out for the Army School in Lisbon in 1955, and despite the assessment from his brief compulsory stint in the Portuguese Youth that he has 'no aptitude for military service', adapts quickly to army life. It's in Lisbon that Otelo has his first significant brush with the opposition – a cousin, already integrated with the democratic opposition, invites Otelo to a dinner with prominent republicans including António Sérgio, an event Otelo finds thrilling. Like most in Portugal, he follows Humberto Delgado's campaign with interest and enthusiasm, witnessing the violence on José Fontana square during Delgado's address in Liceu Camões from his girlfriend's apartment window. Even within the Army School the consensus among Otelo's colleagues is that Delgado was robbed. Late-night discussions in hushed tones express awe and displeasure at how brazenly the state machine crushed a democratic opponent. The following year one of Otelo's professors, Major Pastor Fernandes, is arrested for his involvement in the 'See Coup' and deported to Timor, shocking and further radicalising Otelo and his fellow cadets. Otelo has barely a few months at the end of his officer training before he is sent off to war.

* Now Maputo.

THE CARNATION REVOLUTION

On 4 January 1961, workers employed by the Portuguese-Belgian cotton company COTONANG in Baixa do Cassanje, Angola, begin industrial action demanding better working conditions. Over the following month, the strike spreads and escalates in intensity and violence. The Portuguese military responds with the indiscriminate aerial bombardment of twenty villages in the region, followed by a ground assault that leaves thousands dead. In the Angolan capital of Luanda, while the city is packed with journalists from the international press hoping to see the eventual arrival of Henrique Galvão's hijacked *Santa Maria*, insurgents backed by the MPLA carry out raids on police barracks and São Paulo prison, killing several police. Riots and escalating tensions ensue, with white vigilante groups responding with generalised violence in Luanda's slums. The tipping point comes in March, when thousands of UPA militants sweep through northern Angola, carrying out a brutal massacre of the civilian population and razing infrastructure, a wild and unexpected assault that leaves thousands dead and a panicked, fleeing population in its wake. Military units are deployed from Portugal almost immediately, and the Angolan highlands become the first front in the Portuguese colonial war.

Back in Lisbon, the government's response to the escalating situation in Angola turns out to be the catalyst for mounting frustration among the top brass of the Portuguese military. Having been assigned the position of minister of defence in 1958, General Júlio Botelho Moniz has spent the last three years pushing for serious reforms within the armed forces, which he and several of his colleagues agree are hopelessly old-fashioned and outdated. This perspective, common among a particular generation of senior officers, stems in part from time spent stationed in the US and on NATO bases abroad, where the structure and particularly the efficiency of those other militaries leave a mark on the Portuguese visitors. In 1959 a plan for the reorganisation of the overseas military is approved, aiming to make it 'more adequate for a subversive war' – but financial limitations and the grinding bureaucracy of the Portuguese state means those reforms are never actually put into practice. Lieutenant Colonel Francisco da Costa Gomes, subsecretary of state of the Army, believes that the reforms are necessary to avoid a war – and the events in early 1961 certainly make that argument convincing. By then it's clear to Botelho Moniz and his allies that a large-scale military operation in Angola is not tenable – not simply because the military isn't properly equipped, but also in light of the changing international political climate surrounding colonial policy. This is not a war the armed forces want to fight. Moreover, the military strategy is part and parcel of a political strategy – and Botelho Moniz believes that the political strategy must change. At a lunch meeting with US ambassador to Portugal Charles Elbrick, the ambassador warns the general of the US's changing policy regarding Portugal's colonies, and of a need for Portugal to express willingness to concede autonomy to those territories 'at some indeterminate future' point. Botelho Moniz replies by laying out some threads of his own thoughts on the issue, admitting to the necessity for political change in a government with a broad base of support and 'drastic reforms' in the overseas policy, with the overseas territories granted autonomy 'in a relationship like the [British] Commonwealth'.

This line of thought from Botelho Moniz articulates a particular perspective shared by a faction in the upper echelons of the military – one of a gentle military withdrawal, resolving tensions with the independence movements through political means. The other side of the coin is the approach favoured by a larger faction, and pushed most aggressively by General Kaúlza de Arriaga – that of rapid, overpowering, all-out military escalation, starting with the immediate deployment of ten thousand troops from Portugal to Angola. These factions collide in a 1960 meeting of the Council of National Defence, Generals Botelho

Moniz and Costa Gomes clashing verbally with Kaúlza de Arriaga, and Salazar in the background, monitoring the discussion mutely. In late February of 1961, Botelho Moniz writes to Salazar expressing his deep concerns around the 'gravity of the current international political moment' and calling an escalation of the war a 'suicide mission'. Salazar agrees to meet with the general at the end of March, on two separate days – but other factions hold the dictator's ear, and he ends those discussions clearly unconvinced. Botelho Moniz then tries to persuade President Américo Tomás to take action – and of the need to immediately remove the intransigent Salazar from office. Tomás is also unmoved. Moniz's follow-up plan is to threaten the president with a military takeover of the government. The general begins to mobilise his own contacts, consolidating the units loyal to him and his allies. Behind the scenes of power, Salazar's own allies scramble to his aid, with Kaúlza de Arriaga among those briefing against Moniz behind closed doors. At a second meeting, Botelho Moniz and Colonel Almeida Fernandes confront the president once again, this time putting forward an implied ultimatum – sack Salazar, or the military rebels. Tomás replies with some confidence that neither the Air Force, the Navy nor the Army feel that is the appropriate solution. Two days later, on 13 April, Kaúlza de Arriaga urges Tomás and Salazar to dismiss Botelho Moniz, Almeida Fernandes, Costa Gomes and General Beleza Ferraz from their posts, otherwise both heads of the government would likely be imprisoned, or the country would be facing a civil war. Shortly afterwards, Botelho Moniz receives his letter of dismissal. Moniz is undeterred – he sets off for a planned afternoon meeting with his factional allies, intending to kick off a rebellion.

Anticipating that Moniz would try to go ahead with a planned coup, the government also makes a public radio announcement about the high-profile sackings – publicly severing the chain of command. When Moniz arrives at the site of the meeting, in the Palace of Cova da Moura north-west of Lisbon at 17:00, most of the senior military men he's expecting have been dissuaded from coming. The few who are there defer to the official military chain of command, and agree that attempting a military operation with the government on such high alert, and without the backing of so many military branches, is foolish. Botelho Moniz's *Abrilada* (April Revolt) ends with the moderate faction within the Portuguese military decapitated, leaving a void rapidly filled by Kaúlza de Arriaga and his allies, and setting the tone for Portugal's response on the ground in Africa. When Salazar receives General Arriaga on the evening of the 13th, the dictator remarks that the general looks tired. Kaúlza replies that he had slept little the last few nights. Salazar retorts: 'It's natural, you gentlemen are out there conspiring.'

Otelo Saraiva de Carvalho departs for Angola in June of 1961, part of a contingent that arrives in Luanda expecting an immediate skirmish with terrorists, wild animals or both – but finding only a modest African capital, the heart of the war localised hundreds of kilometres north. The brutality of the Portuguese war effort is made immediately apparent to Otelo – a briefing from headquarters is disseminated, ordering the troops to cut off the heads of the enemy's dead after any upcoming skirmish and to place them on sticks: the display would serve as a warning to the other 'terrorists'. Otelo is repulsed by this order and categorically refuses to follow it, but is urged to pass the option on to his platoon. To his surprise and horror, when he looks for volunteers among his own men he finds that the majority of the soldiers put their hands up enthusiastically – gripped, he realises later, by *Estado Novo* propaganda of a crusade against the enemies of the Homeland. Otelo is an oddity among the overseas combatants – his service weapon is often carried unloaded, as he prefers to de-escalate volatile situations with his words – and he will come to the end of his first commission without firing a shot. In his base in rural Angola, Otelo is surrounded by subtle and less subtle examples of military brutality and excess from both sides of the conflict, from the flinches and averted eyes of the Angolan civilians who fled the UPA's bloody atrocities to the debilitating scars carried by others wantonly tortured by the Portuguese in search of intel against the 'terrorists'. The new crop of soldiers and officers, many of whom had never left Portugal, let alone visited Africa, are seeing the multifaceted reality of Portuguese colonialism, marked as it is by racism, sexism, cruelty and institutional corruption. They struggle to reconcile what they've been told about the local population; framed as savages in a savage land, they turn out to be nothing of the sort, but rather people just like them. Despite the *Estado Novo*'s best efforts, the state propaganda about the colonies begins to chip away, bit by bit.

Over the course of the following year the skirmishes with the UPA and the MPLA in Angola continue and escalate, and the regime commits more units and resources to the conflict. The counterinsurgency campaign within one particular sector of the north Angolan jungle is led by a figure that, among the Portuguese troops, is soon whispered about in awed tones throughout the barracks and military bases. Lieutenant Colonel António de Spínola is fifty-one years old, and leads the men of the 345th Cavalry Battalion like a figure brought to life from the silver screen. His eccentricities are what mark him out – never seen without his cane, lambskin gloves and monocle, he launches into battle at the head of every assault with a vigour that belies his age, an age that nevertheless brands him with the nickname *O Velho*: 'The Old One'. Spínola is a polarising figure – he has a reputation for quick and harsh punishment, and carries out what Otelo terms a 'war of luxury'.[4] Never denied resources, Spínola's vehicle battalion is kitted with special armour and his offensives are backed by helicopter support, granting him an impressive record

84

on the battlefield and the undying respect of his men. His legend has a dark underside too: he is capable of staggering cruelty. Rumours circulate about him shooting, at point-blank range, a local porter who had refused to carry a heavy load of equipment on a mission, the man's load shared out among the remaining terrified crew. A severely injured woman, found by Otelo on the side of the road and later discovered to have been left for dead by Portuguese forces, is shot and buried in the woods on Spínola's orders. Otelo begins to distrust the man.

In December 1961, the Portuguese regime receives the first major blow to its colonial project. In a thirty-six-hour shock campaign, an overwhelming military force launched by Nehru's government occupies the Portuguese Indian territories, neutralising the Portuguese resistance instantly. This isn't a repeat of the storied Battle of Cochin centuries ago – the Portuguese forces are massively outnumbered and completely overwhelmed, and they lose decisively. Goa, Daman and Diu are comprehensively annexed. As late as 1960 Salazar had urged Governor General Manuel António Vassalo e Silva to hold the Indian territories to the last man should it come to a conflict – an order that the governor general is incapable of following when the time comes. On Vassalo e Silva's return to Portugal he is brutally chastised and court-martialled, expelled from the military and exiled. The loss of India casts a pall not only over the regime, but over the armed forces as well – the treatment of the governor general feels like the government is using the military as a scapegoat for its own failings. Vassalo e Silva had lost his career simply for refusing to send his men to die in an impossible situation.

Punctuating the end of an *annus horriblis* for Salazar's regime, on New Year's Eve of 1961 the civilian and military vestiges of the 'See Coup' return, this time in the southern city of Beja. A group of civilians, led by the opposition figure Manuel Serra and the young artillery captain João Varela Gomes, congregate on the outskirts of Beja in the early hours of 1962. Their plan is to take control of the Third Infantry Regiment (*Regimento de Infantaria 3*, RI3), and from there lead a military campaign into the south of the country, building up forces to confront the regime. The revolutionary unit, comprising six officers and roughly two dozen civilians, approaches RI3 in torrential rain. The officers, forming an advance party, manage to convert some of RI3 to their cause, but they are told that notorious regime loyalist Major Henrique Calapez da Silva Martins is spending the night there. Varela Gomes decides that Calapez needs to be arrested and makes his way to the major's room. Calapez quickly realises that something is wrong – he leaves his room wielding two pistols and opens fire. Varela Gomes is hit; the rebel officers make a hasty retreat. The wounded captain is bundled into a car and rushed to a hospital.

Meanwhile, Manuel Serra leads his band of civilians over RI3's fence. After Serra is told what happened to Varela Gomes, the priority becomes neutralising Calapez. The civilians launch themselves through the unfamiliar corridors of RI3's main building, but Calapez is ready for them. After a chaotic gunfight, in which two civilians die, Calapez disappears into the darkness. Unable to find the major, Serra calls off the revolt at six in the morning, by which point Calapez has contacted the police. Over the next few weeks, many of the participants are rounded up and locked away by PIDE, including an injured but alive Varela Gomes. One man who evades PIDE – twice – is General Humberto Delgado. Delgado had entered Portugal under a false identity in order to lead the rebellion that the Beja revolt would spark. Seeing it fail from afar, he swiftly leaves the country again. But as the colonial war carries on, the thinly spread collection of officers critical of the regime remains in the military – and their ideas, percolating in officers' messes, will influence the men of Otelo's generation.[5]

*

In January 1963, having started a campaign of military sabotage the previous year, the PAIGC attacks a Portuguese military garrison in the Guinean province of Tite, and Amílcar Cabral declares war. Portugal is now facing a conflict on two fronts in West Africa, but back in the capital it's not even acknowledged as a war – just the vile actions of insurgents under orders from Moscow, soon to be crushed under the heel of the Portuguese Army. Otelo returns to Lisbon from his first tour of duty in August, his company given a hero's welcome. Having gone to war with some sympathies for the opposition, Otelo arrives home convinced of the ardent need to put an end to the dictatorship. Not fully grasping their motivations before, he now comprehends why military officers threw their careers away in the coup attempts of the last decade. He finds his sentiments reflected in his chats with old friends from the Military Academy, long nights of quiet conversations mulling over the possibilities of a military-led coup – but the conditions, they think, are not yet right. In September 1964, FRELIMO launch a first offensive in the north of Mozambique, and extend Portugal's problems to a third and final theatre of war. And in April 1965, two Spanish teenagers walking a dog find the body of Humberto Delgado, the opposition's 'fearless general', dead for months in the hills near Villanueva del Fresno, his death an obvious political assassination that sends a shiver through Europe.

Portugal's war machine continues to ramp up throughout the 1960s, and with it a steady influx of increasingly young officers and soldiers – all men. When women appear in the theatres of war, they do so only as part of medical staff or as the wives of officers brought over to remain by their husbands. In 1966, 22-year-old Fernando Salgueiro Maia, fresh from the Practical Cavalry School in Santarém, arrives in Mozambique as an ensign and is put to work with the 9th Commando Company, 'The Ghosts', in the northern province of Mueda. Maia is from the first generation of officers to really experience the impact of the war at home – the typically four-year course is shortened to three years by cancelling nine months of summer holidays as the regime scrambles to fill the growing vacancies in the officer ranks. He proves himself immediately: the absence of some superior officers and an undeniable display of talent lands him command of a detachment, an unheard of position for an ensign straight out of officer school. Maia is a born leader – amiable, charming and fearless, he quickly earns the respect of his fellow officers and the conscripted men he commands. He arrives in Mozambique convinced of his patriotic duties to defend the nation. In Maia's eyes, the condemnation Portugal receives from the wider world is driven by envy, and motivated by Cold War machinations. And yet on his first day in Lourenço Marques, he's faced with a troubling reality. Entering a café, he overhears a white Portuguese colonist loudly complaining that his son has been drafted into the military.

'Aren't there any more soldiers in Portugal to come and fight?' the man cries, lamenting that his son is no longer available to 'look after the blacks'. 'Looking after the blacks' seems to be the main concern in Mozambique, where the Portuguese colonial and segregationist politics most resemble those of South Africa. That's in the capital though – in the north, where the fighting is concentrated, the subtle nuances of colonial race politics are overshadowed by the barbarism of war.

The situation in Mueda is intense, so much so that it gains a reputation as 'the biggest hellhole in Mozambique' – the constant jungle skirmishes cause regular losses and almost daily amputations. The Portuguese forces in Mozambique are less well equipped than their FRELIMO opponents for a prolonged jungle war, the independence fighters receiving military support and training from the Soviet bloc. Even in the Portuguese bases the conditions are tough – the rations are repetitive and unappetising, going off quickly in the heat, and standard niceties like mosquito nets have to be bought out of the men's own pockets. Some soldiers start swapping their rations of sardines with the tinned dog food, hoping to give the dogs a bit more energy in the sweltering heat, and are grateful for the variety.[6] It becomes swiftly apparent that there is a deep gulf in knowledge and experience between the officers carrying out missions in the jungle and the ones issuing orders from the safety of command posts and headquarters, whose training sees them applying the tactics of conventional warfare in an insurgent guerrilla context, with disastrous results. No one is a greater target of disdain, however, than the generals and commanding officers back in Portugal, whose advanced age and attachment to military pomp lands them with the nickname 'Rheumatic Brigade'. A combination of bureaucratic cowardice and the drive for career advancement means the reports that make their way to the upper levels of military command in the capital always have the same tone – that the war is going well, that victory is imminent, that all the war effort needs is another small push of men and armaments to finally tip the scales once and for all. The men on the front lines begin to fear the orders of their detached superiors more than the enemy's bullets. The disillusionment among the soldiers and junior officers gradually turns to anger with the regime as a whole, in contrast with the friendship and camaraderie the men experience among themselves, a deep trust that allows them, thousands of miles from home, to share thoughts of change. PIDE/DGS and its informers are still a reality in the colonies and among the military, but that close-knit friendship means the officers' mess becomes a relative sanctuary for free-flowing conversation. In 1968, in the midst of a bitter conversation with his colleagues on the failures of the government and the need for a revolution back home, Maia manifests an idea – 'Me, commanding a squadron of armoured cars down the Avenida da Liberdade... that ought to be pretty.'

Salgueiro Maia returns home from his first tour in Africa in the winter of 1968, dropped unceremoniously in the capital and left shivering in the cold. It's five years after Otelo was received as a hero from his first tour in Angola, and the tone of the reception for men returning from the war has changed, become muted. Maia is struck by the indifference to the war he senses from his countrymen, the complete lack of interest or understanding of what's happening overseas, aided inevitably by a national propaganda machine intent on selling the idea that everything is going well. Hoping to broaden his own understanding of the world and politics, Maia signs up for a Politics and Social Sciences course at the University of Lisbon for the 1969 academic year. His time in academia is short-lived – 1969 sees another bout of protests and academic mourning from the student body, with which Maia stands in solidarity, and he barely manages to attend any classes. In 1970 António de Oliveira Salazar dies, having spent two years out of the public eye, his advisors leading him to believe he still has control over the nation. Later that year Salgueiro Maia receives his promotion to captain, and both he and Otelo Carvalho are separately deployed to Portuguese Guinea, to carry on a war that has now been raging for nine years.

The Portuguese war effort in Guinea has been the brainchild of António de Spínola since 1968, newly promoted to brigadier general and granted the title of commander-in-chief of the armed forces in Guinea by Salazar himself, one of the dictator's final acts as leader. Spínola is the brightest rising star in the Portuguese military, driven by an unquenchable personal ambition. Otelo is now on his third tour of duty and is granted an air-conditioned posting as head of Broadcasting and Media in the Bureau of Civil Affairs and Psychological Action. At the military headquarters in Guinea, he sees first-hand the effect Spínola has on the enlisted men on the front lines. The Old One, resplendent in his monocle, lambskin gloves and cane, commands the battlefields of Guinea with equal parts respect and fear. Otelo, speaking fluent English and French, ends up as the primary liaison for elements of the international press who come to Bissau to report on the war, and becomes intimately familiar with both how the *Estado Novo* seeks to present itself to the outside world and how carefully Spínola crafts his own propaganda. In 1970, Spínola's strategy in Guinea is what might be in modern terms referred to as 'nation-building' – as well as facing off against PAIGC insurgents along the outer edges of the country, the Portuguese military in Guinea organises the construction of roads and schools, investing in infrastructure that increases the quality of life of ordinary Guinean people with the goal of painting the Portuguese as the 'good guys' and turning more of the local population against the PAIGC – or at least, preventing them from taking up arms. Amílcar Cabral, leading the PAIGC insurgency from bases in neighbouring Senegal and the Republic of Guinea, refers to Spínola arriving in Guinea 'with a smile, and blood in his teeth'. In Angola, General Francisco da Costa Gomes employs a parallel political strategy, striking deals with guerrillas more amenable to the Portuguese Army against the threat of the MPLA.

This stands in contrast to the strategy employed by the Portuguese in Mozambique after 1970, under the command of Kaúlza de Arriaga. Arriaga's first major act as commander-in-chief of the armed forces in Mozambique is to put into practice his own personal war philosophy through an incursion into FRELIMO territory, christened Operation Gordian Knot. The operation begins on 1 July – the same day that Agostinho Neto, Amílcar Cabral and Marcelino dos Santos are at the Vatican on an official visit, representing the independence struggles in Portuguese Africa and appealing for aid from the Pope and the international Catholic community. Gordian Knot is the largest operation in the war, making use of eight thousand soldiers (40% of the Portuguese forces in Mozambique) alongside air and Navy support, followed by an intense radio and leaflet propaganda campaign. The military captures multiple FRELIMO bases in northern Mozambique and scatters the resistance – briefly. In the aftermath, the military spins the operation as a great success, but the reality is much more nuanced. Arriaga's mistake is, as General Costa Gomes remarks afterwards, 'the application of concepts of classic warfare to a subversive war'. The effect of scattering the guerrilla fighters doesn't fundamentally change the FRELIMO presence in Mozambique – the command structures remain intact, and the resistance forces use the lessons learned in the wake of the operation to sharpen their tactics. Far from being the clean solution to the Mozambique problem, Gordian Knot entrenches the conflict, hardens the resistance, solves nothing.[7] It contributes to notions, held by Spínola in Guinea and Costa Gomes in Angola, that a purely military response to the war, without a political underpinning, cannot work.

In Guinea, the PAIGC combines its guerrilla tactics with a sophisticated propaganda campaign, aimed at both the Guinean population and the Portuguese Army. In the form of typed pamphlets and radio appeals, the party makes a clear distinction between the soldiers fighting on the African front and the Portuguese regime that sent them there, with a Marxist bent arguing that the Portuguese soldiers have more in common with the guerrillas on the other side than with the rich capitalists who sent them there to die. The campaign is effective – defections from the front-line Portuguese Army are regular occurrences, which the PAIGC incorporates into their propaganda. One such pamphlet, telling the story of three soldiers who surrendered to the PAIGC and were evacuated to 'a country of their choice', bears the title 'FREE! FREE FROM THE CRIMINAL COLONIAL WAR! FREE!', followed by a statement underlining that the PAIGC isn't fighting 'against the Portuguese people, Portuguese individuals or Portuguese families', but 'Portuguese colonial domination'. The PAIGC's propaganda meets a receptive audience on the Portuguese side, in part due to the regime's increasingly desperate attempts to send men to the front lines. Since 1967, conscription laws see the soldier pool draw more and more youth from the increasingly politicised student population, some of whom arrive in Africa as fellow travellers or members of organisations with detailed plans for anti-war agitation within the military.[8]

In his role at the Guinean military headquarters, Otelo Carvalho comes across a copy of an English edition of Amílcar Cabral's book *Revolution in Guinea – An African People's Struggle* which, among a collection of Cabral's essays, contains the political programme of the PAIGC. The book has an indelible effect on Otelo – he finds in it a deep clarity of thought and expression, follows Cabral's arguments for a free, independent, democratic Guinea, and is convinced. He makes the effort to find, in Bissau, the PAIGC's former president, Rafael Barbosa, fresh from an eight-year stretch in a colonial prison and freed, though still under constant watch, by Spínola. Otelo and Barbosa strike up a friendship, Otelo aware of but indifferent to the fact that his regular visits to Barbosa's hut will be made note of by PIDE/DGS. The two men discuss the PAIGC and politics, and Otelo deepens his own understanding of his supposed enemies. Across the Portuguese colonies, officers experience shifts, moments that change them, where the war ceases to make sense. For Captain Vasco Lourenço, that moment happens nine months into his two-year stint in Guinea, stationed barely a kilometre from the Senegalese border. Leading a detachment on a patrol mission, Lourenço's convoy is attacked by a PAIGC ambush. The men ahead of and behind the captain are killed, among them a member of the local militia – but Lourenço escapes unscathed. Sometime later he uncovers a PAIGC informant network operating within that same militia, a network that had been feeding the PAIGC information about the Portuguese Army's movements in the Guinean jungle. One of those informers, he discovers, had died in the ambush. The informer had known that by feeding information to the PAIGC, he was likely putting his own life at risk – and he had done it anyway. Lourenço realises that the Portuguese aren't going to win this war. His men have no business being there.[9]

Along the outer edges of Portuguese Guinea, in spite of Spínola's meticulous war plans, the conflict worsens. The PAIGC are vastly outnumbered by the Portuguese Army, but the numerical disadvantage appears to be their only one. Portuguese Guinea is surrounded by PAIGC bases contained within Senegal and the Republic of Guinea, from which the guerrillas terrorise Portuguese camps with rockets and mortars acquired from the USSR. The roads into the countryside are riddled with mines, and any incursion into contested territory is agonisingly slow as the soldiers move by inches along the gravel, gingerly poking metal rods into the ground and listening out for the telltale sound of metal on metal that usually indicates another one of the enemy's deadly surprises. The *Chaimite* – the colonial war's iconic squat armoured vehicle, workhorse of the cavalry – is as likely to turn into a fiery metal grave as it is to provide protection. Salgueiro Maia is one of the thousands whose days are spent like this, in the blistering heat and suffering relentless insect bites, long days of tedium punctuated by explosions, dismemberment, death. The nights are spent drinking to forget, the air filled with popular folk songs with lyrics adapted to the soldiers' own situation. Among the repertoire is music by José 'Zeca' Afonso, an activist singer and poet whose songs, largely banned by the regime, have been taken up as anthems of the resistance in Portugal. In Guinea, Afonso's '*Os Vampiros*', written in 1963 as an anti-capitalist ballad, is edited to refer to the senior officer class as the titular vampires, who 'only complain, and don't do anything'. Maia is spotted one evening joining in with a spirited rendition of Afonso's classic and is disciplined, a rare mark in an otherwise impeccable record.

Back in Portugal, Marcelo Caetano's limited reforms fail to quell the growing unrest among the population. The resistance to the regime and the war hits a new tenor when several of the radical left organisations that sprang up in the late '60s and early '70s begin to put their ideas of violent resistance into practice. The country is rocked by bombings of ships bound for Africa, airbases and bureaucratic institutions, organised by the Revolutionary Brigades and the PCP-aligned Armed Revolutionary Action (*Acção Revolucionária Armada*, ARA). Among the plethora of new organisations undertaking direct action against the regime is the Unity and Revolutionary Action League (*Liga de União e Acção Revolucionária*, LUAR), a group formed by many of the perpetrators of the hijacking of TAP 114 and led by Hermínio da Palma Inácio himself. LUAR makes a grand entrance on the scene by robbing the Bank of Portugal in the town of Figueira da Foz, proclaiming in printed missives that it intends to use the captured funds 'For the liberation of the people' and sparking a continent-wide chase led by PIDE/DGS and Interpol.[10] The various attacks add another dent to the already stretched infrastructure of the colonial war – but it's not all explosions and bank robberies. In July of 1972, following another of the regime's sham elections in which Admiral Américo Tomás is elected president for the third time (and unopposed for the second), the Revolutionary Brigades dress two pigs in admirals' uniforms and release them in Lisbon, one in Rossio and the other in Alcântara. The pigs are oiled and the police, unable to hold on to the slippery swine, resort to gunning them down in the street. BR follow the stunt by setting off petards loaded with pamphlets decrying the elections in Portugal as a 'mockery': 'Besides that, Tomás's election is filth.* Hence the pigs, symbols of Tomás and the pigs who elected him.'

Even in civil society, the regime faces increasing pushback from elements traditionally aligned with its politics. On 30 December 1972, a group of Catholic activists and their allies, among them

---

* 'Filth' in this case is a translation of *porcaria*, which works better as a pig-based pun.

government civil servants, occupy Rato Chapel, a modest building south of Parque Eduardo VII. The assembled group pass a motion condemning the 'criminal war, with which [the government] tries to annihilate colonial liberation movements', and denounces 'the complicity of the Catholic Church hierarchy' with regards to the war. The vigil lasts just over a day, some of the gathered going on hunger strike, until a brigade of police shock troops force their way into the chapel and end the occupation. As a gesture to the religious significance of the building, the officers remove their riot helmets as they enter, before leading the assembled protestors into vans and carting them off to prison. Unbeknownst to the gathered protestors, two weeks prior to the occupation, Portuguese forces led by PIDE/DGS agents had orchestrated an operation that massacred hundreds of civilians in the Wiriyamu region of northern Mozambique, an unrepentant bloodbath of men, women and children. The military escalation continues unabated. And in January of 1973, Amílcar Cabral is shot and killed at point-blank range by members of his own party in front of his home in the Republic of Guinea.

In April 1973, Otelo and his colleagues stationed across Africa discover the government has called a Congress of Overseas Combatants, set for early June in Porto, ostensibly to discuss the war effort. Looking over the published details, the officers see that the Congress is sanctioned by the highest levels of the military – which can't possibly be a good sign. A large part of the organising committee is made up of former militia officers who had done their compulsory two-year duty in the war in the early '60s and had, largely, returned to civilian life. There is hardly any representation from permanent staff officers – people like Otelo Carvalho, Vasco Lourenço and Salgueiro Maia, for whom military service is a career, and who had faced multiple deployments to the African front lines. The Congress is an obvious attempt by the regime to add credibility to its war policy by showing the armed forces as being its 'enthusiastic adherents' – something that, in early 1973, couldn't be further from the truth. News of the conference spreads throughout Guinea, and the discontent among the permanent staff officers percolates, making its way to Spínola and back to Portugal. The Guinean officers assemble a delegation to send to the conference, intending to disrupt the proceedings and present a different, more accurate perspective from the front lines – but the Guinean group is denied attendance, as are any other permanent staff officers. In Lisbon, Majors Ramalho Eanes and Hugo dos Santos, along with Captain Vasco Lourenço, begin organising a protest movement around the Congress. As part of this effort, the officers in Guinea put together a document, which after an intense two-day hunt for signatures garners the support of four hundred men. The telegram ultimately sent to the Congress reads:

> Roughly four hundred permanent staff officers and overseas combatants with various campaign service commissions, certain of interpreting the feelings of hundreds of other comrades that, for various reasons, are unaware of the Congress, wish to inform Your Excellencies and the Nation as to the following:
>
> 1. Not accepting values nor defending interests other than those of the Nation;
> 2. Not recognising that the organisers of the '1st Congress of Overseas Combatants', and therefore the 'Congress', contain the necessary representation;
> 3. Not participating in the works of the Congress, and not allowing that through their lack of participation, positions or attitudes might be broadly attributed to the combatants;
>
> For all the above-mentioned reasons declare themselves oblivious to the conclusions of the Congress, regardless of their content or expression.

The telegram is signed by Captain Alberto Rebordão de Brito and Sergeant Marcelino de Mata, two officers chosen for having previously received high status commendations and medals, granting them a certain amount of clout. The congress ignores the letter, and goes ahead undeterred. Its conclusions, as expected, do not challenge the *Estado Novo*'s stated military aims. In the hundreds of signatures gathered in outrage, however, is a first real glimpse at the scale of discontent among the junior officer ranks – and a crucial document from which those disaffected officers can continue to recognise each other, and organise.

Salgueiro Maia reaches the end of his tour of duty in May 1973. He and his unit are still at a border base, killing time waiting for the order that will send them home. One morning he hears gunfire in the distance, and through the radio he hears the strangled appeals for air support and evacuation from a unit trapped under heavy fire. The base commander orders the reserve unit out on the evacuation mission. The reserves refuse. Maia volunteers himself and his men, hopping onto a truck and leading a convoy into the dense jungle. The seven-kilometre journey takes them an hour and a half, and they arrive to see a landscape of carnage and pale, shell-shocked faces. Maia stops the first soldier he sees and asks after the wounded – a man who 'looks like a big kid that they shoved into too large a uniform', who waves Maia to a pile of bodies. Five men, horrifically injured and still bleeding, given the barest of medical aid. None of the sixty soldiers under fire knew how to tie a tourniquet, and the air is thick with the smell of blood. Maia and his team do the best they can, staunching the bleeding and speaking soft reassurances to the wounded. The foliage and the enemy fire are too dense for a helicopter. By the time they liaise with the ambulance unit, away from the heat of battle, the men in the back of the truck are already corpses. Maia contemplates the bodies – unbelievably young, their faces frozen in a look of shock, like they don't understand what's happened to them, why they are here. He removes their shoes, wets and closes their eyes, crosses their arms over their chests, does his best to give them dignity in death. Maia doesn't understand what's happened to them either, why they're here. At this moment he only understands sorrow, and rage.[11]

The reward Maia and his unit receive for their bravery is a phone call from Bissau on 22 May, telling them that their deployment back to Portugal has been delayed – they are required for another mission. Guidage, an area right on the Senegalese border, was hit by a devastating PAIGC attack that also managed to take down three Portuguese planes with ground-to-air missiles. Maia's mission is to help evacuate the Portuguese units still under siege in Guidage. When he asks why his unit is being sent, when their current tour is technically over, he's told there's nobody else – command had to choose from units at the end of their deployment, and Maia's has one of the best military records. The journey to Guidage is harsh, the mined roads forcing the armoured convoy into the dense jungle, their progress periodically halted by ambushes and bombs. The month of May sees the death of ninety Portuguese soldiers. Salgueiro Maia and his men return to Bissau over a month later – what was meant to be a six-day mission turned into a forty-day odyssey, and they arrive wild-eyed, unshaven, with their uniforms rotting off their skin. Meant to return home in May, Maia finally makes it back to Portugal in October of 1973. By then, the network of disgruntled officers that had been loosely brought together by the Congress of Overseas Combatants is flourishing into something new, and Maia is more eager than ever to get stuck in with his comrades. In the 1950s, Portugal exported revolutionaries, radicalised under its nose, back to their homes in the colonies. Over two decades later, the colonies pay back the favour: now the Homeland's soldiers return dreaming of a revolution.

Soldiers, officers and civilians in Terreiro do Paço celebrate following the withdrawal of government troops, 25 April 1974.

PART TWO

OPERATION HISTORIC TURN

Be careful with the captains. They are dangerous, given they're not yet old enough to be bought.

Marcelo Caetano, 1974

DESENHO DO CARIMBO QUE REPRESENTA O
TEMPLO DE DIANA EM ÉVORA

A drawing of a stamp, commissioned by Captain Dinís de Almeida of
the Temple of Diana in Évora, developed in order to authenticate
documents from the Movement of Captains, but never used, 1973.

CHAPTER FIVE

A CONSPIRACY
OF CAPTAINS

When the Galeto snack bar and restaurant was first inaugurated in 1966, its white and red neon signs were a beacon for the upwardly mobile, modern families of Lisbon. Its interior walls glitter with brass studs, reflecting the dim, intimate lighting. Its counters are long and narrow, the patrons pressed up against one another as the waiting staff shuffle professionally in the gaps, mixing cocktails and ferrying fried chicken and club sandwiches. It becomes a Lisbon institution as soon as it opens – 'the most beautiful and modern snack bar in Europe' croons an advertisement – and its doors experience a thrum of customers twenty hours a day. It's a place where you can easily blend into the crowd, and where the perpetual music and chatter can mask a delicate conversation.

It's May of 1973, and Captain Eduardo Dinis de Almeida is meeting an old friend in Galeto's smoky haze.[1] He and Captain Curto don't see each other often – their assignments never line up, and they've maintained a friendship through a chain of accidental bump-ins and meet-ups. Now that both are in Lisbon – Curto between deployments, Almeida still recovering from two broken arms and an evacuation from Mozambique – Almeida is keen to gauge his friend's interest in something that's bubbling away behind the scenes.

Almeida starts subtly. 'We've got to change this.' Curto's reply is a smile, not taking the bait. Almeida pushes further – 'We have a small group working…'

'For what? To solve nothing?' Curto replies quickly – 'This all stays the same!'

'It doesn't!' Almeida fires back. 'Do you want to be part of our group? Of a little group we've set up?' Leaning forward, Almeida's tone becomes conspiratorial. 'We're organising to solve the situation.'

Curto doesn't bite, and the conversation quickly changes subject. The two men part ways after a few drinks, Almeida in a funk – this was his first failed attempt at expanding his network. Others will prove more fruitful.

If by the start of 1970 the junior officers in the armed forces are tired of the war, by 1973 that exhaustion has been sharpened to a fine edge, and officers' messes across the armed forces are alive with whispered disgruntlement, rage and conspiracy. Many of those whispers are, for now, the half-hearted blowing off of steam. Almeida first comes across such a conversation in the officers' mess bar at the Santa Clara base in northern Lisbon, where Lieutenant Colonel Pastor Fernandes, the elderly and nearly blind veteran of the failed 'See Coup', surrounds himself nightly with sympathetic allies to complain about the regime and discuss what is to be done in hushed tones. This is the first time Almeida hears a superior officer speak ill of the regime, and speak of democracy as a tangible alternative. Pastor Fernandes' evening bar meetings don't lead anywhere and don't ever feel like they will, but the campaign against the Congress of Overseas Combatants is the spark that pushes some of those disgruntled officers to take the first steps of collective action – and to some that first taste of light rebellion, of pushback against the *Estado Novo*'s stifling presence, is intoxicating. That's the 'little group' Almeida refers to in his meeting at Galeto – and at this stage, there are several 'little groups' forming across the country and the colonies, keen to take action. Those groups don't have to wait long before new circumstances arise that they can organise around.

In 1973 the war has been raging in Africa for twelve years, and the Portuguese armed forces are wearing thin. Salgueiro Maia being called back into action at the end of his deployment is just one sign of a system coming apart at the seams. In the Military Academy, the number of students enrolled in the training for full-time staff officers is just over 14% of the available slots, a void of over four hundred students the regime desperately needs to maintain the overseas war effort. An internal study finds that, should trends continue, by 1977 the vacancies in staff officers will reach 1,200, effectively half of the total officer contingent. The regime, blinded to any options other than the continued war, needs to fill out those numbers. The solution it comes up with is Ordnance 353/73, published 13 July 1973. The timing of the ordnance is no accident – the government saves its more unpopular legislation for the summer months, when the vast majority of people (permanent staff officers included) request their holidays in order to make the most of the beach weather. It takes a little while, then, for the full blow of the regime's legal machinations to reverberate across the Army – the branch of the armed forces affected by the laws.

Portugal's need to plumb the depths of its manpower to feed the war machine means that, since 1961, a conscription system has been in place, pushing the vast majority of young men hitting the age of twenty into a two-year mandatory stint in the Army and thus into the thick of the war. In 1971 the conscription age is lowered to eighteen – and by 1973 a significant majority of Portugal's male population of 'recruitable' age is fighting overseas. A proportion of that conscripted stock is put through a short officer training course and allowed, for the duration of their two-year service, to hold officer rank and command a company. Many of these militia officers are held in some degree of contempt by the full-time staff officers, not having undergone the full four-year training and not having initially chosen the military as a career. Their relationship to the war is different by default, being able to return home after their two- (or, later, three-) year service rather than thrown, repeatedly, into the relentless meat grinder the African front has become for the majority of full-time officers in the Portuguese military. It's militia officers that make up the bulk of those addressing the Congress of Overseas Combatants – their return to civilian life means pushing the argument for continuing the war effort, under the guise of 'not betraying the Fatherland', is easier. As the war progresses and the officer stock depletes, those conscripted officers who had done their duty in the early to mid-'60s and returned to civilian life are occasionally called back in to fill the vacancies, after another short training course. Some are made to do so ten years after their initial conscription, when they are handed the rank of captain and sent, terrified, unprepared and unwilling, into the front to command a platoon of forty men in the African bush.

Ordnance 353/73 addresses staff officer vacancies by allowing militia officers (those already with the rank of captain and under the age of thirty-one) to undertake an intensive two-semester course, followed by a six-month placement in the practical school of their respective field (infantry, artillery or cavalry) which, if passed successfully, grants them the status of permanent staff officer. Moreover, the transition to the permanent staff has the potential of coming with a considerable promotion based on seniority – whereas militia officers can reach a maximum rank of captain, a militia officer with a long enough service record in the field or time since their last deployment could undergo the intensive course and come out having jumped to the rank of major or even lieutenant colonel. It's easy to see how this could provoke discontent. Salgueiro Maia, who took six years to make captain, and Lourenço, who took eight, could end up taking orders from a major whose qualifications include having spent a decade in civilian life.

The Congress of Overseas Combatants and its clear political bent shook up the sections of the armed forces opposed to prolonging the war. Ordnance 353/73 manages to anger the whole of the junior officer class – but the responses are staggered as news percolates across the various sections of the Army. By the time Otelo and the contingent in Bissau hear of the proposed legislation it's already August and the defence minister, Sá Viana Rebelo, is already on the back foot. Numerous officer branches have sent strongly worded letters to the government opposing the ordnance. The first, issued by officers in the Institute for Higher Military Studies, comes out on 17 July, focusing primarily on the issue of full-time staff officers being overtaken in rank – but this isn't, for Otelo and many of his comrades, the principal issue with the legislation. The ability for a militia officer to take a rapid two-semester course and acquire the same status and rights as an officer who had undergone the full four-year course (which is generally regarded as being equivalent to a higher education diploma) has the effect of massively devaluing the latter, and causes an unacceptable dilution of the status of the whole officer class, and the prestige of the armed forces as a whole. The war is a source of perpetual mounting frustration among the officers, a growing powder keg of resentment – this legislation might be the kick needed to propel that resentment into real action.

Minister Sá Viana Rebelo makes a statement on 14 August addressing some of the raised concerns and 'unforeseen effects' of the legislation, promising that the Council of Ministers had already approved an updated ordnance that would be far better received by the staff officers. This is revealed on 22 August – Ordnance 409/73. This new document is a mildly edited version of the previous ordnance, with new wording that prevents majors from being overtaken in rank by any retrained militia officers. The crux of the law, the accelerated and compressed training of officers, remains the same – as do the staff officers' objections. Rebelo's speech, however, shows the regime's hand: the captains' pushback has already caused a backtrack, a real rarity for the typically intransigent government. The officers have power. In Bissau, two dozen officers meet in the games room of the Military Club to discuss the ordnance, and agree that a small committee should go away and draft a letter expressing the Guinea group's disagreement with the proposed law. They meet again a week later to discuss the letter – and when the time comes to determine how it should be signed, the tension in the room is palpable, the dawning realisation that the men in the room are about to take a public stance against the regime causing a few to balk. On the other end of the spectrum, however, is Captain Jorge Golias, who raises his voice against the more timid officers in the room. 'We're wasting too much time thinking about and discussing the contents of the document and the way to send it, when we should be preparing for armed revolution – what matters is putting down the regime, and that's only achievable with a fight.'[2]

The tension in the room increases at Golias' outburst, panicked glances exchanged between captains unused to this degree of open dissent. The meeting concludes with an agreed wording for the letter, and an elected commission made up of officers still early in their Guinea commission so as to allow a degree of continuity. Otelo is tasked with typing up the document and gathering signatures, which leads him on a chase around Bissau to catch as many staff officers as possible – he even makes a stop at the airport to intercept a captain at the end of his commission and on his way back to Portugal, knowing each name adds to the weight of the message. The letter makes its way out of Bissau on 7 September, copied and posted separately to the defence minister, the secretary of state for the Army, the president and Marcelo

Caetano himself, bearing forty-five names,* a large majority of the Guinea-based junior staff officers.

In Lisbon, military headquarters and barracks fill up with circulating pamphlets that begin to show the clear divide between militia and staff officers, with the former's documents denouncing the latter's objections as a 'conservative minority' of wreckers who simply don't understand the advantages of the new laws. The staff officers first brought together to oppose the Congress of Overseas Combatants find a new banner to organise around. There is a sense that this sort of government overstep is exactly what the officers more inclined to rebellion have been waiting for – an opportunity to coalesce the various gripes simmering under the surface into an active fighting force for something more, even if that something remains left unsaid, hovering on the peripheries of conversation like a glittering jewel of possibility. When Dinis de Almeida first hears of the new laws he carries the news like a gift, offering it in hushed conversations to trusted fellow officers, keen to discuss the next steps, anxiously hoping the others see the potential he sees. When he informs Pastor Fernandes of the law, the elderly lieutenant colonel remarks that the junior officers have already committed a crime in the eyes of the state – the crime of being too few.

Almeida is introduced to Captain Vasco Lourenço after one of these conversations, and they recognise in each other an interest that goes beyond self-preservation or careerism – a shared interest in changing the country's political future. They hold a small meeting in Almeida's quarters, in the *Depósito dos Indisponíveis* – a building in the Lisbon quarter of Graça occupied by officers who, for various reasons, are unavailable for action. There are five of

---

* In his recollections after the fact, Otelo claims the document contained fifty-one signatures, but the copy archived by Dinis de Almeida contains only forty-five.

them there – Almeida, Lourenço, and Captains Bicho Beatriz, Lopes Camilo and Rosário Simões, each taking a shift keeping watch by the door so the other four can converse in safety. There is unanimous support for holding a much larger meeting – the question is where. Almeida suggests a homestead rented out by his family in the countryside near the northern city of Évora and it quickly becomes the only viable option, because of its size and seclusion. Lourenço, as the most senior officer in the group, takes charge of organising, and Almeida sets off to get his family's permission to hold a large, illegal meeting on their land.

That conversation doesn't go as expected. Approaching the relevant in-law – an elderly republican with an anti-fascist track record – the reply is quick and jovial: 'I'll only lend it if it's for a revolution!'

'We have a problem with an ordnance...' Almeida replies timidly.

'Ordnance nothing! Only for a revolution! These are fascists and we have to put an end to them!'[3]

Almeida gets the permission without making too many promises. The captains meet again a few days later, making plans for keeping the exact meeting location secret and producing a detailed map that will lead attendees to the right place from the agreed meeting point – the Temple of Diana, an imposing Roman ruin in the centre of Évora. Vasco Lourenço is tasked with standing by his car, which has its bonnet open, as though he's doing some minor repairs on the engine. To anyone who hasn't already been given directions to the meeting, Vasco is the contact in the field with the maps, checking IDs. Attendees are warned not to congregate in groups too large, and to travel separately. There is a serious concern for operational security – as much as the meeting is ostensibly to discuss the new legislation and the captains' responses to it, what they are doing is verging on conspiracy against the government and the military hierarchy, a punishable offence should they be outed. Despite their military status preventing them from suffering the same brutal incarceration and interrogation as civilians, the shadow of PIDE/DGS and its vast spiders' web of informants still looms over them. They come up with a plausible-sounding reason for the gathering – it's nothing more than a countryside barbecue, to say goodbye to one of their own being sent back into the war – a flimsy story considering how many officers are regularly deployed and redeployed to Africa, but good enough. Standing by his car at 13:00 on the dot, Vasco Lourenço almost laughs at the crowd of young men with close-cropped hair he can see meandering around the Roman temple, in groups of three or four, in an awkward pantomime of pretending not to know each other.[4] Dinis de Almeida makes his way around numerous butchers, buying up supplies for the meeting, concerned that even a particularly large purchase of meat from one place might arouse suspicion.

On the afternoon of 9 September, over 140 junior officers, none ranking higher than captain and the majority in their twenties, congregate in the Sobral homestead near Alcaçovas, led there from Évora by a stencilled map. Due to security concerns, and the likelihood that they would be targeted first should the meeting go south, the few majors already involved (such as Hugo dos Santos, instrumental in gathering signatures against the Congress) are not invited to the meeting. As a result of this restriction, the Movement of Captains is born. They hide their cars behind a long house and hold the meeting in a barn filled with dusty farm tools, having arranged a rotating fifteen-minute sentry. There are three broad groups present – the largest is made up of officers angry at the ordnances, propelled to take some form of action by the imminent dilution of their status in the military. These officers bring friends and comrades who, while perhaps not yet entirely committed to the cause, are at least prepared to give the event a hearing and keen for an excuse to socialise. Finally, there's the group around Vasco Lourenço and Dinis de Almeida, men who see this as an opportunity to perhaps push for something beyond military prestige, to challenge the war and even the regime itself.[5]

The meeting starts off simply, the gathered officers electing delegates from each military branch into an organising committee, and agreeing to protect each other in case any of the attendees is harassed for participating in the meeting, a protection that extends to Almeida's family and the owners of the land. They also agree to carry out the meeting to its conclusion, touching on all of the proposed discussion points, even if the barn is surrounded by the police or any other antagonistic forces. The crux of the meeting is touched on next, after a short break where the assembled participants smoke and share out snacks and drinks. They declare themselves unanimously opposed to the published ordnances – even the solitary militia officer who had somehow made his way into the room. The order of the day, around which everyone in this barn can gather, is the destruction of the prestige of the armed forces. The question is what the response should be. The proposals bouncing around the room range from organising an officer strike, to a large demonstration of protest in a Lisbon square, to a strongly worded letter signed by the attendees. The more radical options are met with shock and murmurs – the letter, the most moderate option, is the one chosen, drafted and signed by 136 of those present with the intention of delivering it the very next day. The letter outlines in clear terms the disgust of the staff officer class, and the issues that Ordnance 409/73 (despite the defence minister's insistence) doesn't solve. More important than the letter, however, are the connections – as the main meeting carries on into the evening, groups form spontaneously along the edges of the building, whispering and exchanging details. Along with the delegate structure, these liaisons are the building blocks of the Movement going forward. The gathered officers depart at the end of the night, leaving Almeida and a few others to clean up. They pick their way around the homestead into the early hours, intent on not leaving any trace that the meeting or even anything non-farming related had happened there, filling bags with the discarded cigarette butts of a hundred career officers. When PIDE/DGS visit the property a few days later, tipped off by an officious senior officer in the local area, they find nothing.[6]

The letter and the number of signatures that come out of the Évora meeting are an undeniable show of force. A summary of the decisions taken is circulated widely among the staff officers in Portugal and an additional 190 signatures are gathered in solidarity with the Évora statement. By this point the letter Otelo posted from Guinea has arrived in Lisbon, shortly followed by letters from Angola and Mozambique – separate statements repudiating the ordnances and the perceived attack on the prestige of the armed forces, as well as pages and pages of additional signatures expressing solidarity with the Évora document. The Movement of Captains begins to gain purchase and support from every corner of the Portuguese military. The appearance of these letters sparks a rash of memos and pamphlets, some from high-ranking military officials restating and clarifying the need for the new laws, met by more memos and missives from angered officers refuting those arguments – mostly anonymous. Given the density of circulating information, the Movement decides to put together a regular bulletin, wary that bad faith actors might start disseminating misinformation in their name. The military hierarchy sends delegations to buildings with high officer density, like the Military Academy, ostensibly to listen to their concerns. Behind the scenes, the regime scrambles for an appropriate response, but the scale of the problem is too big to deal with through the usual methods of military discipline – there are simply too many officers to act against. Moreover, the Movement's sharp focus on operational secrecy means the government is unaware of who the chief instigators are.

Those chief instigators, people like Captain Vasco Lourenço and Major Vítor Alves, elected members of the organising committee, begin the important work of broadening the Movement as much as possible, seeing it as an important structure for future organising. The ordnances affect infantry, artillery and cavalry the most, but it's important to get the other Army sections involved as well. In a small meeting shortly after the Évora plenary, with the goal of bringing in more officers from engineering regiments and discussing the influx of signatures, Vasco Lourenço, for the first time, lays his own views out in front of his trusted comrades.

'We're out here with presentations and signatures, but with this we're not getting anywhere. We need to think about doing a coup, nominate a military junta, last a year, have free elections and then whoever wins those elections runs the country!'

Vítor Alves starts picking holes in this immediately. 'Where are you getting generals for a military junta?'

'Look, you haven't got generals, you haven't got brigadiers, you haven't got colonels, you haven't got lieutenant colonels, you might not have majors, but I guarantee I can find you captains!'

'And you think you're capable enough to belong to a military junta?'

'Why not? So I'm here suggesting we topple the government, do a military coup, and you think I'm afraid to go into a military junta?'

'You're crazy!' barks Vítor Alves, and the conversation comes to a quick end.[7] But Lourenço's position, rarely expressed so frankly, is one percolating through the minds of many of the more actively involved in the birth of the Captains' Movement.

Otelo Saraiva de Carvalho returns to Lisbon on 16 September, keen to dive headfirst into the Movement of Captains. He's lucky to land a role as assistant professor of artillery tactics in the

Military Academy – in the heart of Lisbon, and in the eye of the brewing storm he and his comrades seem to have started. His contacts already integrated into the Movement introduce Otelo to Dinis de Almeida, whose youthful enthusiasm he finds infectious. They hear through the grapevine that General Costa Gomes, already in good standing among the captains, has approached Marcelo Caetano expressing objections to the ordnances and had pushed the prime minister to make noises about 'taking a clear position' in a few weeks. They also receive word of a bold new salvo from Angola – those at a meeting of the Movement branch in Luanda decide to threaten mass resignations from their officer posts should the ordnances be enacted. The flurry of activity prompts the Movement's organising committee to call another meeting on 6 October, this time held in four locations simultaneously to avoid too large a gathering. The locations are captains' houses, spread across the Greater Lisbon area, each chosen for having a working landline telephone. There are four agreed-upon options for discussion:

A – Collectively put forward letters of resignation (as the branch in Angola had done).

B – Collectively take a leave of absence from service and quarters.

C – Cease performing any functions but remain quartered.

D – Use of force.

The discussions carry on deep into the night, the pros and cons of each option mulled over in tedious detail. Option D is discounted by all four meetings relatively quickly – it would certainly solve the issue of the ordnances, but there is no broad base of support for such a move. Option C, the de facto officer strike, similar to the proposal made at the Évora meeting, begins to slowly make its way to the top of the list. Vasco Lourenço is adamant this is a bad call – he's convinced the Movement needs to organise further before that sort of public protest can be attempted, otherwise it would be like 'trying to stop a runaway train by colliding with it headfirst'.[8] Taking matters into his own hands, Lourenço calls each of the other houses to see what their discussion is leaning towards. All the other groups also seem to lean towards option C. Lourenço lies to each – 'Well, see if you can hurry up and make a decision – we've already gone for option A on this end.'[9] Lourenço's call pushes the other groups to reassess option A, and as exhaustion begins to set in across the parties, eventually the four meetings consent to Lourenço's line.

The following day in Captain Rodrigo Sousa e Castro's house, the Movement further formalises its organising structure, preparing for the serious administrative task ahead. A form is drafted and distributed widely, laying out the required phrasing for the officers to sign, but leave undated, and return to the Coordinating Committee. The document permits the Movement to date the signed documents and submit them to the government should the demands – the complete repeal of Ordnances 353/73 and 409/73 – not be met. Those demands are also communicated to the heads of the military. The organising committee begins receiving hundreds of signed letters of resignation, which are kept in a safe Major Hugo dos Santos buys for the express purpose of holding on to them. This, as Vasco Lourenço will come to say, is the 'nuclear option'[10] – the mass resignation of officers, particularly the types of officers most commonly on the very front lines of combat, would completely paralyse the Portuguese Army and the war, a route the government cannot countenance. On 12 October, the Army minister suspends the application of the ordnances and orders an investigative commission to decide what further steps to take – a delay rather than a total repeal, but still a significant step forward for the captains.

The Army minister's backtrack causes a split within the Movement's leadership. A more moderate faction, headed by Captain Mariz Fernandes (with connections to General Costa Gomes), sees the concessions as sufficient and begins to make noises about winding down the Movement activity, in a show of good faith. The more radical faction of Vasco Lourenço, Otelo Carvalho and Dinis de Almeida, always intending to use the ordnances as a springboard to organise their officer comrades to greater ambitions, disagrees. There is still enough energy and enthusiasm, under the banner of armed forces prestige, to keep the Movement going, even as its original *raisons d'être* begin to recede through their successes. The erosion of prestige might seem a strange prime mover for a subversive movement. But in Portugal, officers feel embarrassed when they walk down the streets in uniform, frequently subject to civilians haranguing them about the poor course of the war. Restoring their status in the eyes of the population is the live issue that the Movement seeks to harness. As the coordinating meetings continue, the internal politics of the Army begin to bleed through in their interactions – Otelo is regularly pulled aside and told that certain other officers are 'dangerous communists'[11] or, alternatively, working with the chiefs of staff to undermine and destroy the Movement. There are various degrees of politicisation, of ambitions and objectives, and the leadership fight to hold together the alliance they've so carefully assembled. There is an escalating paranoia over who can be trusted, and how to guarantee that the Movement's information bulletins aren't intercepted and copied – Almeida goes as far as to design a stamp with an embossed drawing of the Temple of Diana that they can use to authenticate their messages, but the idea is ultimately dropped.

Wary of the factions forming in the Movement, Almeida seeks out Mariz Fernandes in the Army's Cartography Unit. Fernandes had at various points raised objections to Almeida's tone and presence at meetings, and Almeida hopes to smooth things over. They have an amicable chat, joined by Captain Albuquerque Gonçalves. Feeling confident, Almeida tries pushing a little further.

'We have to stay united; if we are, we might start aiming higher...'

Gonçalves interjects – 'Well, I won't be there if you do. Not that I don't agree, I just don't feel able to.' Pause. 'But I won't be the one to dissuade you from going further. If you feel capable, go. Carry on as far as you can.'

Emboldened, Almeida returns to the seemingly endless piles of correspondence with the ever-expanding branches of the Movement. He is also particularly concerned with the recent spate of violence from elements of the police. The legislative elections, held in October, had led to the usual resurgence of state violence against opposition meetings, various brutal crackdowns that showed beyond a doubt that Caetano had returned to his predecessor's ways of conducting business with his political opponents. Various captains had been caught in the violence, at times specifically targeted, the police saying 'it's captains we're after, you lot are out causing trouble' after the attacked had identified themselves. Almeida has put together a dossier on police violence he hopes to disseminate among his comrades. It seems the eye of state repression is slowly turning on to the Movement.

The Movement's coordination group, taking explicit pains to disseminate as much information as possible and liaise as much as possible with as many officers as possible in the furthest reaches of the Army, is by necessity made up only of men based in Lisbon.

Their meetings are held in the privacy of the most trusted captains' houses, mostly in the suburbs of Greater Lisbon in the parishes west of the city, a slew of homes linked by the train line that follows the river and then the ocean, from Cais do Sodré to Cascais. In the early hours, driving back from a meeting at Dinis de Almeida's house in northern Lisbon towards Estoril, in Vasco Lourenço's car, Otelo turns to his comrade.

'Vasco, suppose that, more or less in the short term, the government retreats, and all the objectives with which we started this fight are achieved, with the repeal of the ordnances, which is possible. Do you think the Movement will fall apart?'

'I have no idea, but my view is it shouldn't,' Lourenço replies. 'There are a lot more issues that can be addressed if we keep up the pressure, that otherwise wouldn't be. What do you think?'

'Like most or all of the other guys, I don't know anything about politics. But ever since I was an officer, my ambition has been to be an active participant in an action that will topple this government. Even if we don't quite know what to do next. It would be marvellous if the conditions are being created to make that happen, and for the honour and historic destiny of taking down the dictatorship and completely change the way things are in this country to fall to our generation.'[12]

Vasco Lourenço glances over at his comrade. 'I don't know if we're going to get that far. Look how hard it is to move beyond just professional concerns. But either way I agree with you, and I'm on that path myself. Have been for a while. I hope we get there.'

The Movement committee decides to open invitations out beyond the junior officers, confident that there are people in the upper ranks who share their views and perspectives for change. They're right. A meeting on 24 November, in a family home behind the children's swimming club *O Século* in Estoril,* has the honour of being for the first time graced with the presence of two lieutenant colonels: Otelo's colleague in the Artillery division of the Military Academy, Almiro Canelhas, and Luís Banazol, a senior officer a few weeks away from redeployment to Guinea. Banazol's seniority grants him a place at the head of the meeting, flanked by Majors Hugo dos Santos and Vítor Alves. Even in conspiracy, military hierarchy reigns supreme. The room is scarcely large enough to hold the forty-odd officers convened from every corner of the country. Mariz Fernandes doesn't attend – the shift in tenor of the meetings away from the strict issue of the ordnances pushes the captain away from Movement activity. Before the meeting, a captain ushers Vasco Lourenço outside and opens the boot of his car. Inside is a bazooka and two grenades. Lourenço pales – 'Are you crazy?! What is this?' The captain replies calmly, 'In case anyone turns up to give us trouble.'[13]

Luís Banazol turns out to be the star of the meeting, and not just for his rank. After the meeting's business – discussions of the ordnances, presentations to the minister, signed statements, the floor is handed over to the lieutenant colonel. He launches into a bombastic speech, beginning with the claim that the captains are focused on the wrong thing.

> We are being strangled by a regime that drives us
> directly towards the abyss, to collapse, as all fascist
> regimes have done, notably those of Hitler and
> Mussolini. The whole world looks at us, staff officers, as

* Unbeknownst to the gathered captains, the home had been used by a group of sailors in the late '60s to screen illegal films like *Battleship Potemkin*. On top of that, one of the residents is a LUAR activist who had been arrested by PIDE/DGS in a raid that also captured Palma Inácio two days prior to the meeting.

real agents of Nazism. Agents of the SS. And we cannot in any way avoid that grotesque image if we don't take the initiative of a rehabilitation, a redemption in the eyes of our people and the other peoples of the world, utilising our force to topple the government.

Banazol continues, demanding an end to the colonial war, and the crimes the military commits in Africa. He concludes: 'Don't have any illusions. The government will only leave with gunfire, and the only ones capable of making them leave are us. No one else. If we don't, history will judge us.'[14]

Otelo scans the room for reactions and sees it split. As well as nervous glances, on some faces there is genuine fear, rejection. In others, he sees the glimmer of excitement, the spark that could become a raging fire if given the right fuel. In the wake of the furore following Banazol's speech, Major Vítor Alves tries to calm the room, and asks the attendees to be careful with what they include in their reports back to their units. Banazol is having none of it – his upcoming deployment is his fifth, and the desperation to avoid another trip to the hell of the war has him grasping for his words not to fall on deaf ears. He threatens to take his own unit from Évora and solve the problem himself before the other senior officers talk him down. But his message hasn't been ignored. Like Banazol, the camaraderie shared by the officers means many see this as a safe space for free discussion – Banazol's idea, in the long term, is taken seriously, as are the deeper political questions of democracy and even self-determination for the colonies. After an involved discussion that carries on into the night, the delegate meeting comes away with an agenda for the next gathering, armed with questions for their branches and working towards a new direction for the Movement. The three options put to the various Movement branches are:

A. Conquest of Power, leading to a military junta that can create the conditions for 'true national expression (democratisation)';

B. Legitimising the government through *free* elections supervised by the Army, giving the government the option of having them without armed forces interference, followed by a referendum on the problem of the Overseas Territories;

C. Raising exclusively military issues, with the goal of restoring armed forces prestige and putting enough pressure on the government to achieve option B.

In addition, the branches are to be asked whether the scope of the Movement should extend beyond the Army, what structure the next coordinating committee should take and whether the Movement should seek the support of generals (and if so, which ones). There is a palpable impatience among the organisers – the next meeting is only a week later in a village near the medieval city of Óbidos, the time and location circulated at the last minute and cryptic enough that Otelo and several of his comrades arrive late. Banazol is again at the head of the table, and the room is split between options A and C – the presence of delegates from parachute regiments tips the scales, marginally, for the moderate option. Banazol rages against the decision, another revolutionary tirade that antagonises the portion of the room still unprepared to entertain his vision of military juntas and storming the seats of power. The parachute regiments provide a tense political edge to the meeting – when the discussion turns to getting support from generals, the vast majority of votes go to General Costa Gomes, with a sizeable number going to Spínola in second place. The third name, exclusively backed by the paratroopers, is Kaúlza de Arriaga, the founder of their corps. The view of many of the more active Movement organisers is that

Arriaga is a committed fascist and regime loyalist – his politics, whenever they've been expressed openly, are antithetical to the direction in which the Movement is heading.

Widening the scope of the Movement to branches outside the Army, and the range of supporters to senior officers, turns the Movement of Captains into the Movement of Armed Forces Officers (*Movimento de Oficiais das Forças Armadas*, MOFA),* initially armed with a new delegate structure with representatives from the main Army branches under an Executive Coordinating Committee. At the helm are Majors Otelo Carvalho and Vítor Alves, and Captain Vasco Lourenço. The new committee has some early teething issues. The democratic focus of MOFA means each military section has to be represented as well as possible, so when Major Manuel Monge can't attend on behalf of the cavalry, Major José Rafael Saraiva is quickly found as Monge's replacement and turns up to a meeting presided over for the first time by a colonel: Vasco Gonçalves. Gonçalves is tall, gaunt, his dark hair a jumble that frames a prominent receding hairline, and he peers out at the room through smart black-framed glasses – and he has a tendency, in private, to go on a little too long about Marxism. When the topics of discussion begin to veer towards the political, particularly towards colonial independence, Saraiva stands up in a huff. 'But, this is treason!' he proclaims, 'treason to the Fatherland, in an exceptionally grave time for the nation!' The room quietens, enough for Saraiva to realise the mistake he's made. He glances around in a panic and follows up quickly: 'But rest assured I won't breathe a word of this to anyone, you have my solemn promise...' He backs out of the door and leaves swiftly.

---

* The scattered nature of the communication throughout the organisation's network means this change in branding takes a while to really catch on, and many of its members continue to refer to it as the Movement of Captains, or simply the Movement.

Colonel Gonçalves laughs at the interaction: 'That's my godson! I did think it was odd he was here. He doesn't think like us. But he won't tell anyone, don't worry.'

While the MOFA committee discusses how to implement option C and what issues to continue to raise, the upper levels of the Portuguese military hierarchy are engaged in a conspiracy of their own. Captains Sousa e Castro and Bação de Lemos are approached by Colonel Jacinto Frade Júnior and informed that a military coup is being planned by four generals – Kaúlza de Arriaga, Silvino Silvério Marques, Joaquim Luz Cunha and Henrique Troni. The political leaning of the coup is in line with Arriaga's politics and to be expected from generals decidedly on the right of the armed forces. Seeing the regime struggling to mobilise effectively for the war, the generals intend to take over and instigate a large-scale rearmament of the African divisions, redoubling the philosophy of 'intransigent defence of the Overseas Territories'. Frade Júnior's goal is to bring MOFA on board. This is Arriaga's solution to the loss of armed forces prestige – winning the war by any means necessary, the Gordian Knot mentality. The captains are told that Arriaga had tried to bring General Spínola on board, but the Old One had rebuffed the general, saying: 'If I wanted to organise a coup, I'd do it myself, and I'd have the whole of the Calçada da Ajuda with me.'* That interaction places Spínola in opposition to Arriaga, alongside General Costa Gomes – both of the 'progressive' armed forces heads need to be 'eliminated'.**

The captains, stalling and unwilling to commit support, request a rundown of Arriaga's intended political programme

---

*   Referring to the sizeable cavalry and GNR units in that area of Lisbon, all of whom are loyal to the general.
**   The conspirators never outright suggest physical elimination, but it is heavily implied.

124

for this coup. What they receive instead a few days later, from Frade Júnior, is a report drafted by the general outlining his involvement in stopping the Botelho Moniz conspiracy in 1961, one which frames him as a saviour of the regime and the Empire. The timeline is so short that the captains involved in these liaisons don't have time to consult with the MOFA Coordinating Committee. They know, politically, that they cannot sanction Arriaga's coup and should if anything try and oppose it, especially given the imminent threat of 'eliminating' their closest allies in the upper ranks. There's a serious risk that if troops are mobilised by the four generals, officers out of the loop might believe the action is MOFA-supported and jump headfirst into the action, and their careful conspiring will have been for nought. Vasco Lourenço organises an impromptu meeting with Costa Gomes in the general's office in Lisbon to warn him of the imminent threat of a right-wing coup, but comes away from the meeting dumbstruck at the general's calm, seemingly unperturbed reaction. Lourenço tries again a day later with Spínola, intercepting the old general and inform- ing him of the impending coup and the potential threat to his life. Spínola is also, seemingly, unfazed – the Old One thanks Lourenço for the information and urges the captain to listen to a speech he plans to deliver in January, which he's sure the captains will support. Lourenço's insistence that there is an imminent threat comes to nothing – Spínola makes his way from the meeting with a brisk handshake, leaving Lourenço, again, dumbfounded.

The seeming lack of action pushes Major Carlos Fabião, involved from the beginning in the liaisons, to act decisively. On 17 December, entering an afternoon class in the Institute of Higher Military Studies, in Belém, Fabião addresses the room. He declares that a coup is being planned, naming the four gener- als, with the goal of taking power and eliminating Costa Gomes and Spínola. Fabião declares that the Captains' Movement has no involvement in the action. He may as well have thrown a grenade into the classroom. The room erupts in furious discussion and the class is ended shortly afterwards – but the pronouncement has the desired effect. With the element of surprise gone, and clearly without the support of a large part of the officer base, Arriaga and his fellow conspirators spend the next few weeks backtracking and denying everything. The generals' conspiracy fizzles into nothing, with only a parting blow delivered to Major Fabião for his whistleblowing, reassigning him to quarters in the northern city of Braga. Echoes of the conspiracy continue to reverberate into 1974, with even the BBC running a story on the 'coup that never existed'. The regime feels the pressure tightening, seemingly from every corner at once.

On 22 December, the government publishes new legislation that effectively repeals Ordnances 353/73 and 409/73, reverting access to the permanent staff to officers who had completed 'normal training', through the regular Military Academy courses. A week later, new guidance comes out massively increasing staff officer salaries across the board – the largest pay rise any of the officers have seen in many years. It's a bribe – at least that much is obvious to the MOFA executive. To their surprise, however, the government payout only elicits a few raised voices from the officer base declaring victory and questioning the Movement's need to exist. Focusing energy on to the issue of prestige has struck a chord – and it doesn't take much to convince their colleagues that the ordnances were only a symptom of a greater problem, one that a pay rise also doesn't fix. The new laws also create the role of vice chief of staff of the armed forces, a position, second in the military hierarchy, conjured from thin air almost exclusively to deal with the question of António Spínola. The general had returned from Guinea in early November and spent several months in an administrative limbo while the regime figured out what to do with him. Spínola's highly crafted image, of a respected and effective military man and politician, means the usual route of pushing him into a National Assembly role or a senior post in military academia is likely to ruffle feathers. It's clear to anyone who's paid attention to the general's ascent that his goal is the presidency, but Tomás taking a third term means the second best choice, for now, is to make him the second most powerful military officer in the country. When Spínola takes on the role officially, on 15 January 1974, he delivers the speech he had warned Vasco Lourenço to watch out for one month before. Among the bureaucratic platitudes and thanks, one line in particular stands out: 'The Armed Forces are not the Praetorian Guard of Power.'

It's a line that resonates almost immediately. One day before Spínola's address, in the Vila Pery region of Mozambique, west of Beira and near the Rhodesian border, a family of white farmers is attacked by an armed group, leaving a woman dead. The action sits among a series of FRELIMO incursions into that part of Mozambique, a region that had until recently been largely untouched by the war. Feeling, for the first time, the conflict on its doorstep, the community of Vila Pery shuts down its commercial establishments the next day, demanding that the Portuguese government reinforce the area and guarantee the safety of the colonists. The strike action spreads – soon, there is an effective shutdown all along the train line running from Beira and the coast to the Rhodesian border. That shutdown accompanies a wave of social unrest, targeted at the regime headquarters in Beira – and the armed forces units stationed there. Angry crowds surround the governor's office and the Army officers' mess, hurling insults and even rocks at the building and the officers, the local police powerless to deal with the size of the crowds. The Movement in Lisbon only hears of the events a few days later – the Telex message from their contacts in Mozambique reads:

...The internal contradictions of the system have started to emerge. The flawed and even twisted information the public receives could only lead to this, as we all predicted. It's hard to see how we get out of this with a modicum of dignity. The prestige we've all been fighting for is seriously affected. Urgent measures are required that can only be taken [in Portugal]...

A follow-up message a few days later nails the crux of the problem:

...Our fears of becoming a scapegoat are being realised. We request urgent measures to prevent the continued staining of the armed forces.

A scapegoat for the failures of the regime is precisely what the armed forces in Africa have become. Twelve years on, with the war having grown ever more intense, a Portuguese victory virtually inconceivable, and a political resolution nowhere in sight, the officers on the front lines find themselves powerless to effect any change. Yet the propaganda arm of the state, still incapable of publicly admitting the war is failing, saddles the Army with the population's ire. The Movement sees an opportunity to assert itself. Otelo quickly drafts a document to circulate widely, one that summarises the events in Beira, and the Mozambique detachment's statements, and urges officers to escalate their concerns with their commanders 'with the aim of obtaining, in the shortest time possible, the necessary reparation of an institution that has, for the last twelve years, silently and loyally, carried out its DUTY, and as such feels undeserving of the reactions to faulty INFORMATION.' The regime reacts with fury to the document, but the anonymous nature of the Movement's missives, an ever-present headache for the top brass, means they have no one to act against. With Costa Gomes sent to Mozambique to listen to the local concerns (both from the armed forces officers and the local population), Spínola is left to deal with the missive – and he clearly emerges, for the first time, as a potential ally of the Movement. Calling Vasco Lourenço and Otelo into his office, the old general informs the officers that he'd covered for them when his fellow generals had come to him looking for scalps. He leaves them with a warning about the tenor of future missives – but also, an implied support for their ideas.

There is an undeniable craving for action among the officers, a dangerous energy that, as yet, has no clear outlet. Feeling, finally, in a position to channel that energy, the Movement sails into uncharted waters. Now they don't need to limit themselves to purely military issues; they can confront the political question. It's time to draft a programme.

Plaque commemorating the 5 February 1974 meeting, where the political programme of the MFA was first developed, erected 1999.

CHAPTER SIX

CONFRONTATION

A short walk from the airport, Olivais district in north-east Lisbon is criss-crossed with streets named after officers – captains, ensigns, sergeants and corporals. The trend began in 1963, two years after the start of the war, an homage to some of the men who had died in that first of Salazar's sorties, 'to Angola, rapidly and in force'.[1] The initiative was taken up in other neighbourhoods around the city, but ran out of steam as the war progressed, and was quietly shelved. Hidden among the overgrown shrubbery on 43 Rua Sargento José Paulo dos Santos is a grey marble plaque. Below a sketch of four men in officers' uniforms, flanked by a carnation and the logo of the MFA, is the inscription:

IN THIS LOCATION, ON 5 FEBRUARY 1974
THE CAPTAINS' MOVEMENT MET
CLANDESTINELY TO DISCUSS THE
POLITICAL PROGRAMME TO PRESENT TO
THE PORTUGUESE PEOPLE
ON 25 APRIL 1974

It's the evening of 5 February, and the chill air shimmers in neon light and cigarette smoke. Most of the officers called to attend this one don't know where it is, but most are used to that by now – there is a grudging acceptance that the security measures are necessary. They meet in small groups, in the places that make up the Lisbon nightlife, still bustling on a Tuesday night – Galeto on Avenida da República, the restaurant at the Apolo 70 shopping centre in Campo Pequeno, Mexicana at the foot of Avenida de Roma – each a short walk from each other, each a place to drink, snack and blend into the crowd, their neon signs like secret beacons of the widening conspiracy. Each group meets their contact, shuffles into cars and drives to the home of Colonel Marcelino Marques, on a street named after one of their many fallen comrades. In total, twenty-six men gather in the colonel's large living room, including some new faces. Otelo Carvalho spots a man he has rarely seen since his days at the Military Academy, but whose reputation precedes him: Ernesto Melo Antunes, bespectacled artillery major, an Army man with rare political bona fides. Melo Antunes, closely linked to Humberto Delgado, had tried to run on the opposition ticket in the legislative elections of 1969 and had his candidacy blocked by the military authorities. The major had followed the Movement at arm's length – unlike many of his fellow officers, the focus on military concerns leaves him doubting that this is the sort of project he can get behind. Soon the Movement will change his mind.

Some weeks prior, Captain José Maria Azevedo, another of the more politically minded of the Movement officers, had been tasked with drafting an early pass at a programmatic document. Vasco Lourenço had warned him not to push the political envelope too hard, and stay broadly within the ballpark of the military issues that had brought them together – it wouldn't do to spook the more timid officers in the group too early. When Azevedo brings his document to the meeting on 5 February, however, his deliberately defanged preamble is dismissed by the attendees as too meek to 'shake up the masses' and drive the Movement forward to a real politicisation – a politicisation which, for many in this room, means pushing for democratic reforms and a clear shift in the overseas policy. Azevedo is furious – at one point he tosses his papers into the air and shouts 'I've had enough of you! I tried to do all of that and you wouldn't let me!' before storming out of the room, chased by Vasco Lourenço. Lourenço eventually convinces his embittered comrade to return – in his view, if Azevedo had arrived with a fully composed political manifesto, the officers might have pulled it back too far in the opposite direction. This way, the committee is turned towards more radical ideas fully convinced they've come up with that renewed vigour themselves.[2] A new drafting committee is formed, and Major Melo Antunes, his interest piqued by the tone of the meeting, joins it alongside Azevedo, Lieutenant Colonel Costa Braz and Captain Rodrigo Sousa e Castro.

The Movement isn't the only one working on a political programme. In the weeks since António Spínola had taken up his position in the heady heights of the military structure, rumours had abounded among those in the know that the general had a book on its way, and that its contents were likely to shake up the Portuguese political landscape. Spínola has been essentially untouchable for years – he's one of the most well-known and well-regarded generals of his time, a status that he exploits to stick his head above the parapet and differentiate himself from the Rheumatic Brigade regime loyalists that make up the rest of the top brass. At the heart of that difference is the opinion, proffered liberally in speeches and articles, that the solution to the war cannot be purely military in nature. The upcoming book has already sparked grumbling behind the scenes. Walking to lunch through central Lisbon in early February, Otelo is waved over by the driver of a shiny Mercedes to find the general sitting in the back seat rolling his window down and poking his monocled head out for a chat.

'Man, can you believe this? The guys tell me they've received various letters from officials protesting my book – they don't want it to come out. Have you ever seen anything like this?'

'I hope the general won't go along with that and publishes anyway. It will help show people that there are generals with different ideas to the government,' replies Otelo.

'Good, I'm going ahead with it. But can you believe it?'

'These are a bunch of cowards, General. What's the position of General Costa Gomes?'

'No worries there. Chico's with me.'[3]

Despite the book's potential controversy, it flies under the radar of the usual censors. Marcelo Caetano can't actively mobilise against it – preventing the publication of a book by a respected general would raise more alarms (and probably result in more black market circulation) than simply allowing it, and besides there are rumours that a French publisher already has the manuscript ready for publication should it be blocked in Portugal. Defence minister Joaquim da Silva Cunha signs off on the book without even reading it, asserting his trust in Spínola's reputation. Costa Gomes writes a glittering pre-publication review, hinting at the book's contents:

> General Spínola very logically argues a balanced solution that we can place roughly in the middle between the two extremes that have broadly been debated: pure, simple and immediate independence in all the Overseas territories, sponsored by the communists and the socialists, and that of homogenised integration of all of those parts, advocated by extremists from the right. We don't need to develop much of an argument to conclude that those solutions should be set aside, the first for being harmful to the national interests and the second for being unfeasible.

Leaning on these two nods, the regime allows the book's publication. Marcelo Caetano receives his copy on 18 February but only gets around to starting it two days later, in the evening. He reads it in one sitting. When he finally puts the book down in the early hours, Salazar's exhausted successor can feel a storm coming.

Portugal and the Future (*Portugal e o Futuro*) hits the shelves on 22 February, and it's an immediate bestseller. Costa Gomes' review turns out to have been burying the lede. Spínola reaffirms his statements on the solution to the colonial problem being political and explicitly not military, and goes one step further, stating that that political solution must base itself on the self-determination rights of the respective African peoples. He doesn't advocate for full independence, but rather a federated system with each of the nations governed by representatives of the black majority – avoiding by all means the creation of 'new Rhodesias'. Spínola also acknowledges that, given the nature and development of the conflict, it might already be too late. The PAIGC, for example, had declared formal Guinean independence in late September of 1973, a claim already recognised by a plurality of world nations that flipped the framing of the Portuguese presence from territorial defenders to unwanted invaders. Even Spínola's intermediate solution might be unachievable. Among the staff officers, Spínola's book unlocks an avenue of thought and furious discussion that many at that point still consider treasonous – decolonisation. Regardless of the viability of his plan or conclusions, having a prestigious senior officer make a compelling case for national self-determination, in a book published on Portuguese soil, sends shock waves through the military establishment. It seems, for the first time in decades, possible to discuss the Homeland and its History.

The Movement's drafting committee, following the saga of *Portugal e o Futuro* with interest, have also been busy. A meeting in late February brings three documents together that read along broadly similar lines, with Melo Antunes tasked with assembling them into one coherent draft. They need to present the programme to as many MOFA representatives as possible, covering as wide a unit base as possible, in all three of the main branches of the armed forces. On 28 February Otelo makes his way to the building at number 9 Rua Braamcamp and arranges to book out its large seventh floor conference space – run by the Sinase company – the only meeting space in Lisbon suitable for the plenary they're hoping to hold. The purpose of the event, says Otelo to the receptionist, is a class reunion from the Gil Vicente high school, to discuss a group holiday. Vítor Alves isn't convinced – the major thinks hiring a room openly like this, under Otelo's real name even if under a false pretence, will draw PIDE/DGS attention, and starts looking for a different location out of town. On the evening of 5 March 1974, over two hundred delegates, representing upwards of six hundred officers in units across the country and overseas, descend on the coffee shops and restaurants of Lisbon. There are twelve meeting points this time,* the officers split up by disciplines, a mammoth logistical task soon to be made even more complicated – Alves was successful, and the meeting point has changed.

At 20:30 Vasco Lourenço and Otelo split up and drive to each of the meeting points in turn, telling the liaison officers the news: everyone is to head to 45 Rua Visconde da Luz, in Cascais. Alves had arranged the use of an architecture studio belonging to the brother of an Army chaplain for the evening's events. The two officers meet again at 9 Braamcamp at the end of their sorties – Otelo, the first there, stations himself by one of the double doors into the building, keeping an eye out for any stragglers that might

---

* Besides the previously mentioned favourites of Galeto, Apolo 70 and Mexicana, there's also the Monte Carlo, S. Remo Café, Pique-Nique, Pisca-Pisca, Smarta, Princesa, Sol-Parque, Canas and Palladium. At the time of writing, only roughly half of these still exist, and most that do are unfamiliar with their importance in the run-up to the Portuguese revolution.

have been given the wrong information and had come there still, but misses that there are two entrances to the building, at right angles to each other. Lourenço makes his way upstairs to pay for the room hire. He approaches the receptionist and tells her the meeting's been delayed, but is met with confusion. 'Delayed?' replies the receptionist, 'but sir, the room is full!' Lourenço is also confused – he walks over to the conference room, and inside he finds several dozen young Army officers, who greet his arrival with bemused grumbling about the late start to the meeting. Lourenço glances around quickly and raises his voice above the chatter. 'Did nobody tell you lot the meeting's been cancelled?' he barks, louder than strictly necessary, all the while pressing his finger to his lips and gesturing at his ears and the walls. There's every chance the room has already been bugged. Continuing his pantomime, he urges the men – now wide-eyed and silenced – out of the room, ferrying them outside to where they can't be eavesdropped on.[4] As much as the Movement's coordination has a shared understanding of the need for operational secrecy bordering on paranoia, that attitude isn't as widespread as they would like, especially among younger and newer recruits. Pulling together all the required officers for a meeting of this size while also stopping them from getting arrested or killed is, as expected, a constant tightrope.

By the time Otelo, Lourenço and their convoy of stragglers arrive in Cascais, they're the last ones there. The architect's studio is a fraction of the size of the room at Braamcamp, and the officers are packed in shoulder to shoulder. It's hot, and the windows are left closed in case the bizarre gathering is spotted from the street, or an ill-timed intervention is overheard by a passerby. There are so many people that Otelo begins to fear for the structural integrity of the floor – but the eagerness he can sense in the room, the willingness to stand the sweat and cramped space and give attention to the MOFA committee, is exciting. The vast majority of those present are Army staff officers – the bulk of the Movement – but there are also twenty delegates from the Air Force, and three from the Navy. Whereas the Air Force's membership has its ties to Kaúlza de Arriaga and sits on the right of the organisation, the Navy officers have historically been the more radical section of the armed forces – and the three delegates are there to see whether the Movement is heading in enough of the right direction, politically, to garner their support. The Navy don't want the Movement becoming 'the docile instrument of certain militaristic factions'. A new set of faces in the room is a small contingent of militia officers. The heated debate over the ordnances had originally put militia officers at loggerheads with the staff officers in the Movement, but since their revocation (and through a concerted effort of olive branch diplomacy on the part of the Movement committee) the two groups had found common cause in the broader issues facing the military. The presence of the militia officers means the appearance, for the first time, of a more organised faction within the Movement – those aligned with General António Spínola.

After a brief introduction, where Vítor Alves sketches out the Movement's activity since the meeting in Óbidos for the newcomers, as well as a few pieces of housekeeping and updating the organisational links, the floor is given over to Melo Antunes. The major takes his position by the whiteboard and begins reading the document that most have come here to consider: 'The Movement, The Armed Forces and the Nation.' Beginning with an appraisal of the decline of the armed forces since the surrender of the Indian colonies, the paper traces a history that everyone in the room is familiar with – the onset of the war, its aggravation and expansion and the political deadlock that keeps it going. Echoing the letters from the comrades in Mozambique, it goes further than ever before:

Conscientious ones in the military know, however, that the solution to the Overseas problem is political and not military, and understand it is their duty to denounce the mistakes they are victims of and that will transform the Armed Forces, once again, into a 'scapegoat' of an impossible strategy: a political solution that safeguards national honour and dignity, as well as the legitimate interests of the Portuguese installed in Africa, but that takes into account the incontrovertible and irreversible reality of the profound aspirations of the African people to govern themselves – which necessarily implies extremely flexible and dynamic political, judicial and diplomatic formulas. This solution must be faced with realism and courage, as we believe it corresponds not only to the real interests of the Portuguese people but also to its true historic destiny and the highest ideals of justice and peace.

This push, acknowledging the right to self-determination of the African people, is in lockstep with *Portugal e o Futuro*. Going further, however, the paper turns inwards, to the regime:

And because we think this, we understand it necessary, as a precondition to the solution to the African problem, of the Armed Forces crisis and the general crisis of the country, that political power bear the maximum legitimacy; that its institutions are effective representations of the aspirations and interests of the People. In other words: without the democratisation of the country it is impossible to think on any other valid solution to the extremely grave problems that assault us.

> It is about, therefore, before and above everything else, *obtaining in the short term a solution to the institutional problem in the framework of a political democracy.*

Antunes goes on to list a series of points that link the national question with the armed forces, a set of goals that lead on from democratisation around reuniting the will and intent of the Portuguese population with the actions of the armed forces. After his presentation, the densely packed room is given a break for discussion – and it erupts in chatter and barked questions from the floor, a mass of voices, each officer in their own way digesting the immensity of the proposals. The way the Movement has been structured thus far has put much of its decision-making and actioning ability in the hands of the elected committee and executive. While the term isn't ever used among themselves, Otelo will come to realise years after the fact that the Movement operates along principles of democratic centralism.[5] Amongst the raised voices, Captain Rosário Simões raises a pertinent point that's on many minds – 'Might the endorsement, which is being given to the Coordinating Committee, include going to the very end, or shall we say, to a brawl?'[6] The suggestion meets with broad support – should the document be approved, the committee is empowered to organise a coup; what everyone understands by Simões' euphemistic 'brawl'.

The discussion break comes to an end soon after, followed by the voting. Unit by unit, the delegates state their positions on the document. There seems to be a majority of support, especially from the Army, but the occasional vocal objections have an impact on the mood of the room. The Air Force delegates are split – there are loud grumbles about the overt politics of the text, and strenuous objections to the lines about colonial policy – this despite the fact that the Air Force had been part of the drafting committee. One delegate from the Navy states that their unit is already further ahead, politically, in its thinking, and can only commit to not actively opposing any initiatives on the part of the Army. The retreat by the Navy and the Air Force causes the rest of the delegates to balk – there are scattered murmurs of apprehension, even the suggestion that the programme put forward in *Portugal e o Futuro* might be enough. The sudden backtracking from previously supportive units is the last straw for Vítor Alves – already stressed from having to host such a chaotic gathering in the cramped circumstances, he utters some words of abuse under his breath and removes himself as chair. Captain Nuno Pinto Soares takes over and manages to smooth things over with the crowd, and a hastily scrawled motion from Melo Antunes about circulating the documents to all units so every officer has a chance to sign up on their own terms seems to satisfy most of the room.

Salgueiro Maia is already thinking ahead. 'When do we need to take action?' he asks the chair. Another voice cuts through the commotion: 'Gentlemen, it's like this! Whoever wants to take this to the very end, risking their lives and taking every risk, signs the papers that are being passed around. Whoever doesn't has no business being here and the best thing they can do is leave!' The circulated papers, bearing a typed preamble handing operational control to the Movement's Coordinating Committee, gather 111 signatures – a majority, if slim, of the units in the room. Major Ruben Domingos, signalling his support for the document, raises two fingers and shouts 'Two votes!' When pressed as to why, he replies 'Two votes indeed! Me and my general!'

'Your general?! But – is he on our side?'

'No,' laughs Domingos, 'but I'll arrest him, so we can say two!'[7]

The meeting disperses in the early morning hours, exhausted men filing out of the small architect's studio into the night, grateful for the cold air, lighting their cigarettes and leaving in clusters of animated whispers, bobbing pinpoints of red light radiating outwards in the dark. What happens next has already been planned out to the smallest detail. Should everyone follow their carefully typed out instructions faithfully, the Movement should have a dossier of supportive signatures to their document ready to present to the military leaders on 18 March, and a delegation from each armed forces branch prepared to address the president directly on 23 March. Two days after the Cascais meeting there are two thousand printed copies of 'The Movement, The Armed Forces and the Nation' ready to be posted to every Portuguese military unit with a postal address. The carefully laid out Movement plans for an orderly escalation are, however, abruptly cut short.

At noon on 8 March, Captains Vasco Lourenço, Carlos Clemente, David Martelo and Antero Ribeiro da Silva receive their literal marching orders: Lourenço and Clemente are being reassigned to the Azores, Ribeiro da Silva to Madeira and Martelo to Bragança. It's a shot in the dark that manages to strike true – while Martelo, Clemente and Ribeiro da Silva are delegated members of the Movement, Lourenço is one of the most important elements of the Coordinating Committee, one of the few whose involvement is clear to even the upper military hierarchy. The news of the transfers sparks an emergency meeting that evening to decide how to respond. From its very first steps, the Movement had stressed the need to stand in solidarity with any comrades against whom the state took any action – the time had finally come to put that solidarity into practice. That sudden demand for concrete action makes the meeting extremely lively and tense – after a few hours they decide to call a demonstration outside the Army Ministry in Terreiro do Paço the next day. By this point the stress has made Nuno Pinto Soares lie down on the carpet with his eyes shut, where he spends a large part of the meeting, and José Maria Azevedo has thrown a pile of books onto the floor.[8] Otelo pushes his comrades with a more radical suggestion still: *ordering* specifically the three comrades set to go overseas not to accept the transfers. Otelo's suggestion is that they effectively kidnap Lourenço, Clemente and Ribeiro da Silva. That proposal is also ultimately accepted, along with the suggestion that the transferred comrades should not spend the night at home – this gets loud objections from both Lourenço and Ribeiro da Silva, the only two actually present in the emergency meeting. Carlos Almada Contreiras, the most vocal of the few delegates from the Navy, offers to visit Navy minister Admiral Manuel Pereira Crespo in his home and demand the transfer orders be revoked. He's sent on his way in the early hours, the group still clinging to the idea that they can, through sheer tenacity, overturn the effective exile of their comrades.

When Contreiras knocks on Pereira Crespo's door, it's three in the morning on 9 March, and the admiral is not best pleased to be woken up. The Navy minister is also intransigent in the face of Contreiras' requests, categorically refusing to intervene in the situation. When Contreiras eventually leaves empty-handed, Pereira Crespo makes a call to the defence minister, Silva Cunha, who orders a full-scale military shutdown across the country – all military units recalled to their stations, on high alert. Phones start ringing throughout the Movement – the targeted officers are warned to leave their homes as quickly as possible. At 05:30 Vasco Lourenço's unit commander knocks on his door. Adélia Lourenço answers – Vasco hasn't come home, she lies. Lieutenant Colonel Ferrand d'Almeida, Carlos Clemente's unit commander, arrives at the captain's home and personally escorts him to quarters – he's pushed directly onto a plane to the Azores that very morning. Meanwhile, Antero Ribeiro da Silva has taken refuge in Pinto Soares' house. Nobody quite knows where Vasco Lourenço is, until Otelo answers his door to find his friend bleary-eyed and shivering. Lourenço had left his home in a hurry, and he's not dressed for an early March morning. Otelo's house is also not the safest hideout, and right now the captain is a de facto fugitive, so the two men travel to Miraflores – Major Manuel Monge has access to an empty flat belonging to his uncle, with a discreet entrance around the back. Lourenço is stashed there with a care package of bread, fruit, beer and cold meats, now wearing a woollen jumper borrowed from Otelo, and suddenly plunged into full clandestinity while his comrades figure out what to do.

Given the full-scale military shutdown in place, the proposed demonstration outside the Army Ministry is cancelled. Instead, getting through to as many units over the phone as possible, the committee suggests a new course of action: officers should approach their commanders and express their solidarity both with the officers being transferred and the Movement which is keeping them, for now, out of the hands of their superiors. The result shakes the regime and the senior officers to their core. Until now unaware of the full extent of the Movement's influence, across the country commanders are being approached by their own men and told, in no uncertain terms, that a stand is being taken against the senior armed forces staff. Most unit commanders don't even know why they're on high alert, and have to be told by their junior officers – a deeply disconcerting experience that causes the brigadier general in charge of the unit in Mafra to burst into tears.[9] Nuno Pinto Soares, however, on account of being on sick leave, doesn't get recalled to his unit and is out of the loop. He appears at noon in Terreiro do Paço in his full uniform expecting a mass demonstration, to find he's the only one there. The captain has to decipher what's going on by asking a passing fellow officer. On the spur of the moment, Pinto Soares marches into the Army minister's office and writes out a letter of resignation, declaring himself to be in solidarity with his comrades.

That evening, the Movement gathers for another emergency meeting, in Captain Luís Macedo's father's house. The decision to hide the officers is weighing heavily on the group, and especially on Lourenço and Ribeiro da Silva, who are exhausted and irritable. Otelo tries to make the case that they shouldn't be given up, but he's outvoted – they are now skirting very close to desertion, and everyone fears what that could imply for the captains' careers and the survival of the Movement. Nuno Pinto Soares volunteers to escort the fugitives to the military headquarters, audaciously arguing that he'll be safe: 'Nothing's going to happen to me, you'll see. I'll hand them over, in the name of the Movement, say what I have to say and leave. You know, my father is very close with [Military Governor of Lisbon] Edmundo Luz Cunha.'

'I have a hunch all three of you will be immediately shipped to prison, but, if you insist, we haven't got an alternative. I'll keep an eye on it from afar and see who's right,' replies Otelo.

Pinto Soares, with the Movement's blessing, intends to impose conditions for the handing over of the prisoners: the cancellation of the transfer orders, and the immediate return of Carlos Clemente, who is already in the Azores. The condition comes with a veiled threat – non-compliance could result in uncontrollable action on the part of officers, including those stationed overseas. Pinto Soares is absolutely convinced that he won't suffer any setbacks himself – so much so that he cheerfully informs Lourenço that he has ballet tickets with his wife for the next day. Lourenço laughs back – 'Buddy, you're definitely getting taken in with me.'

Otelo witnesses the handover from his car, parked out of the way, with sight lines to the back entrance to Vilalva Palace, the headquarters of the Lisbon Region Military. He sees Pinto Soares ring the bell, the doors opening, the three men walking in. He waits for an hour and a half, his suspicions confirmed – nobody's coming back out tonight. It's only the next day that the Movement hears of their comrades' fate. Pinto Soares had spent the night in Vilalva Palace, Lourenço and Ribeiro da Silva had been sequestered with the 7th Cavalry Regiment for the evening. In the morning, they had all – even the recently resigned Pinto Soares – been driven to Trafaria Fort – Lisbon's military prison facility, on the south bank of the Tagus. Although Otelo never really thought the regime would respond any differently, the news of his comrades' arrest makes Otelo unexpectedly emotional. The Movement had pressed the regime hard enough that it lashed out wildly like a cornered animal, and the arrests have a powerful symbolic importance. Otelo dictates a letter to Luís Macedo intended for the overseas comrades, informing them of what the last two days had involved and urging them to start kicking off at their end.

Trafaria Fort has stood on the edge of the Tagus for over three hundred years; its dubious usefulness as a defensive structure leading to its employment as a quarantine hospital, guano factory and, finally, an on-again-off-again military prison, initially for the Navy and then for the Army. If you know what you're looking for, its grey walls and red roof can be picked out in the distance from Belém tower, or the top of the Monument to the Discoveries. Vasco Lourenço and Antero Ribeiro da Silva arrive in its draughty entrance hall with their heads held high, escorted by Cavalry Major Pato Anselmo. Nuno Pinto Soares arrives shortly afterwards. Recognising the captain from the Military Academy, Anselmo greets Pinto Soares with surprise.

'Nuno! Great to see you, but what are you doing here? Who have you had to escort over?'

Pinto Soares replies, laughing. 'I haven't escorted anyone over Pato – I've been brought here myself!'

Anselmo is so shocked by this he bursts into tears, apologising profusely to his old school friend about having to put him in prison. Pinto Soares pats Anselmo's shoulder gently, murmuring encouragement. 'There, there, friend, don't worry, it'll all turn out all right, you'll see.' Lourenço finds the mood in the prison odd, as though the captains are being treated with kid gloves. After the first night, the duty officer approaches the prisoners and asks

146

if everything is okay – whether they had slept well, or if they needed an extra blanket for the night. Lourenço confidently turns on the young lieutenant.

'You guys are anxious. You've been told to treat us particularly well, haven't you?'

The lieutenant denies any special treatment, claims that every officer brought to Trafaria is treated the same, but Lourenço squares up to the man.

'Let me tell you something, man. Listen very carefully. Soon it won't be me in this prison, it'll be the Army minister. I'm only here to see what bed we're putting the minister in when he finally gets what's coming to him. You make sure that when the minister comes here, you put him in the same bed I'm in now. Do you understand, officer?'[10] The lieutenant rushes off, tail between his legs.

If Vasco Lourenço wasn't already fired up from being arrested, the trepidation with which his captors seem to be approaching his situation fills him with confidence. When the escort party arrives to take him and his comrades to the airport, he demands to make a phone call to his wife. His request is denied, but Lourenço stands firm – 'Either you let me talk to my wife or you'll have to drag me out of here in a straightjacket. And let me tell you boys, you'll need twelve of you to put me in that straight-jacket.' There's a wild energy here, and the escort team don't really know what to do with this – Lourenço is a large, visibly powerful man, and he looks like he means business. They eventually lead him to a telephone, where he can explain what's happening to his wife and ask her to bring him a bag with a few things from home. Adélia meets him a few hours later at Portela airport – when his captors try to keep them apart, he just has to bark the word 'straightjacket!' at the officers to have them back down. When he walks into the airport proper the first thing he notices are the figures skulking in the shadows and around the edges of the terminal, their eyes trained on him, men with a certain bearing whom he immediately recognises as PIDE/DGS agents. Lourenço is very much past the point of caring about his reputation – 'I can see you!' he shouts at a man peeking from behind a pillar, 'I can see all of you! I know who you are!' Lourenço rants at his escort all the way to the plane steps, trailed by a cordon of military officers and secret police astonished by his open defiance. With a last kiss and goodbye to Adélia, he leaves for the Azores, a political exile in all but name.

Meanwhile, Otelo and the rest of the Movement are still scrambling. Another bit of news comes in that hints at the regime's next steps: the National Assembly has organised a session, on 14 March, where the generals making up all three branches of the armed forces intend to declare their continued support for the government, and specifically its overseas policy. It's a clear response to *Portugal e o Futuro*, and Spínola is worried – there's every chance the regime will use the opportunity to dismiss him and Costa Gomes from their posts. Spínola's suggestion, communicated to Otelo through his aide-de-camp, is, once again, to hold a protest in full dress uniform. At the same time as the Movement is having to ramp up its activity, a new face arrives on the scene: Major Luís Casanova Ferreira, recently returned from another commission in Bissau, a charismatic firebrand who, while not already integrated into the Movement structures, is known to be a regime critic and extremely keen to get involved. Barely a few days after his initial contact with Otelo, Casanova Ferreira is already raring for action, and responds to Spínola's suggestions with contempt.

'Don't forget, we've already had three prisoners! Meetings don't accomplish anything any more! We have to have a fight!' Otelo is sceptical, and tries to bring the major down to earth, with no luck. Casanova pushes on: 'Assemble the gang from half a dozen of the strongest units. Tomorrow morning, my place. You'll see how it is.'[11]

CONFRONTATION

The meeting goes ahead as suggested, on 12 March, at Casanova Ferreira's house, north of Belém. There are six units represented – each of the Practical Schools of Cavalry, Artillery and Infantry, plus the 5th Infantry Regiment and the 1st Lisbon Artillery Regiment, a sizeable contingent of forces. There is broad support for immediate action, and Casanova Ferreira rolls with it – they decide to put together a plan of operations and present it to the other comrades the next day. The afternoon is spent cobbling a plan together – Otelo, Casanova Ferreira and five other MOFA officers, tossing ideas around like children preparing a raid on a sweet factory. They're finally doing it! Casanova Ferreira wants to start the whole thing off with a quarter-ton bomb dropped onto the National Assembly building, 'to completely scrap that shit in one go'. Otelo, not entirely convinced, interjects with regular questions but is swept up in the excitement. The plan of operations is beaten out on a typewriter in a few hours, a rough outline that assigns each of the units they think are Movement loyal to important strategic points throughout Lisbon. The list of steps to take after the coup is long, and vaguely defined – controlling information, dissolving the government and imposing a military junta and essentially generating a new political system from scratch. It seems like a vast undertaking in the time they have, but Casanova Ferreira and Manuel Monge insist on ploughing ahead, and their bright-eyed, infectious enthusiasm drags the rest of the officers with them.

The next day, the plan of operations weighs heavily in Otelo's coat pocket. He drives to Santarém first, to present it to the Practical Cavalry School. Salgueiro Maia is out on training exercises, but Otelo addresses a room of young captains and lieutenants who seem keen to hear what he has to say. They're also smart – the plan is flawed and vague, and the timeline seems incredibly short. The sticking point comes when he's asked whether the paratroop regiments are on board – the Movement hasn't had a chance to show them the plan, and they're not yet confirmed. One of the cavalry officers agrees to liaise with the paratroopers and bring a delegate along to an afternoon meeting with the rest of the strong units. That meeting goes even worse than the morning one – after Otelo reads out the plan of operations, the parachute unit liaison captain, Cristóvão Avelar de Sousa, categorically refuses to have his men follow the plan. 'What you have there isn't a plan of operations, it's nothing. It's completely inconsistent. We like to act seriously, when there's a serious plan and serious possibilities of success.' Dropping a bomb on the National Assembly? There's no way anyone in the Air Force would ever agree to that. Otelo protests, insisting they need to take action before Spínola and Costa Gomes are sacked by the regime, but Avelar de Sousa cautions him to be patient – they'll have more chances in the future, with a better plan. The stoic withdrawal of the parachute regiment – an 800-strong unit without which their already flimsy plan is scuppered – brings Otelo, Casanova Ferreira and the other more enthusiastic comrades back to earth. With the immediate plan killed off, they're left with the option of letting the parachute regiment come up with their 'serious' plan – Avelar de Sousa agrees to put something into action in ten days, and the meeting ends on that hopeful note.

Not everyone is on board with cancelling the coup. Captain Virgílio Luz Varela, highly decorated militia officer and primary Movement contact at the 5th Infantry Regiment (*Regimento de Infantaria 5*, RI5) based in Caldas da Rainha, just under a hundred kilometres north of Lisbon, is a diehard Spínola supporter and unwilling to let his general take a fall without putting up a fight. He's waiting for Casanova Ferreira at the major's house on the morning of 14 March. Luz Varela declares his unit is still operational, and if the Movement's demobilisation order isn't withdrawn they'll march on Lisbon alone, whatever the consequences. Casanova promises to try and rework the operations plan into something actually usable, but he needs time. Varela agrees to a week – in the meantime, RI5 remains ready to leave. Casanova Ferreira joins Otelo in the Military Academy to watch the live broadcast of the Rheumatic Brigade's pantomime of allegiance to Marcelo Caetano. It's exactly what they expected – Spínola and Costa Gomes are missing, and the session is taken up with speeches from tedious, decrepit generals reaffirming their undying support for the overseas policy, Caetano graciously 'accepting' the declarations of discipline and loyalty. A key line: 'The country is assured it can count on its Armed Forces. And at all its levels *there cannot be any doubts* as to the attitude of its commanders.' The next morning, the confirmation comes through – Spínola and Costa Gomes have been sacked.

15 March. In the northern city of Lamego, east of Porto, officers in the Special Operations Training Centre (*Centro de Instrução de Operações Especiais*, CIOE) approach their commander and declare themselves opposed to the removal of the two generals from office. Their commander takes their side, and soon the Lamego barracks is in a direct confrontation with Porto Region Military HQ. By the time the Movement committee hears about it, it's nine in the evening – the phone rings at Manuel Monge's house where he, Otelo, Casanova Ferreira and a few others in the inner circle are having a debrief. They're told by Captain Ferreira da Silva that it looks like Lamego might be 'on wheels'. Casanova Ferreira is ecstatic and grabs for Otelo's copy of their plan of operations. If the Lamego unit is on the move, they'll have backup. The coup is back on. Captain Marques Ramos is told to drive immediately to Caldas da Rainha with a copy of the plan and order them into Lisbon to take the airport. Casanova prepares to leave for Santarém to mobilise the Practical Cavalry School. Otelo is told to mobilise various artillery and infantry units, but begins to balk – all the units, raring to go the day before, have

been demobilised, and the Cavalry School is unequipped and unwilling to participate without the parachute regiments. He's talked down by his comrades – it's now or never.

Otelo rushes to meet Vítor Alves – since Vasco Lourenço's arrest, Alves and Otelo are the two men at the top of the Movement command structure. Alves hears the news and pulls back – the plan is too risky, too quick off the mark – he doesn't think it's a good idea and he will only go so far. He stands quietly, anxious, as Otelo puts on a thick green jumper over his uniform and packs his pistol. The two men hop into Otelo's car and drive wildly around the outskirts of Lisbon, stopping at the houses of various trusted officers to tell them what's going on. At two in the morning an artillery captain's wife greets them at her door – her husband's been called back to his unit, there's been another military shutdown and everyone's being brought back in. The government knows something's wrong, and is mobilising. Otelo makes a call to the Practical Artillery School. He barks an order into the phone – 'Listen, everything's kicking off, Lamego's on the move, you have to send a battery now and park it on Salazar bridge. I'll meet you there in a few hours.' The reply from the terrified captain on the other end confirms Otelo's fears – it's the weekend, there's nobody there, not even enough men to form a platoon. Otelo tells the captain to do what he can, knowing it's now unlikely to come to anything. He makes the hour-long drive to the Practical Infantry School at Mafra, and has a similar conversation with the duty officer – all the officers are on training exercises miles away, there isn't anyone around to put together a fighting force – they'll need a few hours to even get access to any vehicles. The officers in Mafra are told to put something together and get it on the road – they'll hear from Otelo soon. As the major leaves the school, he begins to feel the panic setting in – everything they've worked for is about to come apart at the seams.

Meanwhile, in Santarém, Major Casanova Ferreira is coming up against the same problems as his comrade across the country.

On his way to Santarém, he and Major Monge had stopped at Spínola's house to alert the general and urge him to take on a leadership position – which he had categorically refused. Now Casanova faces a more concerning refusal from one of their own comrades. Salgueiro Maia is adamant – the Practical Cavalry School needs forty-eight hours to prepare a mobilisation, and since the last one was cancelled, they're simply not ready. They only have two armoured vehicles in any condition to put on the road. In a panic, the two Movement officers burn any compromising documents in a bidet, convinced the day's actions will lead to arrests. The only officer to have any success is Captain Marques Ramos, who had arrived in Caldas da Rainha at 11:00, with Virgílio Varela there to greet him. They round up a gang of captains and lieutenants and push into the unit commander's office, declaring RI5 under the control of the Movement and that they're mobilising it to take Lisbon. The commander reaches for his pistol – half-heartedly – and is quickly disarmed. The Movement officers lock the commander in his study, but make one crucial mistake – he's left in there with his private telephone, which he uses to sound the alarm to his superiors. When RI5 finally make contact with CIOE in Lamego to coordinate action, the news isn't at all what they're expecting – Lamego's 'on wheels' doesn't mean they've mobilised at all, just that they are ready to go. The excitement around CIOE's stand-off with the Porto Region Military had generated an unstoppable rumour mill that had sent the Movement into a spiral. There's no going back for RI5 – they've arrested their unit commander, they can't exactly return and apologise. Surely Lamego is the exception – surely at this very moment all the Movement's might is descending on Lisbon, ready to topple the regime once and for all. But when, at four in the morning, the 5th Infantry Regiment opens its gates and files out onto the motorway towards the capital, they do so alone.

Brigadier General Pedro Serrano demands the surrender of the besieged 5th Infantry Regiment in Caldas da Rainha, following their aborted coup attempt on 16 March 1974.

CHAPTER SEVEN

GENERAL PLAN
OF OPERATIONS
(HISTORIC TURN)

Lisbon's Military Academy sprawls over a large area in the centre of the city, between the university complexes to the north in Campo Pequeno and the bustling Pombaline downtown. The Academy was built up over years in the vast palatial estate created for and only briefly occupied by Queen Catherine of Braganza in the seventeenth century. The palace's farm and open land have been replaced by a circuit of stone buildings, recognisable as part of the military complex by their distinctive pinkish-red colour. It's an imposingly sober place, whose storied history underscores the sense of prestige and heritage its students carry with them when they finally leave its draughty corridors for military life. The Captains' Movement can trace its origins in more ways than one to the Military Academy – the people each officer met there, the camaraderie they formed and its totemic role in the fight against Ordnances 353/73 and 409/73. On the morning of 16 March 1974, the regime hopes it can become the place where the Movement falls.

It's half past midnight, and the officers' mess in the command building on Rua Gomes Freire is unusually full of officers and whirring with conversation. Colonel Leopoldo Severo finds the presence of several men not linked to the Academy strange, but asking what all the commotion is about yields no results. He retires to his office. An hour and a half later, the Academy is surrounded by the National Guard, weapons raised and on high alert – the lockdown measures that had started as soon as RI5's commander had sounded the alarm had spread here, where, in the government's eyes, the conspiracy was based. It was, at one point – Major Manuel Monge had come here after splitting up with Casanova Ferreira to try and wrangle his contacts and pull troops to the capital, but his efforts, like those of Casanova and Otelo, were fruitless. Having left the Academy before it was surrounded, Manuel Monge and Jaime Neves head to Casanova Ferreira's house to liaise with the major after his return from Santarém. Unbeknownst to Monge, his own house is in the process of being raided. An officious elderly general from the Rheumatic Brigade had finally given PIDE/DGS the permission they needed to come after military officers (on the suspicion of being Spínola supporters!) and Manuel Monge is one of the first on agent Óscar Cardoso's list. Major José Maria Azevedo is the only Movement associate still in Monge's house, accompanied by his wife – he escapes the PIDE search by hiding on the roof terrace, while his wife is introduced to the secret police as simply 'a friend'. Otelo witnesses the raid from his car – intending to stop at Monge's house to look for the major, he decides to drive away from the scene after spotting the agents making their way into the building.

Monge and Casanova, realising that RI5's mission is doomed to fail, have by this point set off on the motorway to intercept the regiment before they can get hurt. The armed might of the state has already mobilised – there are several GNR, tank and artillery units amassing on the roundabout on the southern corner of Portela airport, where the motorways from the north begin to join Lisbon proper. Monge and Casanova sight the convoy barely three kilometres from the edge of Lisbon, and they have to veer their car over to the opposite lane to intercept it. It's there, on the road, that Captain Marques Ramos is told the news – nobody else is coming, and the regime is ready for them. With heavy hearts, Monge and Casanova take command of the RI5 convoy and turn it around, fearing for what might be waiting for them when they return to Caldas da Rainha. Meanwhile Otelo and Captain Germano Miquelina Simões are sitting at a café, within sight of the roundabout where the government is concentrating its forces. As much as he's frustrated at what's going on, Otelo can't help himself from assessing the government's response and filing the information in his mind. What he learns is important – despite the show of force, excessive for facing off against the one regiment they believe is on its way, the response is sloppy, uncoordinated, the officers poorly briefed and in some anxious disarray. Even in terms of sheer firepower it's not *that* impressive, and Otelo knows a few of the units present are loyal to the Movement, even if the circumstances have meant turning their weapons, potentially, on their own. With enough of a plan, a big enough mobilisation, the regime can actually be challenged.

It's ten in the morning by the time RI5 make it back to their base in Caldas da Rainha. All of the unit commanders had been arrested when the regiment had mutinied – Major Manuel Monge takes on the sober responsibility of command. At eleven, the power inside the barracks is cut, along with the water supply and the telephones. Over the next few hours the 5th Infantry Regiment's building is surrounded, bit by bit, with armoured cars and military divisions. Among them is a division from the Practical Cavalry School, who had been told in no uncertain terms by Salgueiro Maia not to act against RI5 – 'take their side even, if you can'. That last request is far-fetched, but in any case unnecessary – Monge has ordered his men not to open fire under any circumstances. When the siege commander, Brigadier General Pedro Serrano, arrives to demand their surrender, he stands on the bonnet of his jeep, shouting through the iron gate of the unit courtyard.

'Open the gate, in the name of authority!'

'You might have authority,' replies Monge calmly, arms behind his back, 'but in our land authority is very poorly constituted.'

'You have a quarter of an hour to open the gate, or you risk bloodshed.'

'You're not the one who's going to make me open this gate. We will only take orders from our general Spínola!'[1]

Monge's bravado notwithstanding, a quick consultation with the remaining officers reveals the situation as hopeless. RI5 surrenders shortly afterwards – the officers who had led the coup are shipped off to Trafaria, the remaining junior officers and soldiers to the military prison at Santa Margarida. Otelo returns to the Military Academy on the evening of 16 March – his absence has been noticed, but he manages to convince his unit commander that he had left Lisbon to a place off the grid and thus hadn't received the order to return to the Academy when the military went on high alert. Despite having spent the last day driving around and making contact with a whole array of officers, Otelo appears to have escaped the government's attention. In fact, that appears to be true for most of the Movement – as Otelo gets brought up to speed by his comrades at the Academy, it seems the only officer from the Coordinating Committee to have been arrested among the dozens is Manuel Monge. The government missive, broadcast on the television news on the afternoon of the 16th, ending with 'order reigns throughout the country', suggests largely that the regime believes the immediate threat to be over. But there is now a ticking clock on the Movement – if they're going to do something, they have to do it quickly. And now they have a new incentive: getting their comrades out of jail as fast as possible.

GENERAL PLAN OF OPERATIONS

In the 18 March issue of the newspaper *Diário da República*, covering Sporting Lisbon defeating Porto 2-0, comes a cryptic message that seems intended for the captains:

> The many northerners that marched on Lisbon at the weekend, dreaming of victory, ended up retreating, disappointed by the defeat. Their adversary in the capital, better organised and equipped (and above all informed of their strategy), counting on faithful assistance, aborted the intentions of the men of the North. But, paraphrasing what an astute commander once said, 'a battle has been lost, but not yet the war...'

In the days after 16 March, the regime spends some time meting out punishment to its military detractors in the only way it really knows how: reassigning them to posts far away from where they were based, hoping in that way to break up the various organisational tendrils of the Movement. This is what happens to a large part of the CIOE unit in Lamego – their confrontation with the Porto Region Military is enough to merit such measures, but no more. The same happens with Dinis de Almeida – a minor disciplinary issue has him spend three nights in prison before being transferred to Figueira da Foz, where he immediately starts proselytising for the Movement. On the evening of the 18th, Otelo meets Vítor Alves, Ernesto Melo Antunes and Ernesto's wife Gabriela, at the Café Londres on the corner of Praça de Londres. It's here that Vítor Alves makes an important request to Melo Antunes: take the rough outline of the political programme that was shared with the Movement in Cascais and make it into something detailed and real. Melo Antunes is undeniably shaken and pessimistic about the turn the last few days have taken, but ultimately agrees to the task. He has to do it quickly, however – after various attempts at securing a transfer, he's finally being reassigned to the Azores (unlike Vasco Lourenço and the dozens of other officers who suffer similar fates, this transfer is entirely self-imposed). That programme is delivered to Vítor Alves a few days later, to be worked on further. It will prove to be a uniquely important document – both for what it contains, and what it doesn't.

The decisive meeting of the Movement comes on 24 March, in the home of Captain Candeias Valente, in Oeiras. Valente is replacing Miquelina Simões in the Movement command structure, after Simões had been hit by the wave of transfers. Having allowed the designated time to pass for the parachute regiments to put their promised plan into action, the Movement committee decides no such action is forthcoming, and to take matters into their own hands. The trepidation that had been the hallmark of the early Movement meetings is gone – everyone here has their heart and mind set on instigating an armed revolution. Otelo takes on the task of redeveloping the plan of operations they had cooked up just two weeks prior, and becomes the operational commander of the coup. Vítor Alves, bearing the programme drafted by Melo Antunes, takes on the political wing of the operation. It's agreed that, based on Otelo's reworking of the plan, the coup will take place sometime between 20 and 29 April. It has to be in that time frame, because the period before 1 May is the one where PIDE/DGS is likely to be busiest rounding up Communist Party members and other left activists, on the suspicion of planning subversive actions on May Day. From this moment forward, there are to be no more open communications among the Movement – no more pamphlets or missives. The regime is to be left believing that its punitive countermeasures were successful, and the Movement has been wiped out. Otelo has a mammoth task ahead – they don't know how the 16 March operation has shaken up the officer structure, and whom they can still count on to be ready, able and willing. To be sure of success, they have to look at the task as rebuilding the Movement from scratch, approaching everyone with a concrete plan of action and getting full commitment.

In the early days of April, Otelo begins writing the document he titles 'General Plan of Operations (Historic Turn)'. It's a sprawling thing. Expanding on the rough ideas he and Casanova Ferreira had cooked up, he spends days scribbling notes by hand in his neat, flowing handwriting, crossing out or annotating in the margins when more information emerges that changes the plan. Vítor Alves and a small network of contacts bring him as much information as possible about the make-up of the 'enemy' units – the police, the Portuguese Legion, PIDE/DGS, the government military response systems already in place. On top of these are the military units that are known not to be aligned with the Movement at all – the 2nd Lancers Regiment, effectively a military police force, is a maybe. The big one is the 7th Cavalry Regiment, located in the heart of Lisbon and led by several well-known regime loyalists, with the ability to mobilise at very short notice. This unit is made up of armoured vehicles – *Chaimites*, M47 tanks, heavy artillery batteries. The best way to deal with these is to remove their commanders, and for that they need a group of specialised commando units. In fact, having control of a swathe of small tactical units for various missions seems immensely useful, such as taking targets like the PIDE/DGS headquarters that are less likely to be heavily armed and armoured. Otelo spends days chasing down contacts he thinks might be suitable for the task, but the first few fall flat – the officers he approaches either have too few men, don't have faith in Otelo's plan, or, in one case, claim not to know 'anything about politics'. Finally, a colleague points him to Infantry Major Jaime Neves, who starts to look like the only viable option. Neves is competent – his record in the field shows as much – but he has a reputation as an immoral, corrupt philanderer. The meeting between the two, in the back of Otelo's car, is fraught – Neves insists the Movement should seek to be led by Kaúlza de Arriaga, which puts his own political leanings in a clear light. Otelo dispels this notion immediately; Neves was at the packed-out meeting in Cascais and knows the Movement has its own chosen generals. Eventually Neves agrees to source and coordinate a group of commando units for Otelo's missions – an assignment Otelo will come to regret.

There is a cavalier frankness to the way in which Otelo Carvalho assembles the adherents to his plan of operations, one that Vasco Lourenço, in the years after the revolution, will come to call 'completely insane'.[2] The pressure of putting together and distributing his plan of operations in his limited time (while also fulfilling all of his duties as an artillery instructor in the Military Academy) means a few of the usual, more cautious tactics simply fly out of the window. Otelo's days in the first weeks of April are spent making contact with officers – some he knows and trusts, some he is introduced to, some he simply doesn't know at all – and presenting them, openly and frankly, with the plan of operations. He doesn't mince words – his approach to Major Garoupa, a former artillery colleague and a man deeply integrated into the workings of the regime, is 'I am working on a plan of operations with the goal of toppling the government, and I need you to give me information.' It says as much about how the political landscape within the armed forces has changed since the Movement was first brought into being as Otelo's own instincts that none of the people he approaches denounce him to the nearest authority – even if they themselves are reticent or even categorically against participating in a military coup. The roots of military camaraderie run deep, and the pervading sense that something needs to change has become unshakeable. Thus, piece by piece, the plan moves from something abstract and imagined to tangible and real as Otelo assembles his broad team from among the disaffected Portuguese armed forces. At the heart of this team is the Army. As much as the different branches of the armed forces came together towards the latter stages of the Movement, and the Coordinating Committee contains several crucial, involved members from the Navy and the Air Force, the Army's size and involvement from the very beginning means Otelo can only fully count on Army detachments. Importantly, the Navy, the Air Force and the parachute regiments have been convinced into a position of neutrality: they will not oppose any operations put into action by the Movement. And within the Army, the combination of manpower and the element of surprise has the Movement outnumbering the regime's forces.

By 15 April Otelo's plan of operations, twenty-six handwritten pages, is passed on to Lieutenant Colonel Amadeu Garcia dos Santos, whose job it is to elaborate the communications protocol for the operation, and to assemble the infrastructure for Otelo's command post. On 20 April, Vítor Alves has a typed version of the political programme, fine-tuned over the course of multiple meetings of the drafting committee and anyone else with political nous that wanted to participate. The programme attempts to lay out the essential political foundation of the steps after the coup – the government to be dissolved and replaced with a temporary military administration, the organisation of free and fair elections, abolishing state censorships and freeing political prisoners. It's a developed version of the document Melo Antunes had read out at the meeting in Cascais, and the aspects relating to self-determination of the African nations, during the detailed drafting process, had continued to be the source of conflict with the few Air Force delegates who deigned to appear. In addition to his responsibility for organising the granular details of the coup, Otelo is also the Movement's liaison with General Spínola, and there's a general understanding that, as one of the Movement's 'chosen generals', it's imperative to keep him in the loop. Spínola can't be involved directly – there's still too much heat around him from the events surrounding his removal from office and he's certainly under constant surveillance – but Otelo can maintain communication through an intermediary on Spínola's staff. It's through this intermediary that the general is given a look at the programme, with the goal of ultimately placing him into that temporary military leadership. Colonel Vasco Gonçalves, another of the ideologues heavily involved with the programme's drafting, uses his own connections with Costa Gomes to try and get that general on board – a process that gets nowhere. The Movement, led from the beginning by junior officers, finds itself incapable of letting go of the shackles of proper military hierarchy in the search for 'chiefs'.[3] Under the proposed structure of the temporary regime after the coup, General Costa Gomes is set to take the role of president, and the intention is to put Spínola in the role of chief of staff of the armed forces – number one in the (newly constituted) military hierarchy.

António Spínola had spent some time in the aftermath of 16 March cursing the 'snakes and lizards' of the Movement for their inaction – the radio silence from the leadership had worked, and much like the regime the general had come to the conclusion that the captains had wound down their activity. Being approached with the manifesto delights the general, and Spínola takes a pencil to the Movement's document, shaping it to his own views. Some of the suggestions are straightforward, and are taken on board without dispute: the Movement of Armed Forces Officers is shortened to Armed Forces Movement (*Movimento das Forças Armadas*, MFA), the temporary military government is given the name Junta of National Salvation (*Junta da Salvação Nacional*). Other edits and redactions, however, give a glimpse into Spínola's own hang-ups. The programme makes numerous mentions of democracy, and pushes for an active removal of fascist or far-right organisations from political power, or even from participation in the democratic process. Spínola draws lines and crosses through these sections – in his view the country's political direction should remain out of the programme. He also raises questions about the complete abolition of censorship, and the release of *all* political prisoners, which seem to him excessively radical positions.[4] One of the additions Spínola makes involves the total removal of power and rank from any senior armed forces elements that had participated in Marcelo Caetano's pantomime of loyalty at the National Assembly on 15 March – having been scorned by the military establishment, Spínola prepares the scene to take his revenge on the Rheumatic Brigade. After a series of back and forth exchanges and edits (and some key redactions), Spínola approves the MFA's programme and agrees to form a part of the Junta, in principle. Should the coup come off.

Otelo storms ahead with the plans. By 20 April, every unit on his list, up and down the country, has a copy of their mission, and the detailed communications protocol that will guarantee unified action. Not everyone in Otelo's orbit is as optimistic as he is. Vítor Alves has never been sure of the plan – in his mind, and among a scattering of others on the committee, it seems a better idea to organise a mass show of force, assembling all their loyal units in one central location and placing an ultimatum in front of the regime. Otelo is adamant this would be suicide – the regime would be able to siege any Movement force stuck in one place, all the while massing their loyal units and even potentially those of fascist Spain and NATO. Otelo's strategy has always been an employment of force that neutralises the regime's own, one that acts so quickly they don't have time to respond. The General Plan of Operations has the MFA achieving victory in less than a day. Vítor Alves, stroking his beard, asks the question he's been fearing: what does Otelo reckon are the chances of success?

'Taking into account the unknowns, I guarantee our chances of success at 80%, for a victory achieved twelve hours after H Hour.'

Alves is astonished. 'Wow! If you'd said 20% I would have found it sensational! Don't you think you're being too optimistic? I hope, in any case, that you've prepared for the alternative.'

'Alternative? What alternative?' Otelo replies cheerfully. 'I have to confess I don't have any other plan prepared. To think of an alternative is to admit possibilities of defeat. I don't make those admissions. I have to say, mentioning a success chance of just 80% I was playing to your perspective. We're going to win, and in the timeline I've said.'[5]

That frank optimism has been Otelo's line when questioned by his units – that there's no need for a plan B, because they're going to win, and win quickly. When the questions persist, he quips back: 'If we lose? You say in your interrogations, when you get arrested, that you had nothing to do with it. That there was an artillery major named Otelo, crazy in the head, that thought of bringing this government down and convinced you to join his war. Tell them it's all his fault.' That doesn't stop many of his officers from developing their own fallbacks, in many cases contingencies that involve retreating to a fortified location and, if necessary, fighting until the last man. Everyone knows that, whatever happens, once the operation starts there's no going back. But Otelo does have one final ace up his sleeve. In a quick and impromptu meeting with artillery major Alexandre Aragão, soon set to return to Bissau, he sets out his only plan B: should the coup fail in Portugal, the MFA in Guinea are to launch their own operation and topple the military command structure there. He hopes Caetano's government won't survive the coming days, but if it does, a rebellion in the overseas territories will be the final blow.

All the MFA units enter a state of alert on the morning of 22 April. The only missing piece of the puzzle is the information about when the operation is to be carried out. Assessing how much remains to be done, Otelo sets what he calls H Hour for 03:00 on Thursday 25 April. They now need to figure out one clear way to tell all their forces that everything is going to plan, and to carry out their missions. One of the key points of failure of 16 March – the one that ultimately led to the arrests of their comrades

– was the lack of collective action. The regiment from Caldas da Rainha left for Lisbon hoping that they were part of a larger force, but there hadn't been any coordination to that end. The Movement is set on not repeating that mistake. Carlos Almada Contreiras, their main liaison with the Navy, puts forward an interesting suggestion. While on a recent trip to Madrid, Contreiras had been given a book by an exiled Chilean monk, who had left his home country following Pinochet's rise to power.[6] The book – *White Book of the Change of Government in Chile*[7] – details how Pinochet's units had used radio signals consisting of specific popular music to coordinate elements of the coup. Doing the same in Portugal might be a viable way to send out a wide, coordinated signal without the regime catching on to anything untoward happening. The radio station Rádio Clube Português is already on Otelo's radar as a hub to send out communications on behalf of the MFA, and it has a wide reach. Otelo has a connection there – João Paulo Dinis, one of RCP's presenters, was a conscripted corporal under Otelo's command in Guinea. With his packed schedule of coup planning, Otelo sends the Air Force captain José da Costa Martins (already assigned the task of coordinating the occupation of the RCP station) to liaise with Dinis.

Costa Martins has never met João Paulo Dinis. Knowing that the presenter has an interest in new music, he arrives one morning with a collection of Israeli music on vinyl, hoping to use it as an icebreaker. Dinis meets him in the long hall at the centre of Rádio Clube Português' offices on Rua Sampaio e Pina, and immediately the captain puts him on edge.

'Look, come outside with me for a moment,' mumbles Costa Martins, suddenly conspiratorial. The two men step outside. 'Let's go over to my car. I want to talk to you.'

João Paulo Dinis climbs into the passenger seat of Costa Martins' Mini, but keeps one leg on the pavement through the open door – ready to make a quick escape if needed. Costa

Martins fumbles through an introduction, flashing his military ID. 'We need you. To give a signal. We're going to do a movement. Do you understand?'

Dinis looks back blankly. 'Look, I'm not sure who you are or what you want. You could be a PIDE agent for all I know…'

The accusation gets an explosive reaction from Costa Martins. 'I'm not! Hell! Don't even think that! No way! You can believe that I'm not!'

'You might say that but I don't know you from anywhere.'

'But you know Major Otelo Saraiva de Carvalho, right?'

The name of his old commander changes Dinis' demeanour slightly, but he's still sceptical. Costa Martins proposes to arrange a meeting between the former corporal and the major, to clear up his intentions. Dinis agrees. 'Today's Monday, so I guess we could meet on Friday?'

'Friday?!' replies Costa Martins. 'No, it has to be today!'[8]

At midnight on 22 April, Otelo and Costa Martins are waiting for João Paulo Dinis in the restaurant at Apolo 70. They spot the musician Zeca Afonso, sitting at one of the tables like a good omen. When Dinis joins them fifteen minutes later he greets his former officer like an old friend, but the conversation, over cold beers, soon becomes tense. Otelo explains what they're doing, and what he needs from Dinis – a radio signal that will launch the coup, broadcast from the powerful antennae at RCP. Dinis is hesitant – the news of the 16 March failure doesn't fill him with confidence – but Otelo convinces him this is the real deal, a carefully planned operation unlike the adventurous cock-up in March. Another problem – Dinis isn't on RCP's full-time staff, he's only a collaborator on one of their programmes. The station he actually works at is Lisbon Associated Broadcasters (*Emissores Associados de Lisboa*, EAL) – he doesn't know who'll be on duty at RCP on the night of the operation. Otelo suggests he find out – it may well be an ardent anti-fascist they can pull to the cause. The men finish their beers and make the short drive to Parque Eduardo VII, leaving Dinis to take the short walk to the radio station alone. He comes back with mixed news – the presenter on the evening of the 24th will be Joaquim Furtado – apparently a nice guy, but not someone Dinis knows personally. Time is of the essence – they don't have the luxury of tracking down Furtado and convincing him to play the signal. Dinis instead agrees to broadcast from EAL – but what should the signal be? Otelo and Costa Martins are keen that it be a song by Zeca Afonso. The musician's poetic, subtly anti-regime music was a constant presence for the officers in Africa and is barely tolerated by the state, many of his songs on national ban lists. Using his music would be a powerful symbolic gesture, certainly for the officers who know its meaning. Dinis, already nervous about his task, counters with a song he knows won't raise any eyebrows – Portugal's 1974 Eurovision entry '*E Depois do Adeus*', a national hit that's already a regular on the airwaves. Otelo agrees – in any case the actual signal is to be João Paulo's preamble, specifically the phrase 'it's five to midnight'. Any changes to the plan will be communicated in person. Before the men go their separate ways, Dinis has one pressing question: 'What happens if this fails?' Otelo doesn't hesitate: 'It's not going to fail, man!'

There's another problem: the Associated Broadcasters only have a range of one hundred kilometres, covering the Greater Lisbon area but useless for reaching any units further afield. Otelo takes the last-minute decision to have two signals, one for the Lisbon area that kicks off the bulk of the missions, and one played shortly afterwards for everyone else. Through contacts made by Captain Almada Contreiras, the Movement have an in with the people who run the Rádio Renascença show *Limite*, and can arrange for a song to be played. In this case, Otelo is insistent it be one by Zeca Afonso. At the top of the list is '*Venham Mais Cinco*' ('Let Five More Come'), but it's a no-go: it's one of the many tracks on the radio ban lists for having lyrics the regime deems too provocative. Another, favoured by Otelo, is '*Traz Outro Amigo Também*' ('Bring Another Friend As Well'), which has the added, playful layer of urging the officers to bring their friends out onto the streets. Captain José Santos Coelho, another of the men charged with occupying RCP, has another suggestion: '*Grândola, Vila Morena*', recently played by Afonso at the Recreios Coliseum to a receptive crowd. The song contains the line 'the people are in charge', which echoes the political goals of the operation. They settle for '*Grândola*', which is left in the hands of Carlos Albino, Álvaro Guerra and Leite Vasconcelos to be played just after midnight on the chosen date. As with the first signal, the actual cue for action is less the song and more its prerecorded introduction, Leite Vasconcelos reciting the first stanza.

On the afternoon of 23 April, Otelo drives to the top of Parque Eduardo VII and parks on Avenida Sidónio Pais. He takes out a briefcase and walks over to a bench, where he can overlook the park. It's a cold day. A casual observer wouldn't necessarily remark on the number of figures, in their late twenties or early thirties, wearing identical shoes and trousers and walking with the clipped confidence of military men who seem, despite their similarities, to be taking meandering paths through the park.[9] These are the MFA's liaison officers, tasked with collecting the Final Instructions and the Annex of Transmissions, the radio cues everyone is expected to listen out for. They also contain the sign and countersign for MFA units to recognise each other in the field: 'Courage', and 'For victory'.[*] One by one, the officers sit on Otelo's bench, and he hands them a folder that also includes a copy of the fascist newspaper *A Época*, which is the shibboleth for the units receiving the

---

[*] The original plan of operations, handwritten as it is, grants a glimpse at Otelo's flair for the poetic. Scribbled out next to the final sign and countersign are a first, rejected pass: 'Immense faith in victory', and 'guarantee of a better future'.

instructions on the other end. There are two liaison officers for each MFA unit, who receive their folders separately and travel to their destinations over different routes, a redundancy measure in case anyone is caught. It's a long afternoon of handoffs, and it's late evening by the time Otelo drives back to his home in Oeiras. He's decided not to spend the night there – if something goes wrong, they'll certainly be after him – but there's something he has to do first. His wife, Dina, is there when he arrives. He sits down next to her on his couch. Despite the many Movement meetings at their house, despite his whirlwind schedule over the last month, he's never clued her in on what the Movement is doing.

'I won't be sleeping at home, but I won't tell you where I'm sleeping. It's a question of security, because they might come here and arrest me. But I want you to know that I'm launching a military operation to topple the government.'

Dina's eyes widen. He calms her down enough to say: 'H Hour is the day after tomorrow, at three in the morning. At four our first communication should be out, through Rádio Clube, to take advantage of the news hour. If it's read out, it's a good sign. It means we have the broadcaster and everything's going well.'

'And if it's not?'

'Wait for the next news segment. If instead of our communiqués you start hearing another kind of news, praising the regime and talking about another aborted coup, that means we lost the fight.'

'And then?'

'And then, I don't know what could happen to me. I assume I'll be fired, handed over to PIDE, spend a few years as a civilian in Caxias or, who knows, take a one-way trip to Tarrafal. One thing I guarantee you: I will never fight a war overseas again.' The mood is tense, and Otelo senses that that last flurry of information was too much. 'But don't start worrying about that. I'm certain that, in a few hours, we'll win this war. We control almost

171

all the units in the country, the gang is on formidable form, we have the element of surprise on our side. It's easy!'

Dina holds it together enough to crack a joke. 'You mean we're not going to the opera tomorrow?' He'd forgotten. They have tickets to *La Traviata*. It'll have to be for another time.

Otelo kisses his sleeping eight-year-old son on the head, and embraces his wife one final time. 'Until Friday, my love. I'll be here to have lunch with you.' He exits the house with his uniform in a bag. He remembers, too late, he's left his pistol behind. Walking back into the house, he sees his wife on their bed, arms wrapped around her knees, sobbing heavily.[10]

On the afternoon of 24 April, Ernesto Melo Antunes' mother-in-law receives a telegram in her home in Ponta Delgada, from an unknown source. It reads:

AUNT AURORA TRAVELS USA 25 03 00
A HUG
COUSIN ANTÓNIO

She thinks to herself, 'That's odd.' The Aunt Aurora she can remember, wizened and barely mobile, would scarcely leave the house, let alone take an overnight trip across the Atlantic. When Melo Antunes receives the telegram, however, he clutches it like a delicate prize. It's the code he and Otelo had agreed before he'd left for the Azores. He shows the letter to Vasco Lourenço, and the two men smile in anticipation. Tomorrow. It's happening tomorrow, and they need to prepare.

Meanwhile, Otelo has arrived at his command post, a room set aside by Luís Macedo in the 1st Engineering Regiment (*Regimento de Engenharia 1*, RE1) building in Pontinha, a few miles north-west of central Lisbon. RE1 is chosen for several reasons, but high among them is its complete loyalty to the MFA. The command post is set up in a spare classroom within the unit, which Captain Luís Macedo, Otelo's second in command and one of the regiment's officers, has set aside. The room is taken up by a large empty table, which is flanked by three more: one piled high with assorted radios, the other two with banks of civilian and military telephones. In a corner stands a metal cupboard, filled with pistols and grenades. Lieutenant Colonel Garcia dos Santos' communications protocol is elaborate – every MFA unit and target has been assigned a code name, so the regime is left in the dark in case it manages to listen in to any of the radio or telephone chatter from the revolutionaries. The command post is given the name OSCAR – a play on Otelo's initials.

The key to an effective military operation is knowing what your enemy is doing. That notion lies at the heart of the technical crown jewel of the coup. Garcia dos Santos has known for some time that there's already a plan in place to connect a phone line from the Transmissions Regiment on Rua dos Sapadores to the Military College in Luz, just past the edge of the north circular. There's an underground cable doing part of the journey – but they need to make the rest of the connection through overhead wires. Garcia dos Santos gives Captain Veríssimo da Cruz and militia quartermaster Carlos Cedoura the task of finishing that link to the Military College, and then extending it to RE1 in Pontinha, with the utmost urgency. The first part is easy – the twenty-one soldiers they manage to rustle up for the job make their way up the motorway, simply attaching the long loom of telephone cable to preexisting military pylons. It's when they get to the Military College that things get hairy – not only are they doing this without any real permission from the higher authorities, but the way to Pontinha is completely lacking in the infrastructure needed for an overhead phone line. In the dead of night, metre by metre, the soldiers make do; they climb rooftops, run cable through balcony railings, toss it over tree branches, all the while under the bemused eyes of Lisbon's denizens who, thankfully, decide not to question why the military is running cable over their homes at such odd hours.

It's early afternoon on 24 April by the time Cedoura's men arrive in Pontinha with the end of the phone line and a supplementary bank of telephones. Luís Macedo isn't expecting them, and comes close to arresting the young quartermaster, until Garcia dos Santos' name is mentioned. A few hours later, Garcia dos Santos himself arrives in a truck, giving Macedo his second surprise of the day: he needs to set up a thirteen-metre-high antenna. Macedo balks – if the unit is being surveilled, suddenly raising such a tall structure is sure to arouse suspicion. They agree to build the antenna up to the height of the regiment's walls, and only finish its construction after sunset.[11] Combined, the telephone line and the antenna give the MFA's command post the ability to liaise with any and all loyal units in the field, as well as listen in, with help from allies in the Transmissions Regiment, to the regime's own communications: anything from the police, GNR and Portuguese Legion to the military authorities and Marcelo Caetano himself. Carlos Almada Contreiras, trained in transmissions, finds himself in the basement of the Naval Ministry, at the centre of all Portuguese naval communications and with a direct line to Vítor Crespo, the Navy's man in the command centre. The Navy is still on the books as a neutral agent regarding the Movement's activities, but Crespo is keen to at least try and mobilise the small corps of marines (*fuzileiros*) the Navy has in reserve to take the PIDE/DGS headquarters and Caxias fort – two targets that have fallen out of the operations plan.

The communications set-up is the most high-tech element of the whole operation. Inside the command post, Otelo lays out the most low-tech element on the central table: a large, detailed map of Portugal's roads. It's the only such map he could find, issued by the Portuguese Automotive Club to its members, and already covered in scribbles and labels, the result of a month's work. It's not like the military maps the men from Guinea are used to, but it'll do. Beside it sits a 1:25,000 scale map of Greater Lisbon, sourced by Luís Macedo. When Vítor Crespo wanders into Pontinha in the early evening of 24 April, he's shocked by how shoddy the set-up is – Otelo has to convince him that they have all the tools they need to make the operation happen. Whatever jitters the officers in this room might have, whatever apprehension about the success of the coming day, there's little the men in this room could do to stop it, even if they wanted to. Over the past month Otelo has assembled a formidable machine, one with hundreds of moving parts and contingencies, one designed for the express purpose of hitting the oldest surviving dictatorship in Europe exactly where it's weak, and shattering it forever. In a few minutes that machine will be fired up and set loose. All there is to do now, is wait.

A mural of Captain Salgueiro Maia on Avenida de Berna,
Lisbon, painted in 2014.

CHAPTER EIGHT

'IT'S FIVE TO ELEVEN...'

Just up the road from Parque Eduardo VII, past a smaller park which hosts the Gulbenkian Arts Centre, stands the church of Our Lady of the Rosary of Fátima, a white, austere building with narrow windows and subtle detailing. Its modernist architecture jars with many of the older, classical churches dotted around the city and it earned its place in the history books as the first church commissioned by Cardinal Manuel Gonçalves Cerejeira, patriarch of Lisbon, Portugal's leading clergyman during the *Estado Novo* and personal friend of António Salazar. In the 1930s, Avenida Barbosa do Bocage, the street that leads up to the church, was where Salazar would regularly come for Sunday Mass – at the home and chapel of his friend Josué Trocuado. This routine would be shaken up on 4 July 1937. As Salazar exited his vehicle, a bundle of dynamite that had been planted in a nearby rubbish bin exploded, shattering windows and damaging the fronts of houses all along the avenue and its arterial streets. The bomb was intended for the dictator, but its hasty placement meant it resulted in no deaths or injuries. Apocryphally, Salazar dusted himself off and said, 'Well then, let's get to Mass.' This would not turn out to be the only attempt on the dictator's life – but it was the one that came closest to succeeding.

The architects of the 4 July bombing were a heterogenous grouping of anarchists, communists and miscellaneous rebels. The police crackdown in the aftermath of the bombing led to the deaths of two men who were likely not even involved, killed by PIDE's brutal interrogation methods.[1] In the intervening years most would be captured, imprisoned, tortured, some at the Aljube prison in Lisbon, some in Peniche, Caxias, the penal colony in Tarrafal.[2] They would have no way of knowing that thirty-seven years later, within spitting distance of their assassination attempt, something would happen that would smash Salazar's legacy in a way their bomb never could. Parallel to Avenida Barbosa do Bocage is Avenida Elias Garcia. At number 162, just around the corner from the big white church, sits a seven-storey building, unremarkable but for the brown granite pillars that hold it up, its surrounds paved with a pattern of cobbles typical of older Lisbon streets. In 1974 the top floor of this building hosts one of the stations for EAL, one of numerous local radio stations with a broadcast range covering the Greater Lisbon area.

It's the evening of 24 April, and EAL radio host João Paulo Dinis is nervous. He knows he is risking his job, his freedom and potentially his life. He has one task tonight – making sure that a certain song is played at a certain time from this specific location and that he introduces the song with a very specific phrase. Two days prior, he'd had one of Otelo's messengers arrive to tell him that the time slot needed to be moved back an hour – 22:55 is when it all happens. Captain José da Costa Martins of the MFA sits behind the wheel of his Mini Cooper, parked in front of the church next door. He wears a black wool coat, hand-knitted by his mother. At his waist is a Walther pistol, and on the back seat sits a closed leather briefcase containing a sub-machine gun and several hand grenades. Sitting next to him is his girlfriend of three years, Aura, who cradles a battery-powered radio to her chest, listening intently. Costa Martins had picked her up after dinner earlier in the night, his mind wandering – 'It's all going to blow up tonight, Aura,' he'd said. 'Tonight?!' she'd cried. He had urged her to go home – she had insisted on being with him. He's not used to saying no to her, and so here they are together, grateful for each other's warmth as they wait for the song that'll change everything. Aura doesn't know what's in the briefcase behind her, but she can guess. Costa Martins is there in front of the church as much for his own peace of mind as anything – if something goes wrong with this first step, he might be able to step in and fix it, though he hopes he doesn't have to. He is one of hundreds of MFA officers stationed at street corners and in command posts, barracks and assorted houses and cars, holding their breath, tuning their radios, and waiting.

In his command post at the Engineering Regiment building in Pontinha, Otelo Carvalho is surrounded by comrades – Major Sanches Osório and Lieutenant Colonels Garcia dos Santos and Fisher Lopes Pires. Lopes Pires fiddles with his Philips radio. The room fills with cigarette and pipe smoke. At 22:48, mere minutes before the expected signal, there's a sudden problem – the radio station suffers a technical fault that cuts off the transmission. For seconds that seem to stretch indefinitely, Otelo listens to the hiss of static, frozen in place – 22:50… 22:51. Costa Martins exits his car and paces back and forth on the street, as Aura's eyes widen. 'What is this shit? What is this shit?' he repeats into the night. Did Dinis bottle it? Is he about to blow the whole operation? Did PIDE figure out the plan, cut off the signal? He reaches for the briefcase in the back seat. Aura's eyes are frozen, staring straight ahead through the windscreen. Suddenly, seamlessly, the signal returns. Costa Martins stops, the briefcase gripped tight in his hand.[3] In Pontinha, Otelo releases a breath he hadn't realised he was holding.

At 22:55, as if read directly from the secret missive each soldier had received, the voice of João Paulo Dinis crackles on to radio sets across the Greater Lisbon area.

It's five to eleven. With you, Paulo de Carvalho and the '74 Eurovision Song Contest: E Depois do Adeus…

'Alea jacta est," whispers Otelo.

The first note of *'E Depois do Adeus'* is a thundering drumbeat, followed by a rising melody, Carvalho's mellifluous voice kicking in almost immediately. It's a swaying, triumphant ballad about love and loss, sung in Portuguese with a Sinatra-esque twang and backed by a full orchestra. In the BBC broadcast of Eurovision 1974, as the singer takes his applause, host David Vine seems thrilled for him – 'My goodness, what a performance, he's sold that song well!' – but Carvalho's stage presence and pitch-perfect delivery aren't enough to prevent him from drawing dead last with Norway, Germany and Switzerland** – unsurprising given the winners this year are a plucky Swedish quartet with what would become a timeless tune: 'Waterloo'. But ABBA never triggered a revolution.

The MFA officers, to widespread relief, had received their first signal, which meant that at least that part of the operation had gone to plan. For the men listening within the broadcast range of the EAL tower, this is all they need to carry on their respective jobs. Captain Costa Martins waits for the song to finish, leaving the melody hanging in the night air. He exchanges glances with Aura, who smiles nervously, her eyes damp with tears of relief. Martins returns his briefcase to the back seat, climbs back into his car and drives off, with his own operations to undertake in the city. Under the cover of night, Lisbon springs into action.

April 2014. North of the building that once housed EAL, across the road from the church of Our Lady of the Rosary, is a tall glass building that belongs to Lisbon University's Faculty of Social and Human Sciences. Seen from the west, the building

---

*   'The die is cast' – a phrase attributed to Julius Caesar when he crossed the Rubicon.

**   Portugal would not win the Eurovision Song Contest until 2017, and in fact holds the record for most appearances in the final without a win.

(officially Tower B) is meant to suggest the image of an open book. The campus gets regular visits from the ducks that live in the nearby Gulbenkian Institute's garden ponds. On Avenida de Berna, on a bare white wall against the side of the university building, four graffiti artists don gas masks, prepare their stencils, and spray. This is the Underdogs art collective from Porto, commissioned by the university to create a mural celebrating forty years since 25 April.[4] On the left side of the mural, the Portuguese shield appears, contained within chains and crossed bones. On the other end, a heart over crossed rifles, their barrels bent sideways, rendered useless. Symbols of Portugal before and after the regime. Between them, the stoic face of Captain Fernando Salgueiro Maia, framed by two long rifles with carnations in their barrels and a pattern of raised fists, painted in the colours of the Portuguese flag. Over the next several years the mural will suffer wear, bits of the stone will chip off, the colours will fade away. For now, as the Underdogs carry out their meticulous work, the carnations are a vibrant red, and Salgueiro Maia stares out at Lisbon rendered larger than life, as he is remembered, for actions he carried out forty years ago and only a few kilometres away.

24 April 1974. Approximately seventy kilometres away, at his home in Santarém, Salgueiro Maia has left his wife Natércia by the radio and slipped out to the Army Cavalry School (*Escola Prática de Cavalaria*, EPC) under the cover of night. He has told her the signals to listen out for – a small token, so she can at least try and follow along with the day, and know things are going according to plan. She takes comfort in the fact he's taken a bundle of handkerchiefs, for his sinus infection, and a handful of cigarillos. She sees the cigarillos as a sign of his optimism – Fernando rarely smokes. At EPC he is joined by several other officers, some from other regiments, sent here to reinforce the MFA presence. Captain Joaquim Bernardo replaces the duty officers with men he trusts, in preparation for the evening's events.

Earlier in the day, unexpectedly, the garrison commander had left Santarém for Lisbon, leaving the second commander, Lieutenant Colonel Sanches, in charge. Before '*E Depois do Adeus*' graces the airwaves, Sanches is at dinner close to the EPC building, at the home of Captain António Garcia Correia. Correia's objective is to inform Sanches of the evening's plans, and hopefully convince him to sign up to the Movement. He describes the order of operations – the objectives of the mission, and the EPC's specific duties – but omits the fact that the operation is actually already under way. Sanches is less than convinced – he rebuffs Correia. In a huff, he makes his way back to EPC with Correia in tow. On arrival, he is immediately aware that something odd is happening. The officers who were on duty when he left for dinner have been replaced with different men, captains. Turning to Captain Pedro Aguiar, who now bears the duty officer armband, Sanches shouts: 'You're not the duty officer, take that armband off at once!'

Aguiar replies, 'I will not! It was placed on me by Captain Bernardo, and only he can order me to remove it.'

Lieutenant Colonel Sanches immediately summons all the officers to a meeting. To his immense surprise, almost all the officers of the EPC contingent appear – despite the fact that, at that time of night, barely any of them should be there.

'What's going on here?' he demands.

'What you're looking at, sir, is what I was telling you about back at my house. Today's the day – the EPC is ready to leave,' replies Garcia Correia. The second commander announces his intention to get on the phone and report what's happening to the military headquarters in Tomar. Captain Bernardo grabs his arm. 'You're not calling anyone. Central command is under our control. You either come over to our side, or you lose control of the School.'

Sanches continues to refuse. Outnumbered by the men in the room he consents to being locked in his office, his means of communication removed. Gathered now with nervous energy, the men in Santarém have a few hours to wait until they need to kick off their own actions. The MFA officers now in full control of the EPC flick the radio to another station, Rádio Renascença, and await the second signal, the one intended to put boots on the ground across the country.

At Rádio Renascença's offices in downtown Lisbon, the intern Paulo Coelho has temporarily taken over the job of radio announcer from Leite Vasconcelos on the programme *Limite*, and is really screwing things up for everyone. He is unaware of the deal, cooked up between the MFA leaders and their sympathisers at the radio station, to play an eleven-minute recording at 00:20 that includes the necessary signal. Just before 00:20, Coelho puts on an advertisement reel. Thinking quickly, after the first advert concludes, Manuel Tomás in the technical booth nudges the sound technician's hand, hard – this causes the tracks to switch to the 'correct' one.[5] Finding the sudden transition unusual, the on-duty colonel from the government censor's office pops his head in, and is quickly reassured that there was simply a minor change in schedule. Across the country, Leite Vasconcelos reads out the opening stanzas of José Afonso's 'Grândola, Vila Morena', his voice overlapping with the sound of feet marching on gravel, the rhythmic opening notes of the song.

José Afonso's deep warbling voice follows Vasconcelos', transforming the words into a cry, an appeal, a chant. His voice is joined by others, a choir set to the pounding rhythm of stamping feet, evoking workers in the dusty fields of Alentejo. The song is structured as a call and response, the response stanza delivered in reverse and in chorus, the words speaking of solidarity, equality, friendship. The song's lyrics manage to just barely skirt the pens of the government censors, its resonance as a protest song buried in metaphor, a promise to a town whose history of struggle runs as deep as the roots of an ancient oak – a promise to keep up the fight.

When Afonso played 'Grândola' at the First Meeting of Portuguese Song on 29 March, less than a month ago, the reports from government agents in attendance made a note that the audience screamed the lines about popular power with particular gusto.[6] Where the choice of 'E Depois do Adeus' was, as Otelo put it, a mere 'banality', 'Grândola' is a clear statement of intent from the MFA leadership. The civilian late-night listeners who might be tuned to Rádio Renascença shortly after midnight will not know the meaning behind the song until much later. José Afonso's voice echoes into the night, from cafés and car stereos, and on to Fisher Lopes Pires' radio in Pontinha, where, on hearing the first few seconds of Vasconcelos' voice, the room breaks into spontaneous applause. The men grab each other, smiling. 'No going back now,' someone says. Someone else shouts, 'Now it's in God's hands!' Ten minutes later, a convoy from the Practical Artillery School in Évora leaves its garrison, heading to its final destination high up on the hill that holds the statue of Christ the King, overlooking the Tagus.[7]

Back at the EPC, Salgueiro Maia orders the duty corporal to wake the soldiers. Room by room, the corporal orders lights to be switched on, men to leave their beds. 'Captain Maia wants to address you all,' he says. Most of the men think they're being woken for some form of training exercise. They gather in the largest room the EPC has – over five hundred men, expectant and alert, lined up against a concrete wall. Salgueiro Maia meets their gaze.[8]

'In life,' he says, 'there are moments that, by their importance, transcend us. So, in the face of the denial of freedom and the injustice we have reached, the lack of hope in better days, it's time to change this regime. Not by going back to the previous regime but, by granting them freedom and democracy, guaranteeing the people a choice in their collective destiny.'

The tension rises in the room as the men begin to realise what is being proposed. The last few weeks of preparations, of vehicle tune-ups and equipment checks, the ramped-up training regime the soldiers have been subjected to over the last forty days, suddenly begin to make sense.

Maia continues. 'Gentlemen, there are various kinds of state. Liberal states, social democratic states, socialist states, and so on. But none is as bad as the state we live under now! So, whoever wants to come with me, let's go to Lisbon and end this son of a bitch of a situation. Opportunities to enter into the annals of history only arise once in life. Anyone who's willing to join me, arm yourselves. Whoever doesn't want to go can stay here.'

Maia isn't sure how many of his men will be willing to go ahead with the mission. He makes it clear that there will be no repercussions for those who don't wish to participate. What he isn't expecting, what nobody in the MFA is really expecting, is for every one of the 500-strong EPC unit to volunteer, enthusiastically. Maia's men in the EPC are young, and they've heard enough about the situation in the colonies to know they don't want to go there. To the officers here who have survived the war, the men they are arming look like children. Walking past a particularly cherubic pair of trainees, Maia shouts: 'Come on, guys! Let's get some helmets so these kids at least look like soldiers!'[9] The EPC unit only has enough vehicles ready to take 240-odd men into Lisbon – the rest have to be left in Santarém. Despite Maia's best efforts to squirrel away ammunition, there isn't enough to go around – some of the men have to carry empty rifles. The degradation of the military garrisons in mainland Portugal means that many of the rifles they are taking are leftovers from the Second World War – unlikely to be useful in a pitched battle anyway. Maia hopes none of these guns will need to be fired today.

Preparing the EPC detachment takes a few hours – mission details delivered in hushed tones, the syncing of radios. Maia patiently corrects the mistakes of the young men under his command as they prepare for war, just as he did in Guinea. At roughly 03:20 Maia's battalion of men and vehicles is ready to leave Santarém. Maia asks Captain Bernardo whether 'the other guys are out' – referring to the other MFA missions across the country. The memory of 16 March, of the Caldas regiment making their way to Lisbon blind and with no backup, weighs heavily on their minds. Bernardo doesn't know, but tries to encourage Maia – 'If they're not out already, they certainly will be when they know the Cavalry is on the road!' The men hug each other. 'Good luck, Fernando. It's all gonna be OK, you'll see,' Bernardo says.

'Take care of that bum leg,' replies Maia, referring to the wound Bernardo had received in Guinea, one that had taken him out of active duty for several years.

Running in through the EPC gates, Lieutenant Alfredo Assunção is just in time to hop into Maia's jeep at the front of the convoy. He sports a black beret and a striking black moustache. Assunção is Maia's second in command for this operation, but despite the urgency of the morning's preparations, he's managed to sleep through his alarm. At 03:30 the convoy begins its eighty-kilometre journey into Lisbon. Natércia Maia sees the convoy leave through the gaps in the Persian blinds on her window, kept only slightly open for fear of PIDE surveillance. Salgueiro Maia and Assunção sit in their jeep in silence, alert, pensive. This is new for them. Unlike their time in Africa, they head out this morning with no guaranteed base to return to should their mission fail, without the apparatus of the state behind them, without the excuse of superior orders. All they have today is each other, the unshakeable knowledge that the men they travel alongside have their back, a trust built up over years in the colonial war. The war they have committed themselves to end.

Maia's recruitment of five hundred soldiers to the MFA cause is the sort of thing that is being repeated in military barracks across the country, as Otelo's plan of operations fully kicks into gear. In most of those garrisons, it doesn't take very much at all for the MFA officer present to convince the other officers, if not the garrison as a whole, to either join up with the operation or at the very least allow it to take its course. Any resistance, when it does appear, is usually in the form of an altercation with higher-ranking officers. Like in Santarém, the immediate solution is to lock those officers in a temporary brig, under guard, until the mission is accomplished – or they fail.

Two hundred kilometres north of Lisbon, in the coastal town of Figueira da Foz, Captains Dinis de Almeida and Fausto de Almeida Pereira had heard '*Grândola*' on the radio and retired to their quarters, setting an alarm for 02:30, as per their portion of the plan. Their part in the morning mission is to commandeer Heavy Artillery Regiment 3 and take a detachment to secure the political prison in Peniche, before continuing south to liaise with MFA forces in Lisbon. Dinis de Almeida is armed to the teeth when he enters the duty officers' room at 03:00 on the dot – zero hour for many of the MFA operations. He has a pistol in his right hand and another bulging from a holster around his waist, next to a dagger. A G3 rifle strapped to his back pokes out from behind his military cloak. He would look almost comical were it not for the look of sober resolve on his face. The duty officers, Nunes and Santos, look up surprised.

'What's going on?' asks Nunes.

'The Armed Forces Movement controls this barracks now,' replies Almeida.

Nunes pauses, confused. 'What's that?'

Almeida sighs. 'Look, now's not the time to explain. You should be able to figure it out... it's like what happened at Caldas, but this time to win.'

Nunes wants nothing to do with it. 'I'm the duty officer, you have to arrest me, I'm not getting involved in this... You have to arrest me.'

Almeida almost laughs. Both of the day officers are old friends of his. He went to school with Nunes. The whole situation seems absurd. 'Arrest you? Why would I arrest you? Take your gun out, you and your assistant – put them on the table. Pretend you're under arrest! If things go wrong tell them I disarmed you. You can just watch!'

Behind Dinis de Almeida, Fausto de Almeida Pereira notices that the barracks' commanding officer is leaving the officers' mess and alerts his comrade. Dinis de Almeida steps out and levels his G3 rifle at Colonel Aires de Figueiredo. Figueiredo stumbles, shocked, and begins to reach into his coat for his pistol. With his finger on the rifle's trigger, Almeida shouts: 'Careful, Commander, you're being detained!'

Figueiredo freezes. 'You're making a mistake, Dinis de Almeida, you're making a mistake here...'

'I'm not making a mistake, commander. You are under arrest. Please accompany me, without resisting, to the day officers' room.'

The commander is led at gunpoint to the room that contains Nunes and Santos, who are sitting calmly smoking cigarettes. He surveys the room, noting the day officers' pistols that have been left on a table, within reach of the men who seem to be offering no resistance to their imprisonment.

'Why don't you do something?' Figueiredo barks at Nunes. Nunes can only shrug sheepishly.

Dinis de Almeida maintains the fiction in front of the colonel that Nunes and Santos were disarmed in the course of the barracks occupation, and places him in a makeshift brig for the duration. The MFA officers begin running around preparing the regiment for its mission. Unlike the relatively breezy time Maia seems to have had in Santarém, Dinis de Almeida and his fellow officers struggle with the command role that's suddenly been thrust upon them. Several times Almeida loses his temper at his comrades as the preparations take longer and longer. At one point Almeida finds himself having to fill out reams of paperwork. The barracks quartermaster is unable to let go of military bureaucracy despite the revolutionary situation. He's requiring Almeida to sign out each individual rifle as they are handed to the sleepy queue of soldiers. 'Otherwise I'm screwed, otherwise I'm screwed!' the quartermaster cries. Almeida shouts back at the man, 'Stop this charade! There's no time! Give each of them a gun, and I'll sign for them later, and I'll take responsibility for any that get lost!' Another delay is caused by the search for the key to the munitions depot, which had inexplicably vanished. Eventually, Heavy Artillery Regiment 3, joined by a few other detachments that they have also armed, make their departure from Figueira da Foz.[10]

Back in central Lisbon, a short walk from the EAL radio station where 'E Depois do Adeus' was broadcast, west on Avenida Elias Garcia and then south on Rua Marquês Sá da Bandeira, is a small square – Largo São Sebastião da Pedreira. On the northern corner here is the Vilalva Palace – an eighteenth-century building that radiates colonial opulence, its face adorned with a bust of Camões. Behind the palace sits the park which now houses the Gulbenkian Institute and museum, the green land once part of the palace grounds, fully encircled by a stone wall and filled with exotic trees. In 1946 the building was gifted to the state, and transformed into the headquarters of the Lisbon Region Military – hence the green and gold fence that surrounds it, and the wrought iron sign above the main gate that reads Exército Português (Portuguese Army).

At the same time as Salgueiro Maia is leaving Santarém, a force of one hundred men led by Captain Bicho Beatriz surrounds Vilalva Palace. As the local military headquarters, this is a point of immense strategic importance to the MFA. It's from here that the government would try and coordinate its units in the metropolitan area. An almost identical manoeuvre is taking place simultaneously around the military headquarters for the city of Porto. Despite the time of night, Vilalva is staffed by enough of a military presence that surrender isn't immediate. Seeing the MFA forces circle the building, the Region Military units take up a position in a line behind the iron gates, a look of grim resignation on their faces. Bicho Beatriz walks over to face the gates, entering into a dialogue with the men, attempting to avoid a shoot-out. He calls for the duty officer, but the man refuses to appear. Over the course of the next hour of dialogue, the men guarding the palace are convinced of the futility of their efforts – one by one, they drop their weapons and abandon their posts. When Bicho Beatriz finally forces the gate open, he does so with no resistance from inside. The MFA men eventually find one of the duty officers, aspirant Santos, next to a telephone, a look of utter panic on his pale face. The other officer in the building has taken off his stripes, so as not to be identified as such. The delay in securing the building has given the loyalist unit time to call the chief of staff for the Region Military, Colonel Duarte, who makes his own call by waking General Edmundo Luz Cunha, commander of the Lisbon Region Military. The sieges of the two military headquarters in Lisbon and Porto are the first signals to the government that something's afoot.

Bicho Beatriz's unit is a detachment from the 5th Chasseurs Battalion (*Batalhão Caçadores 5*, BC5) which, based just up the road from the top of Parque Eduardo VII, has been given multiple objectives in the immediate area. A few minutes from Vilalva Palace, while Bicho Beatriz is still in the negotiation phase with the government defence forces, another detachment from BC5 positions itself in front of the imposing stone building across the road from the northern edge of the park. This is Lisbon penitentiary, a vast prison complex whose buildings form a six-pointed star, visible only from above. Unlike with Peniche, Caxias and Aljube, political prisons that the MFA intends to liberate, the MFA seeks simply to keep the prison's GNR units inside and away from the action. Within a few minutes of BC5 taking positions in front of the building, they receive a clear message from inside the prison – the GNR's mission is protecting the prisoners, and they do not intend to interfere with the MFA. It's of minor strategic interest – what will come to be much more important over the next several hours and days is the broadcasting building of Rádio Clube Português a few minutes away, off Rua Castilho and adjacent to Parque Eduardo VII's western edge.

Rádio Clube Português is integral to the MFA's plans, and as such the building has been under constant surveillance for days. MFA-loyal officers from the 10th Commando Group (GC10) have been stationed in vehicles and patrolling the nearby arterial streets since 21:00 the night before, in civilian clothes, their cover as late-night wanderers and café patrons only slightly marred by their identical trousers, shoes and socks. They periodically have coffees at the snack bar Pisca-Pisca* on the corner, where they can keep an eye on the entrance to the radio station. A casual observer might have found it strange when, at 00:20, 'Grândola, Vila Morena' seemed to play from multiple car radios in the vicinity, the cars' occupants breaking out in smiles, claps and tears of joy. A few hours later, shortly past zero hour, vehicles from BC5 make their way down Rua Castilho and form a barricade at either end of the road, as well as along Rua Sampaio e Pina, where the radio station is located. Among them is Captain Costa Martins in his wool coat and Mini Cooper, making sure the mission is going to plan. Shortly before, Costa Martins had insisted to Aura that it was time to say goodbye for the evening, and with a final kiss she had hailed a cab home. Seeing that the barricades are in place and watching from a

---

* Pisca-Pisca is no more, but a bakery/snack bar does still exist on the corner of Rua Sampaio e Pina and Rua Rodrigo da Fonseca.

distance as the commandos make their way into the RCP building, Costa Martins drives off, in the direction of Portela airport.

Major Costa Neves, one of the more senior MFA members, is in charge of the critical RCP mission. With a squad of commandos behind him, he enters the building and informs the doorman that this is a military coup – a message that quickly disseminates throughout the building. Within minutes the commandos have swept the offices, stationing themselves in their pre-arranged posts and disconnecting all telephones not needed by the officers. Radio host Joaquim Furtado, just turned twenty-six, is in the radio's Telex room preparing the 04:00 news segment. Buried in his work, he doesn't register the figure of Captain Santos Ferreira walking into the room for a few seconds – only the expectant silence makes him look up. He's taken aback to find an unfamiliar man in military fatigues, holding a pistol. Santos Ferreira is clearly nervous – Furtado asks him politely what's going on, and receives a vague reply about a military operation. The men look at each other in silence for a few seconds and, feeling Furtado poses no threat, Santos Ferreira leaves. To a man as clued up as Furtado on the political situation in Portugal, 'military operation' could mean anything – but the first thing that crosses his mind is the hard-right faction of Kaúlza de Arriaga, rumoured by the BBC to be organising a coup against Marcelo's liberal reforms. The thought makes him nervous.[11]

Joaquim Furtado exits the Telex room and wanders out into the long corridor that cuts through RCP's offices. He sees more soldiers milling around, and taking advantage of a pause in the officers' work he grabs Captain Santos Coelho and asks about the exact nature of the military operation. Santos Coelho summarises it quickly: 'Look – this is a coup to topple the regime, have free elections, end the colonial war, free political prisoners and put an end to PIDE and censorship.' Furtado could not have hoped for a better summary. His mind reels, the scope of the operation too enormous to comprehend. The regime seems too powerful to crack – could these men do it? The morning's programming isn't interrupted just yet – as the staff are informed of the plan, and of their part in the morning's mission, the late-night radio show *The Night Is Ours* continues to play out to unsuspecting night owls. None of the RCP staff put up any resistance – their reactions are surprise and anxiety. At 03:32, Santos Coelho makes a call to Otelo in Pontinha, using the code his target has been assigned: 'This is Group 10. Mexico has been conquered without incident.'

Back in Pontinha, the MFA's command post has had a tense few minutes waiting for the first calls to come in confirming successful missions around zero hour. One of the first was at 02:50, with the capture of 'Monaco' – the state television broadcaster RTP, by the Practical Military Administration School (*Escola Prática de Administração Militar*, EPAM). The mood in the room takes a serious blow with the arrival of Major Jaime Neves and his commando teams, who have failed in several of their missions to capture the commanders of the regime-loyal 7th Cavalry, 3rd Lancers and 1st Artillery regiments. Neves looks fresh and reeks of aftershave – the suspicion is he and his units have been sitting on the sidelines, waiting to see which way the wind blows on the operation before committing.* Slowly, more units begin to phone in, and the command post's mood lifts. Suddenly, the Engineering Regiment whose building Otelo's team is occupying receives a phone call. Captain Luís Macedo enters the command post and informs Otelo that it's the chief of

---

* On 25 November 2020, a tweet from Colonel Rodrigo Sousa e Castro accused Jaime Neves of having been at a strip club on the evening of 24 April. The major's inactivity on the day of the revolution has been further corroborated in reports such as that in *Operação Viragem Histórica* and by Vasco Lourenço in the interview.

staff for the Region Military – what should he say? 'I was about to tell him to piss off!' laughs Macedo.

'Are you crazy?' replies Otelo. 'Don't do that. Tell him everything's fine. Agree to do whatever he wants.'

Macedo gets on the phone with Colonel Duarte and puts on his most convincing impression of a young, clueless officer.

'Good evening,' he says cheerfully.

'Who's this?' replies Duarte.

'This is officer aspirant Santos, day officer for the RE1. Who's speaking?'

'Listen, mister officer aspirant, this is the chief of staff of the Lisbon Region Military – is everything all right there in the unit?'

'Everything's fine here, Colonel – is there a problem?'

'Are you sure everything's fine? Nobody strange has turned up around there, trying to get in? Where's your commander?'

'No, Colonel, everything's normal here. Our commander left yesterday afternoon.'

'Well, mister officer aspirant, you will call your commander immediately and tell him to return to the barracks, and from now on your Regiment is on lockdown. Nobody leaves, and only members of the Regiment are allowed in. Understand? And only take orders from me or your commander when he arrives.'

'Yes, Colonel, I'll call the commander right away.' Macedo hangs up the phone, stifling a laugh.[12]

Having made his way by car away from the barricades around RCP, Captain Costa Martins pulls up a few miles away at the Air Force base next to Lisbon airport. To his surprise, the area is empty. He is expecting to liaise with a detachment from the Practical Infantry School (*Escola Prática de Infantaria*, EPI) from several miles away in Mafra, carrying the firepower thought needed for the MFA to take the airport, but they are nowhere to be seen. Unbeknownst to him, the school's detachment is stuck, their attempt to drive hefty armoured vehicles through Lisbon's narrow streets marred by some badly parked cars and poor local knowledge, requiring them to double back laboriously. Not letting the complete absence of backup stop his mission, Costa Martins takes his briefcase and walks into the airbase. As an Air Force pilot with credentials he makes his way past the doorman without issue, and finds, to his delight, that the duty officers are both of a lower rank than him and asleep on the job. They wake up, startled and embarrassed, and ask Costa Martins if there is a problem. 'Nothing special,' quips the captain, 'just a revolution.' He tells the officers that the building is surrounded – he doesn't want any resistance, and he's in charge of the airbase from now on. The day officers are completely on board with this – so much so that, after a few more minutes of conversation and asserting the objectives of the revolution – Costa Martins considers the airbase converted to the MFA. He glances at his watch – it's well past the time the EPI should have arrived. He looks out of the window at the aircraft parked by the base – prepared to steal one and fly to Algeria, if things go wrong.[13,14]

Things are getting tense in Pontinha. The EPI's failure to arrive at Lisbon airport is delaying the operation – the MFA can't broadcast its first missive on the radio until they know the airport is secured. Having set the time for the first signal at between 03:45 and 04:00, Otelo decides to delay until 04:30. Across town, Captain António Rosado da Luz receives a phone call from Pontinha. He is given his first mission of the night: liaising with Costa Martins and giving him backup at the airport. Driving on the motorways along the edge of the city, he gets the sense that he's being followed by a sports car. He slows down, gives it a chance to overtake – it doesn't. Definitely PIDE, then. Luz slams on the accelerator and speeds down the motorway, the car behind him giving chase around the winding streets and roundabouts of Encarnação, in the vicinity of the airport. At one point, having temporarily lost sight of his tail, Luz performs a manoeuvre learned from years of bingeing trashy action flicks in his youth: he veers into a parking space, switches off the engine and dips his head out of view. A few seconds later, the driver of the mysterious sports car races past, none the wiser.[15]

Rosado da Luz arrives at Portela airport a few minutes later, and spots the tall figure of Costa Martins straight away. To his surprise his fellow captain isn't alone – sitting around him on the black plastic chairs of the airport's designated 'meeting point' are several police officers, looking up at the captain, who is soliloquising. Luz approaches carefully and pulls the captain aside, passing on Otelo's message – that the EPI is running late, but otherwise everything is running more or less to plan. Costa Martins replies that he's aware, and the nearby airbase has been neutralised – as well as the local police force. Martins had, identifying himself as a military captain, disarmed the police officers one by one, telling them afterwards that the revolution was on the move. It's at this point – shortly after four – that the EPI finally arrives, soldiers and officers piling in through the airport's doors. Costa Martins runs up to the airport's control tower backed by infantrymen and barks an order to the air traffic control crew to implement an immediate NOTAM (Notice to Airmen) that Portuguese airspace is closed – all traffic is to be diverted to Madrid and Las Palmas. All planes, military or civilian, are grounded, and no one has permission to land. Costa Martins gets on the phone to Otelo at 04:20: 'This is Lima Two. New York is occupied and under our control.'

'Great!' cries Otelo. 'We were worried about you. Well done. It's all going well.' Fisher Lopes Pires dials the number for Rádio Clube Português. 'Hello, Mexico? You can transmit the first message. New York has just been occupied.'

Back at RCP, the 10th Commando Unit has had a tense time getting set up. The plan is to broadcast the first communiqué from the MFA followed by the national anthem – but when they ask for a recording of the national anthem, the officers are informed the station doesn't have one. It's the sound technician Franklim Rodrigues who has the idea to find a recording of an old radio show in the archives that contains the national anthem, and set up the broadcast so it plays at the right point. The plan also involves playing marching band music in the periods where the MFA isn't speaking – but the only marching band music available to them is a British Royal Marines album, which they grudgingly prepare. Over the next several hours, the men following the radio broadcasts will become intimately familiar with the song 'A Life on the Ocean Wave' by Henry Russell.[16] The MFA in the RCP building asks Joaquim Furtado if he's willing to read out the typed document with their first message to the country. He agrees. In Pontinha, the hubbub of men's voices is shushed as their attention turns to the radio.

This is the Command Post of the Armed Forces Movement. The Portuguese Armed Forces appeal to all Lisbon residents to return to their homes, where they should remain with the utmost calm. We sincerely hope that the gravity of the hour we face is not besmirched by any personal accident, which is why we appeal to the common sense of the heads of military units, such that any confrontation with the Armed Forces can be avoided. Such a confrontation, besides unnecessary, can only lead to serious individual harm that would create divisions between the Portuguese, which we must avoid at all costs.

Despite our express intention of preventing even one drop of Portuguese blood from spilling, we appeal to the civic and professional spirit of the medical class, hoping that you might rush to the hospitals to provide your eventual support, which we hope, sincerely, will not be required.

The needle drops on the national anthem. The MFA has made its first appearance before the nation. The command post in Pontinha is buzzing with enthusiasm. A few minutes later, they receive a call from Bicho Beatriz, who has successfully captured Vilalva Palace: 'Canada has been occupied without incident.' Fifteen minutes later, RCP broadcasts another message:

> *This is the Command Post of the Armed Forces Movement. The Armed Forces Movement advises all militarised and police elements to be prudent, in order to avoid any dangerous clashes. There is no intention to spill blood unnecessarily, but that will occur if there is any provocation. We urge you to return to your barracks and await orders from the Armed Forces Movement. Any officers that attempt, in any way, to pit their subordinates into a fight with the armed forces shall be dealt with severely.*

This is the last one Costa Neves has pre-prepared; all additional broadcasts from the MFA are dictated over the phone by Lopes Pires. The national anthem is played again. Somewhere else in Lisbon, the director-general of PIDE, Silva Pais, wakes Prime Minister Marcelo Caetano and urges him to leave his home and take shelter in the GNR station by Carmo Convent. The call is intercepted, and Otelo makes a note of the change in the government's plans. On 16 March, the government has sent Caetano to hide out in a base in Monsanto – Otelo had stationed some artillery units in sight of that base, in order to bombard it should that become necessary. This new move changes things.

It's around 05:30. Salgueiro Maia's convoy has entered the outskirts of Lisbon. Against all odds, they've made it here without any breakdowns or issues. The unit passed multiple police and GNR vehicles on the way, but to their great relief nobody stopped to ask what multiple armoured vehicles were doing on their way to the capital. Arriving at an intersection just off the motorway, Maia feels the jeep stop. He waits for a few seconds, then asks: 'What's the matter?'

'Nothing, sir, just a red light,' replies the driver. Maia laughs. Of course, the driver is stopping at the red lights. 'The revolution isn't about to be held back by a red light. Let's go.' The convoy carries on into the night, heading towards a river glimmering in the moonlight.

Captain Salgueiro Maia moves away from an armoured vehicle on Terreiro do Paço, 25 April 1974.

CHAPTER NINE

DAWN IN TERREIRO DO PAÇO

Most visitors to central Lisbon will end up at the Praça do Comércio (Commercial Square) at one point or another. It's hard not to – the square is on the edge of the Tagus, at the vertex of many of the city's arterial roads. Its yellow and white arched buildings around its edge have hardly changed over the last three centuries, but the businesses using them remain in flux. Restaurant parasols rim the square like neatly trimmed hedges, sharing the space with the (separate) museums of Lisbon, Beer and Cod, and a facade advertising that the building contains 'THE SEXIEST WC ON EARTH'. Seagulls fill the air with screams, vying for food with the city pigeons. To many of the locals, it's still the Terreiro do Paço, a name that translates from old Portuguese as the Palace Yard. Even the nearby metro station bears the old name, but there is no palace here any more. One of the deadliest earthquakes in modern history laid waste to the square's eponymous Ribeira Palace – an earthquake whose impact reverberated through to the twentieth century.

1 November 1755 – All Saints' Day in the Catholic calendar. At around 9:40 that morning, a shock wave from a tectonic shift in the Atlantic Ocean, two hundred kilometres south-west of Lisbon, shook the city for some minutes. Deep fissures appeared across the city centre. People fled to the open spaces of the docks and found themselves wedged between a landscape of crumbling

buildings and a rapidly receding sea, revealing a muddy river floor containing centuries of accumulated detritus, cargo and ship-wrecks. Minutes later, a towering wave swept up the Tagus from the ocean at alarming speed, battering itself against the city. Second and third waves followed, water moving so quickly it outpaced even riders on horseback desperately racing to higher ground. Across Lisbon, candles that had been lit for Mass toppled over, causing fires to break out. Flames engulfed whatever survived the rushing water and collapsing city. It was a disaster of biblical proportions in more ways than one – tens of thousands of lives were lost, and swathes of irreplaceable historic documents destroyed, including records of Vasco da Gama's voyages to India.

The reconstruction effort that followed the great earthquake would permanently reshape the city. Downtown Lisbon was completely razed and rebuilt from scratch under the careful supervision of the Marquis of Pombal, in a new configuration that featured modern wide boulevards and squares, arranged at right angles. The difference between Lisbon's reconstructed and clearly planned Baixa Pombalina and the organic, narrow wind-ing streets of neighbouring Alfama is clearly visible today, as are the ruins of the ancient Carmo Convent, left untouched as a monument to the disaster, a wreck of shattered stone arches clinging to a hill like the skeleton of a long dead beast. The Praça do Comércio is a jewel in the crown of the rebuild effort – a 175m by 175m paved square. At its centre stands an equestrian statue of King José I trampling snakes underfoot, the first statue of a king to be commissioned and built in Lisbon.* In reality José I was permanently psychologically scarred by the earthquake. He refused to spend any time in walled buildings, leading him to

---

* This statue of King José is the origin of a riddle that relies on the Portuguese words for 'right' and 'straight' being the same: '*direita*'. So – 'Which one of King José's horse's legs is the right one? The left.'

relocate his royal courts to a complex of tents in hilly Ajuda, a suburb of Lisbon at a higher – and safer – altitude than his old palace.

The Marquis of Pombal demanded buildings be made to last the ages, and left an enduring legacy of metal and stone, still standing tall in modern Lisbon. The road that frames the Praça from the south is the Avenida Ribeira das Naus, part of the long road that loops around the southern perimeter of Lisbon and past the river's edge, where two tall columns jut vertically out of the river either side of a set of stone stairs, sometimes barely visible underneath the briny water. This is known as the Cais das Colunas ('column dock'), a preserved relic of the palace grounds that would have once welcomed nobles and dignitaries. The northern corners of the square hold the entrances to the Rua Áurea (gold) and Rua da Prata (silver), between them the ornate arched entrance to the bustling Rua Augusta, which reaches northwards at a gentle incline to Rossio square and aligns perfectly with the statue of the king atop his horse. Cutting across the northern edge of the square are a set of busy tramlines that stretch westward to Rua do Arsenal and eastward to Rua da Alfândega.

In 1974, Praça do Comércio is an administrative hub and one of the regime's centres of power, both real and symbolic. Symbolic because of its association with the imposing majesty of Empire and the unmistakable Portuguese-ness that the Pombaline architecture elicits, its image on every other postcard and souvenir tile. Real, because it holds the headquarters of the Army and Navy ministries, in the western complex of perfectly preserved stone buildings that stretches from Rua do Arsenal all the way to Avenida Ribeira das Naus. Just up the road, around from the Rua Áurea, is the Bank of Portugal headquarters. Further up still, just off from Rua Augusta on Rua São Julião, is the Marconi building, a hub for the government's wireless communications and satellite networks, the system through which the regime talks to its agents in the colonies. From a strategic perspective, the square forms a bottleneck into the heart of the city to anyone trying to access it from the Tagus or via the motorway that winds its way along the edge of the river.

The alarm has already been rung for the government loyalists, many of whom were woken in the early hours after news of MFA action in Porto spread through the regime's channels. At 05:00 the ministerial buildings in Terreiro do Paço are occupied by General Andrade e Silva, the ministers of defence, the interior and the Navy, the sub-secretary of state for the Army, the newly appointed head of the armed forces, Joaquim Luz Cunha, and his brother the military governor of Lisbon, Edmund Luz Cunha, the last of these finding himself unable to contact his official command post in Vilalva Palace, occupied as it is by the MFA. With them are two platoons of military police from the 2nd Lancers Regiment, most of whom have been stationed outside the building in defensive positions.

At around 6:00 the sun is not yet risen, and a layer of mist clings to the river, held there by the morning chill. Salgueiro Maia and his company of men roll down Rua Áurea, finally within sight of their destination. The plan of operations is simple and clear, and Maia splits up his soldiers and armoured vehicles along the narrow streets that run parallel to the square. Within seconds the Bank of Portugal and the Marconi building are surrounded. He and his remaining men filter into Terreiro do Paço and begin setting up a perimeter. By now the government is well aware that something serious is happening, even if they do not necessarily know the full scale of their problem. There is a real risk of a confrontation, and Maia knows that his unit is more visually imposing than it is an actual fighting force. As they file into the open space of Terreiro do Paço, the first government forces the soldiers come across are a squad of police officers. These officers defer immediately to what they take as a 'legitimate' military force and put themselves to use creating civilian roadblocks and guiding traffic away from the area. The EPC squad has effectively created a seal from Rua São Julião all the way to Avenida Ribeira das Naus, and within minutes MFA men are on every street.

It doesn't take long for Maia's first real test. Shortly after his column's arrival in the square, a detachment from the 7th Cavalry Regiment (*Regimento de Cavalaria 7*, RC7), a unit which completely escaped MFA interception, creeps in from Rua do Arsenal. Commanded by ensign David e Silva, this is a small platoon of armoured vehicles, some fitted with light machine guns. Silva pulls up next to Salgueiro Maia – they know each other from the Practical Cavalry School. Maia asks him in an ostensibly casual way what brings him to Terreiro do Paço. Silva says he's been sent by the government to defend the ministries. Maia replies, 'There is no government any more, and the ministers have been arrested by us. You're better off joining us.'

The stakes are high: this is Maia's chance to avoid a difficult armed engagement. He knows that many in the military may not be convinced MFA sympathisers, but that there is enough discontent within the ranks that the right pressure can bring his fellow officers onside. It pays off. Silva doesn't put up any resistance; he orders his unit to disperse throughout the square and reinforce critical strategic positions. Most of the men under David e Silva are none the wiser to the fact that they've suddenly switched sides. As a precaution, Maia orders them to turn their radios off.

As Maia's armoured vehicles and men turn their attention to the ministerial building, the military police brought in during the early hours to guard the ministers find themselves in a bewildering predicament. Luckily for them, Maia makes things easy. As he approaches the doors to the Ministry of Defence, he realises he knows the cadet in charge, having once been his instructor. Maia orders his unit to disperse, and the 2nd Lancers Regiment fall into line immediately, becoming Maia's second converts. They rush to secure the ferry port just south of their position. As Maia is giving orders to the squaddies, a brigadier general sidles up to him.

'Come with me,' he says.

'Why?' replies Maia.

'The Defence Minister wants a word with you.'

'I don't think so,' Maia says, grinning. The brigadier general is surprised.

'You don't understand,' he says, 'the minister just wants to thank you for the excellent work you've done in securing the square.'

Maia laughs. 'The minister doesn't need to thank me. He is in fact under arrest, by order of the Armed Forces Movement.'

The brigadier general pales. He's stammering, unsure of what to do. After a few seconds of this, Maia says, 'Look, you better get out of here, or I'll have to arrest you too, and that's frankly a waste of resources, because then I'd have to order some men to keep an eye on you.'[1]

The brigadier general makes a swift exit. The doors of the ministerial complex are sealed from the outside, locking in the government ministers and the seven policemen who happen to be inside. Officially arresting the regime's bigwigs is a problem for later. Having completed his immediate task, Salgueiro Maia radios the MFA command post in Pontinha and gets through to Otelo Saraiva de Carvalho. 'This is Charlie Eight. We have occupied Toledo and control Brussels and Vienna.'

The fortuitous conversion of David e Silva's RC7 detachment proves a source of confused frustration for the scrambling government forces, as Silva radios his superiors to report he has arrived at Terreiro do Paço, and his men are in position defending the government buildings. At the same time, the ministers inside the complex have just been informed by phone call that the MFA have their building under siege. The government radio chatter is starting to reach a fever pitch – the sudden coordinated MFA manoeuvres across the country, combined with the numerous units that have gone inexplicably quiet, means the regime are struggling to make sense of what the actual situation is on the ground and whom they can still trust. The sky over Lisbon is beginning to lighten. In Pontinha, Otelo Saraiva de Carvalho rolls up the blinds of his HQ and stares out into the dawn, blinking. He is a tired man surrounded by tired men, who take a moment to stretch and rub their bleary eyes at the morning light.[2] He looks up to see a Boeing 747 descending over the horizon, coming in to land at Portela airport. Suddenly, the enormous vessel veers sharply to the left, swings around in a long arc, and starts to climb in the opposite direction. Costa Martins has done his job, and the MFA have control of Portuguese airspace.

Across the river, in the parish of Almada, journalist Andrade Santos is woken by a phone call. A friend across town on an early shift had tuned in to Rádio Clube Português, heard the MFA missives and called. Phones are starting to ring across the country, people cottoning on to the fact that something is happening – something big. Andrade works for the Reuters news agency in Lisbon. Like a few others in the press, he has known about the secret gatherings of captains since September of 1973. What he doesn't know is that he's about to get the scoop of his life. Santos hops onto the ferry at the port of Cacilhas and alights shortly afterwards at Terreiro do Paço, now filled with armoured vehicles. He is surprised at how easily he can make his way past the military cordon – the Army isn't usually known for its particular generosity towards the press – and finds himself face to face with Captain Salgueiro Maia – at that time an unknown figure to him.

Maia greets him politely. When asked what's going on, Maia replies matter-of-factly: 'We are here to topple the government.'

After a few minutes of conversation, Santos asks Maia if he has anything that can explain what could lead just over two hundred men from Santarém to try and take on the oldest military dictatorship in Europe. Maia reaches into a pocket and pulls out a crumpled piece of rose-coloured paper: the political programme of the MFA, and hands it over. Santos now has only one thing on his mind – getting to the Reuters office and getting the message out of the country. Nervously, he asks Maia if he's allowed to leave. Maia laughs: 'My man! Do you think that we, who are here to give freedom back to the Portuguese, would start by removing it from you, a journalist?' Santos dashes off, barely believing his luck.[3]

Andrade Santos' swift write-up of his encounter with Salgueiro Maia is the first piece about the coup to make its way out of the country. The 2013 Swiss comedy film *Longwave* (*Les Grandes Ondes (à l'ouest)*) is one of the few foreign-language films that depicts the Portuguese revolution. At its centre is a well-meaning but unexceptional Swiss radio crew, sent to Portugal to do a fluff piece on the country to promote tourism. The crew find themselves witnessing the revolution in real time, becoming one of the first to report on it to the outside world. The film is a slapstick farce, the revolution a dramatic background to Billy Wilder-esque romantic intrigues, and it is fiction – but it does contain a kernel of truth. In 1974 Portugal is a political pariah, as the prolonged colonial war shreds its dignity and credibility in the eyes of the global community. For the international press, Portugal is a backwater barely worth covering, and a particularly unappealing assignment given the constant presence of state censors breathing down journalists' necks. The foreign press in Portugal on 25 April 1974 are young, under-resourced and inexperienced. When Werner Herzog is flown in to cover the revolution, he remarks that they are 'almost all ill-equipped to take on the situation'.[4]

The same can't be said of the Portuguese press on the ground. Forty-eight years of censorship, of secret police interrogations

208

and shredded documents and redactions and the brazen warping of the truth have made a certain class of Portuguese journalist hardy and hostile to the regime. Over the past few months, as the MFA organised their networks behind the scenes, they have been, quietly, sneaking hints to like-minded friends in the press that something is brewing under the surface. It's not much, as operational security still takes precedence – the secret meetings between captains at barbecues in the Portuguese hills, the growing politicisation of the armed forces, their responses to Spínola's book, and to a select few, the cryptic suggestion to make sure they're in the country at the end of April. One of these journalists is Adelino Gomes, who arrives with photographer Alfredo da Cunha at Terreiro do Paço at around 7:00 and discovers Salgueiro Maia, his old schoolmate from Leiria, is in the process of giving orders to a column of tanks in the middle of the nation's capital. Gomes approaches Maia and requests permission to take photographs and speak to the soldiers. 'Go ahead,' says Maia, 'that's part of the reason we're here.' Maia's tone is calm, conversational, his dry wit coming through even as he finds himself in the eye of a storm of his own making. Gomes and Cunha begin covering the unfolding events, and over the course of the next several hours they are joined by some of their colleagues in the press.

As Lisbon wakes up in earnest, the soldiers' occupation of the square is starting to gather a curious crowd of onlookers, managed for the moment by the police. It is a combination of locals who have been alerted to the MFA's radio broadcasts and early shift workers bemused at the way their commute has been disrupted by armoured vehicles. A quartermaster escorts an agitated woman to Salgueiro Maia; she explains that she is a cleaner at the Terreiro do Paço post office and needs to get to work urgently. Maia replies with almost prophetic confidence: 'Don't worry – today, and every year going forward, 25 April will be a national holiday.' Unimpressed, the cleaner wanders back to the ferry port shaking her head. As the crowd gathers at the edges of the square, the nervous tension carried by Maia's men begins to dissipate. The civilian onlookers are smiling, chatty, cheering the soldiers on, gesturing with thumbs up and peace signs, speaking to the soldiers as friends. It is one thing to believe that the people are behind you, it is entirely another to see it so clearly. The ones who have come here have deliberately chosen to ignore the MFA's warning to stay off the streets – they are here to witness, and make, history.

Salgueiro Maia radios the command post in Pontinha and requests the presence of a higher-ranking officer. Despite his current position as the commander of the occupying military force, of a rebellion that makes rank irrelevant, his years of Army training and idealistic concept of honour make him feel uncomfortable arresting government ministers as a mere captain. Inside the ministerial building, however, the regime's men are not sitting idly. With no possible exit via the building's main doors, General Andrade e Silva has put the few remaining military policemen locked in with him to work, smashing a hole in the brick wall from the first floor of the defence minister's office into the library of the adjacent Navy minister's office, an empty building so far left unguarded. The ministers, generals and admirals make their way through the hole and quietly out to the internal courtyard of the ministerial complex, on the other side of the buildings from the square, and pile into a Mercedes van. They drive west, away from the revolutionaries, to the headquarters of the 2nd Lancers Regiment in Ajuda, a barracks Silva trusts to still be under government control. They have come to the same region of Lisbon to which, two hundred years ago, a traumatised King José I fled. Now the strategic heads of the Portuguese military set up a command post intending to fight back, desperate to prevent the structures of the *Estado Novo* from collapsing around them.

Prime Minister Marcelo Caetano is by now ensconced in the GNR station at Largo do Carmo. He calls General Silva in Ajuda.

'So, General. Is this the so-called unimportant, easily controlled little movement?'The general reassures Caetano that there is a plan for a response. He pulls together information about the government forces he still has at his disposal, and sets in motion what he believes to be a strategic master stroke; on paper, he has enough units to completely surround the square and, if necessary, bomb the revolutionary forces into dust. The phone call between General Silva and the prime minister is intercepted by the MFA and transmitted to Otelo in Pontinha, who listens to the general's plan with stoic delight. Otelo has known all along that placing Salgueiro Maia's impressive-looking detachment of men and armoured vehicles in the capital's most famous square would prompt the government to concentrate their remaining forces there. Meanwhile, the MFA's operations around the rest of the city and country mean the square is barely more than a symbolic asset, a diversion. The government have taken the bait, but it remains to be seen how Maia holds out against the forces levied against him.

The first of these is another detachment from RC7, a reconnaissance platoon of Panhard light machine gun cars led by Lieutenant Colonel Ferrand d'Almeida in an Army jeep, which rolls timidly from the west up to the square on Avenida Ribeira das Naus. At this point the MFA soldiers have amassed quite the crowd of onlookers, and d'Almeida finds himself not only facing off against a squad of confident soldiers but also a cheering, joyful crowd of civilians. He tries, feebly, to order his men to push back the crowd, to start making arrests. His young subordinates refuse. Salgueiro Maia makes his way alongside d'Almeida's column of tanks and introduces himself. D'Almeida is clearly nervous. Maia points out the obvious – that d'Almeida and his men are under the sights of many light machine guns, and it would be absurd to try and start a fight. More to the point, he says, it would be a shame to start killing each other after the losses suffered in the colonial war. Faced with the choice of taking on a superior force or surrendering calmly, the lieutenant

211

colonel chooses the latter. He exits his jeep and lets Maia lead him around the ministerial complex and further into the square.

Colonel Álvaro Fontoura, in charge of the Army minister's office, left behind by the escaping ministers, witnesses all this from the window of the Defence Ministry. He shouts down to d'Almeida, ordering him to come up and rescue him. D'Almeida replies: 'I can't come. I am under arrest, my colonel.' The Panhard tanks roll fully into the square, joining the MFA forces to the cheers of the crowd, which is growing ever larger. The soldiers are no longer able to contain the waves of civilians who have come to have a look, and nor do they want to – the crowd shouts in acclamation, chanting 'Victory! Victory!', and becoming more emboldened by the minute. What started as a military operation is beginning to look more like a bizarre street party where some of the attendees happen to be dressed as soldiers.

It's at this point that Colonel Correia de Campos, the superior officer requested by Salgueiro Maia to take control of the ministerial building, arrives in Terreiro do Paço. He is escorted by Jaime Neves and Luís Macedo – there for the colonel's security, but also giddy with excitement and eager to leave the stuffy command post. Otelo has let them leave HQ on the promise that they report back with news. The senior MFA men let themselves into the Army Ministry with ease, and climb up to the first floor, where they discover the hole in the wall and find the ministers gone. It's a loss they barely register – making their way through the crowd of civilians has filled them with an immense joy. Standing in an abandoned office, looked down upon by a framed photograph of António Salazar, Macedo makes an excited phone call to Otelo.

'Hello, Tiger. Dragon here. Listen, can you guess where I'm calling you from?'

'I have no idea, tell me,' replies Otelo.

'Oh, man, from the office of the Army minister. It's a cool office, luxurious, with a heavy, padded iron door. But look, despite all our security measures, the guy hit the road. He broke through a hole in the wall with some other guys; we don't know where they've gone.'

'So you haven't arrested anyone?'

'Not any ministers or government types, no. Just office staff. Small fry.'

'OK. Send them here when you're done. Listen – how are things going over there?'

'It's going great over here, man! The guys just arrested Ferrand d'Almeida who turned up acting like an idiot, window shopping, got done straight away. Listen – can you imagine what it feels like to be a guy standing here at the window of the minister's office, looking out over a sea of people shouting and cheering the MFA?'

'I can, I can. Thank you for passing on that feeling.'[5]

It's easy to forget, given their relatively high ranks and impressive strategic coordination, just how young even the more senior members of the MFA are. These conversations give a sense of that youth – they are light, informal, peppered with slang, uninterested in the pomp and circumstance of military hierarchy and often irreverent. Otelo's numerous phone calls throughout the day are less the short communiqués of a commanding officer and more calls between friends, belying his genuine affection for the men who have thrown their lot in with him.

As Correia de Campos is securing the ministerial complex from within, Salgueiro Maia is informed by one of his quartermasters that a squad of armed men from the Republican National Guard is setting itself up around the corner to the east. Unknown to Maia, this is part of General Andrade e Silva's pincer manoeuvre. Maia strides over to see what's going on, and finds the guardsmen are generally men in their fifties, equipped with old Mauser pistols. In a course of events that is by this point becoming increasingly familiar, Maia knows the GNR squad leader, a lieutenant and former subordinate of Maia's from the Cavalry School. Maia gives the man a big hug. A journalist standing nearby and narrating events into a handheld recorder does a double take. 'Now I really don't know what's going on,' he mumbles. 'The leader of the revolting troops is hugging the GNR.' Maia asks the lieutenant what he's doing there; the lieutenant replies that he's been given orders to take the square. Both men understand the balance of forces – there is simply no way this paltry group of men near retirement, their weapons left over from the Second World War, has any chance of taking on the armoured company they've been sent up against. Maia advises the lieutenant, as a friend, to take his men back to their headquarters. The lieutenant agrees, grateful for the option.

Shortly afterwards, another salvo from the government, where it becomes clear that the counter-revolutionary forces are being assembled and sent in without any warning of the situation on the ground. A squad of military police on motorcycles rolls towards the square from the east, followed by a truck full of men and a column on foot, their white helmets glinting in the sun. Two MFA light tanks stationed by the river swivel their turrets towards the motorcycles. The riders raise their hands instinctively in surrender and, in a sequence worthy of a Benny Hill sketch, topple over, skidding forwards on the cobbles. The truck brakes and veers away to avoid a collision, causing its passengers to be flung over each other and fly out of the side into an undignified heap. The footmen drop their weapons and throw themselves to the ground in immediate surrender.

It's becoming increasingly obvious to the regime that their fighting force on the ground is struggling, as several of General Andrade e Silva's retaliation manoeuvres have either failed or not materialised at all. On the Tagus a new player pulls into view: NATO frigate *Almirante Gago Coutinho*, called back from a routine dawn patrol mission, its heavily armed frame a menacing presence to the MFA soldiers in what now feels like a very exposed square. Unbeknownst to the soldiers in the square, the vice chief of staff of the Armada has ordered the commander of the *Gago Coutinho* to anchor in the Tagus and prepare to open fire on Terreiro do Paço. The ship's two sets of twin-mounted 50-calibre cannons are visible from shore, eclipsing anything the MFA has at its disposal.

As the ship arrives in the Tagus it doesn't stop, but speeds up – seeing the situation in the square, the commander raises an objection to the bombardment, given the large crowds of civilians. Aware that there is the possibility of enemy retaliation, he wants to stay a moving target, and orders the vessel's guns to swivel upwards, a clear indication that they are no threat. What actually takes place on board the *Gago Coutinho* is unclear. Accounts range from a rebellious crew refusing to follow the commander's orders to fire even a warning shot over the city, to the commander himself simply ignoring the orders from high command, whether due to the threat of retaliation or the bloodbath of his fellow men that would result.[6] Ultimately, the frigate's guns remain silent. High above, on the hill where Christ the King stares out over the city, an MFA detachment from the Practical Artillery School consisting of several long-range cannons tracks the *Gago Coutinho* on its journey through Lisbon's waters.

It is now nearly 9:00 in the morning. The sun is riding high on the horizon, taking the morning chill away from the square and dissipating the gentle mist on the water. To the west of Terreiro do Paço is a point where Avenida Ribeira das Naus loops around the edge of the ministries to join up with Rua do Arsenal. Ensign Fernando Sottomayor is there, behind the gun of an M47 Patton tank, one of four. This is the final detachment from the 7th Cavalry Regiment, under the command of Brigadier General Junqueira dos Reis, second commander of the Lisbon Military Region (RML), the man with the dubious honour of being the front-line commander of the regime's dwindling forces on the ground. Reis is from a different generation of officer than Otelo and Maia; he is older, a thin man with a greying moustache and a renowned short temper. He is a true regime loyalist, and the fact

215

that he's been pulled out of bed to deal with what he considers a rabble of treasonous troublemakers has him on edge. The mood is tense. Sottomayor turns to Colonel Romeiras Júnior in the vehicle next to him, and asks him if he thinks there's a way out of the impending confrontation. The colonel seems lost in thought, staring out at nothing in particular. He has tears in his eyes. 'What if we're all friends?' he asks vaguely.[7]

In between Junqueira dos Reis' forces and the ongoing rebellion in Terreiro do Paço, Rua do Arsenal is filled with civilians, unaware of the stand-off they find themselves between. Sottomayor receives permission to fire his machine gun into the air to disperse the civilians. The rattle of the gunfire as it echoes down the stone street is deafening, and within seconds Rua do Arsenal is empty. A few hundred metres in front of Sottomayor, in the square, Ensign David e Silva grabs his radio, which is still tuned to RC7's frequency, and says: 'Oi, careful, I'm out here.'

Sottomayor replies, 'It's OK,' out of his commander's earshot.[8]

The sudden gunfire causes several of the MFA's armoured vehicles to roll out and take positions on Rua do Arsenal and Avenida Ribeira das Naus, facing the government forces. The appearance of these vehicles sends Junqueira dos Reis into a rage – he had assumed he would be able to take the square easily with his four tanks, but it's clear that the MFA has the means to put up resistance. He orders Sottomayor to escort him around the corner to Ribeira das Naus to see if the situation is any better there.

Meanwhile, in Terreiro do Paço, Salgueiro Maia is preparing for the worst and hoping for the best. The appearance of this latest detachment from RC7 isn't like the other government forces he's had to deal with. So far the MFA has had a strong numerical advantage, both in terms of men and vehicles. Maia has been lucky that the regime has made the same mistake as the henchmen in a kung fu film, coming in one by one in a way that means they can be handled individually. Had the regime coordinated its deployments better, Maia's numerical advantage might be less obvious and the officers less susceptible to peer pressure. This new force is different. The MFA in Terreiro do Paço had a decent chance against the Panhard AML light machine gun cars, but the M47 Pattons that Junqueira dos Reis has at his disposal are proper combat vehicles with big cannons, capable of shredding armour and doing serious damage in the square should it come to that. Maia sees the two M47s roll into Ribeira das Naus. Alongside them are Brigadier Junqueira dos Reis and Major Pato Anselmo in a jeep, a few smaller armoured cars and a platoon of men on foot. Maia makes a decision. He orders the vehicles in the square to position themselves with their wheels facing east – if things start to go seriously wrong, they might have to make a hasty retreat back to Santarém. He knows if it comes to that, he won't be with them.

Salgueiro Maia steps out from behind the armoured cars at the south-western edge of Terreiro do Paço. He walks forward on Avenida Ribeira das Naus with his arms outstretched. He holds a white handkerchief in his right hand, and he carries a hand grenade in his back pocket. He knows there is a chance that he might be captured there and then, and if so he would rather make himself a martyr to the Movement than be taken prisoner. He stands a hundred metres from the government's tank column. The brigadier steps out of his jeep and shouts for Maia to turn his tanks around. Maia replies that he can't do that – he asks the brigadier to come and speak to him face to face, in the no-man's land between the two forces. The brigadier refuses – 'You come here, now!' he shouts. Maia shakes his head and stays put. The brigadier is visibly enraged – he is screaming at Maia to surrender and reinforce his M47 detachment. Seeing that this is failing, Junqueira dos Reis grabs the radio on his jeep and has a brief back and forth with someone on the other end. He puts his radio down, turns to Sottomayor's M47 tank, and shouts: 'Open fire!'

Salgueiro Maia hears the order being given, and freezes in place. He fights every instinct he's built up from active combat in the colonial war. He knows the optical sights on an M47 have a magnification of seven. He knows that he has two options here – duck and cover, and risk the hunter's instinct of the man behind the gun – or look calmly down the barrel of the cannon and put his faith in the knowledge that it's more difficult to shoot someone who means you no harm. Inside the M47 tank, Fernando Sottomayor sweeps the cannon towards the river, hoping desperately that he can follow the brigadier's order without hitting anything. Through his scope he sees the *Almirante Gago Coutinho*, he sees sailing boats, he sees an enormous cargo ship in the distance. 'Stop playing around, soldier, and point that at the enemy!' barks the brigadier. Sottomayor swivels the gun back towards the square. He sees the same vehicles he's spent years fighting alongside. He sees a vast crowd of civilians, smiling, singing, stretching all the way to the ferry port in the far distance. He sees the face of Captain Salgueiro Maia, his superior and former instructor from the Cavalry School, meeting his gaze. The brigadier screams again: 'Shoot!'

'No, I won't,' replies Sottomayor. The brigadier lets out a frustrated roar. He grabs Sottomayor, pulls the service pistol from the ensign's holster and levels it at his head. Junqueira dos Reis repeats the order. Sottomayor sits still and silent. The brigadier orders Sottomayor to exit the vehicle. Sottomayor does so and is dragged away by two military policemen. 'You've just ruined your life,' the brigadier shouts as Sottomayor is bundled into a car. Reis turns to give orders to the corporal in Sottomayor's tank, but before he can get a word out the corporal shouts: 'I'm not doing anything without orders from my ensign!' Enraged, Reis approaches the second M47 tank. Corporal José Alves Costa is behind the tank's machine gun turret. Reis climbs up next to him and points at the gun. 'Do you know how to use that, corporal?'

The corporal stammers a reply. 'A little. This isn't my normal post. I don't really know how to use this.'

'Open fire, straight ahead. Open fire,' says the brigadier.

'I'll see if I can, but I don't know...'

'You either open fire or I put a bullet in your head.' The brigadier raises his pistol.

Before he can level it at Costa, the corporal dives into the tank and closes the hatch above him. He shouts to his fellow soldiers in the vehicle: 'Quick, lock the doors!' Outside he can hear Junqueira dos Reis hammering at the hatch, his demands that they come out and follow orders now muffled by a thick layer of metal. Inside the tank nobody can harm them. They will remain ensconced in there for several hours, refusing to come out.

Junqueira dos Reis stares down the causeway at Maia. He raises his pistol and fires several shots into the air, hoping to provoke a response and perhaps knock his men back into action. The shots ring out over the water. The MFA stare back silently. Reis hops back into his jeep and drives away, pulling back some of his remaining men and leaving Major Pato Anselmo to look after what are now two virtually immobilised and useless tanks. Salgueiro Maia watches him leave, his heart pounding.

Meanwhile, on Rua do Arsenal, Lieutenant Alfredo Assunção is slowly, with his arms outstretched, approaching the second tank column, left in the hands of Colonel Romeiras Júnior. Assunção has known Romeiras for some time – on his return from his posting in Guinea, Romeiras had invited him to a command position in RC7. Knowing the school in Santarém had a more active MFA presence, Assunção opted for that instead. As he reaches the tanks, he quickly explains to Romeiras that Generals Spínola and Costa Gomes are involved in the insurrection, hoping that this will convince him to switch sides. Junqueira dos Reis returns from his failure on Ribeira das Naus as this conversation takes place. Spotting Assunção, the brigadier starts punching and slapping him in the face. 'What's this insurrectionist doing here?' he demands. Reis turns to his men and starts demanding that they shoot Assunção on the spot. Before they can react, Romeiras

Júnior steps in and orders his soldiers to stand down. The brigadier shouts at Assunção – 'Those were the slaps your father should have given you!' Romeiras urges Assunção to get out of there.

Returning to the square, Assunção liaises with Salgueiro Maia. Besides the beating Assunção is still smarting from, things could have gone much worse. Maia is thrilled – the brigadier's subordinates refused to shoot him. This is the last evidence he needs that what they're doing today will succeed. On Rua do Arsenal, Brigadier Junqueira dos Reis pulls his vehicles back, looking to regroup. Major Pato Anselmo has been left alone in charge of the regime's tanks and men on Ribeira das Naus – there seems to be one more opportunity to weaken the government. Colonel Correia de Campos, back from the ministerial buildings, tells Fernando Brito e Cunha to go and convince the major to surrender. Brito e Cunha is, unlike many of the uniformed MFA men in the square, in a grey suit and tie. A former artilleryman in Guinea, Cunha is an MFA loyalist who left the Army after his return from combat, but remained involved in preparations for the coup. Now Salgueiro Maia hands him a Walther pistol and jokingly asks him: 'Do you still know how to use one of these?'

Cunha strides over to Pato Anselmo's position and greets the major, who is himself in a black anorak. In the middle of the street, they could be mistaken for two regular civilians having a quiet conversation on a chilly Lisbon morning. Cunha introduces himself and gives Anselmo his options – join the Movement outright, or surrender himself and be taken prisoner. The third option, he says, is the gun. Pato Anselmo opts for being taken prisoner. In a gesture of goodwill, he orders his remaining vehicles to turn their turrets out towards the river.[9] Anselmo is bundled back towards the square, wiping tears from his eyes. He is followed by soldiers from his detachment, who have chosen of their own accord to join in with the revolutionaries. As they make their way into the square a loud cheer rises up from the waiting crowd. The soldiers smile, wave – one of them raises his hand in a V for victory. This moment is captured by the photographer Eduardo Gageiro: a man in military fatigues and helmet, with a pair of Aviator glasses, surrounded by vehicles of war and smiling at the camera, his hand raised in a V for victory.

Brigadier General Junqueira dos Reis withdrawing his units means Salgueiro Maia's mission in Terreiro do Paço is complete, a resounding success. He radios in to Otelo in Pontinha, and receives a new, surprising instruction: he is to mobilise his unit and travel to the GNR barracks in Carmo Square, where Prime Minister Marcelo Caetano has sequestered himself. Leaving a small detachment behind, Maia hops into his *Chaimite* armoured car and leads his convoy, heading north. The gathered crowd follows alongside and behind the soldiers, moving as one. As he rolls onto the cobbled street, stone eyes look down at Maia from the top of the vast marble arch that frames the entrance to Rua Augusta: seven-metre high sculptures representing Glory, Valour and Genius. Beneath them, four figures, spectres of Portugal's past: Nuno Álvares Pereira, Viriathus, Vasco da Gama and the Marquis of Pombal. Four symbols of the Empire Maia is about to destroy.

Soldiers and crowds mingle in central Lisbon as the MFA's coup unfolds, 25 April 1974.

CHAPTER TEN

THE TIME HAS COME

The building at number 9 Rua Braamcamp, on the corner of Rua Castilho, turned heads when it was inaugurated in 1971. Its concrete facade would place it at home on a list of brutalist buildings, with one prominent characteristic setting it apart – each window above the second floor is framed by an odd array of rectangular white tiles that dangle in the sun. From a distance the design has an almost Islamic look; on closer inspection, the tiles are arranged in a pattern around each window, suggesting a head sporting a neat, white fringe. The resemblance to a row of fringe haircuts is what gives the building its nickname, *Franjinhas* – 'little fringes'. It won the prestigious Valmor prize for architecture, but went down poorly in the pages of the popular press.

On the morning of 25 April 1974, Celeste Caeiro is on her way to work. Celeste is forty years old – short, with a tight mop of greying hair and thick round glasses, she heads from her tiny downtown apartment to the self-service restaurant Sir on the ground floor of the *Franjinhas*, where she works as a cleaner. Celeste knows the owner is preparing a celebration of sorts – the restaurant first opened exactly one year ago. The cunning marketing strategy for today, she's heard, is to offer gentlemen customers a free glass of port, and give ladies a carnation. The flowers arrived yesterday, dozens of large bunches in anticipation of the lunch rush. As she arrives, Celeste is surprised that the restaurant is dark, the door closed, with no sign of the cheerful decorations she was expecting. She pokes her head in and sees the owner hunched by the radio, which is tuned to Rádio Clube Português, the room strewn with large unopened bunches of red and white carnations. His expression is grim. 'What's wrong?' she asks.

'We won't be opening today, Celeste.' He gestures at the radio. 'Something's happening in the centre, some sort of military operation. They're telling people to stay home.' They stand for a few moments in the dark restaurant, listening as the radio plays the military tunes the MFA has lined up for the gaps between their missives. 'You'd better go home too, Celeste,' the owner says. 'Here – take some of these with you.' He gestures at one of the large piles of flowers strewn around him. Celeste grabs a bunch and leaves, facing the notion of an unexpected day off, curious about the events that have caused it. She walks to the metro station at Marquês de Pombal and travels two stops down, to Restauradores.

Back at the entrance to Rua Augusta, Salgueiro Maia's convoy slows as the crowds surge into the narrow street, waved away feebly by the captains in their vehicles. The floodgates have opened: the mass of people that had gathered around Terreiro do Paço has swollen to the point of absurdity, and any of the captains' pleas for calm and order have been drowned out by the deafening sound of cheers and song. One refrain in particular carries, loud and clear, like a background rhythm, a drumbeat that merges with the sound of the rumbling engines that make their way up the narrow street:[1]

VITÓRIA
VI TÓ RIA
VI   TÓ RIA
VI   TÓ RIA
VI   TÓ   RIA

The crowd is young, smiling, jubilant; it's a victory march mixed with a street party mixed with a football crowd that's just won a trophy, smatterings of applause directed at the MFA tanks periodically replaced with guttural roars, cheers, whistles, spontaneous renditions of the national anthem. Years of stifling oppression and state violence have built up an unbearable pressure within the hearts of Lisbon's population and, suddenly and dramatically, that pressure has an outlet. Journalist Adelino Gomes is among the crowd – he had arrived earlier, during the occupation of Terreiro do Paço, and now follows the convoy briskly, stopping occasionally to speak his startled impressions into his recorder and point his microphone into the crowd. Some of the chants have a clear political bent, the more radical among the youth starting chants that are taken up and ripple through, echoes of long-held demands. 'Free all political prisoners!' shouts one voice; 'Down with fascism!' comes another. One young man, in a manic state, grabs Gomes' microphone and begins screaming 'I am a communist! I am a communist! I am a communist!',[2] free to express his most closely held secret for the first time. The government hasn't fallen yet, but the sense of change is undeniable and overwhelming. People approach the MFA tanks and their operators, swept up in the moment, pull them up onto the vehicles, suddenly transforming the military convoy into something that looks more like a popular street parade.

In her song '*Cheira a Lisboa*', Amália Rodrigues, Portugal's undisputed queen of Fado, sings that Lisbon smells of the coffee shops of Rossio. This early afternoon, just gone noon, Rossio smells of gasoline and blistered asphalt as Maia's convoy enters the square and begins to veer left, trying to fit its enormous frames into the narrow Rua do Carmo. The square seems to vibrate with the rumble of the M47 tanks. Maia spots a column of infantrymen from the 1st Infantry Regiment, packed into the backs of transport trucks, rolling into the square from the other end. He exits his jeep to speak with the commander. It's another push from the government – they've been sent to stop Maia's column, but the commander says they're with the revolutionaries. Maia orders them to follow along, and the convoy gains several dozen more heavily armed soldiers. Celeste Caeiro is here now, among the crowd, clutching her bunch of carnations in her hands, her eyes wide as she watches her city taken over by machines of war she's only ever seen on grainy footage of military parades. One of the M47 tanks passes a few feet in front of her, and the man atop it looks down, smiling.

'What are you doing here?' she asks the man, with a sudden surge of courage.

'A revolution!' he replies.

'For better, or for worse?'

'It's to end the war, and PIDE. It was still night when we left the barracks.'

'Well,' Caeiro says, 'do you need anything? What can I do to help?'

'Do you have a cigarette you could give me, madam?'

'No,' replies Celeste, 'I only have these carnations.'

'Well please give me one, that'll do as well.'[3]

Celeste passes a flower up to the soldier, who trims its end and slides the carnation into the barrel of his G3 rifle. In this moment there can be no clearer statement of purpose from the revolutionaries, and they have found their symbol. Better flowers than bullets. The other soldiers follow suit, taking Celeste's gifts, offered enthusiastically, the red and white flowers adding a splash of colour to their drab green uniforms. The crowd that surrounds Celeste sees it, and understands: they jostle to Rossio's flower markets, grab more carnations, rush back and distribute them among the convoy. Soon most of Maia's men are sporting a flower on their person, in their lapels or their uniforms, and the people flocking the streets raise more carnations aloft, following the cars like a springtime procession. In Rossio, a new chant has emerged among the cacophony: 'Down with the colonial war!' A young man locks eyes with Adelino Gomes and shouts 'Freedom! Freedom for the press!' And, louder, a strangled voice from within the throng, 'We've won! We've won!', followed by another unintelligible roar. The question on everyone's lips is, has the government fallen? Gomes doesn't know, but the leisurely way the convoy is making its way through Lisbon seems to suggest it has.

Back at Rádio Clube Português, the MFA communications continue broadcasting out to the country. The success of the vast majority of the operation means the 11:45 statement is positive:

In the course of the actions carried out in the early morning today, with the goal of toppling the regime that has oppressed the country, the Armed Forces announce that they dominate the situation throughout the country, and the hour of liberty will soon be upon us.

Climbing up Rua do Carmo and turning right on Calçada do Sacramento, Salgueiro Maia's column finally arrives at Carmo Square at 12:30 and prepares to lay siege to the GNR headquarters they believe house Marcelo Caetano. The headquarters, a white three-floor building with arched windows and a small upper floor balcony, stands next to the entrance to the ruins of Carmo Convent on the eastern edge of the square. Along the other edges are apartments, and within a few minutes windows begin opening as Maia's men, allowed entry by the local residents, seek a better vantage point on the GNR building. If Maia thought his mission was going to be a simple military siege, it has become considerably more complicated: the square fills almost instantly, the crowds surrounding his vehicles and climbing onto whatever structure might get them a better view of the action. Carmo Square's cobbled pavement is broken up, periodically, with trees, and soon those trees are filled with the more adventurous members of the public, all set to a constant roaring soundtrack of raised voices. Maia parks his jeep in front of the GNR headquarters and climbs out. There's a tense waiting game to be played here, and he knows any threats he can make against the GNR are tempered by the presence of the crowds – any exchange of gunfire will descend into carnage. He intends to avoid that at all costs.

Far from being just spectators, the people of Lisbon are keen to get involved in whatever way they can. As the EPC regiment settles into its siege, awaiting orders on its next steps, the crowd begins to ferry gifts to the soldiers – bread and cured hams, cheese and fruit, bottles of water, all graciously accepted by the men, most of whom have been awake since the very early hours and whose reserves of adrenaline are starting to give way to exhaustion. Beyond these simple acts of kindness, however, information on what is happening around the square filters in to Maia, as though the crowd is acting like a vast neural network that reaches to every corner of the city. Maia is informed by the civilians that Brigadier General Junqueira dos Reis has set himself up around the corner in Camões Square with what remains of the 7th Cavalry Regiment and another detachment from the 1st Infantry Regiment. Also that a GNR unit have positioned themselves up along Rua Nova da Trindade, and that a police unit in full riot gear is marching up from Chiado. In terms of sheer firepower, Maia is once again outnumbered, especially facing off against what he assumes is a heavily armed GNR unit inside the building in front of him. The government forces, however, have no chance of seeing the square. Having found their champions in the MFA forces, the crowd have formed a vast protective shield around Maia and his men, shouting at whatever looks like government forces to give up, to turn back, putting their mass of bodies in the way of any perceived ingress from the enemy. Several hours ago the regime was outnumbered by the MFA units – now, they're far more outnumbered by the people of Lisbon. Bit by bit, the government forces surrounding the EPC on the nearby streets begin to dissipate. Maia receives a delegation from the remains of the 1st Infantry Regiment, who announce they've joined the revolutionaries. Their men begin to mingle with the civilians, sharing in the food and drink.

Taking the opportunity of a break in the action, Adelino Gomes approaches Salgueiro Maia. 'Just a minute, Captain Maia, just a minute. Can you tell me what's going on at this moment?'

'We're surrounding the Carmo quarters and awaiting orders as to what to do next,' Maia replies. 'The 1st Infantry Regiment, who were ordered to detain us, have joined us, so we also have to find a mission for them, because they're just standing there doing nothing.' The two men laugh at that. There's a levity to the way Maia speaks. 'So for now, we're just waiting for orders.'

'And do you know who's in there right now?'

'The assumption is that Marcelo Caetano is in there and...'

'And Américo Tomás?'

'And Américo Tomás, that's right."

'You haven't got into phone contact with them so... how are you going to parlay? Will you try to speak to them personally or...'

'An emissary will be sent to the door, to start a dialogue.'

'And at the moment you don't know who that emissary is, or when he gets here?'

'I'm awaiting orders,' Maia affirms.

'And you haven't had any contact at all with the Carmo quarters? You don't even know if they're preparing a reaction?'

'A reaction is impossible. There's no force that can face ours.'[4]

Back in Pontinha, Otelo needs to urge this siege along. He makes a phone call to the GNR in Carmo, requesting his old geography professor from the Military Academy, Colonel Ângelo Ferrari, now chief of staff of the GNR. He reaches the colonel, eventually.

'This is the command post of the Armed Forces Movement. I'm calling to tell you the following: we know Dr Marcelo Caetano and a few other ministers are taking refuge there. On the other hand, if

---

* This turns out, in fact, not to be true.

you take the time to look out of the window, as I imagine you already have, you'll see that Movement forces, in this case the Practical Cavalry School, completely dominate the situation in Carmo Square. There is no possibility of a counter-offensive on your part. Victory is ours. I demand that you surrender, and hand over the ex-president of the Council to the commander of our forces.'

The voice on the other end is panicked. 'But where are you calling from? What command post is this?'

'I've told you and I repeat, this is the command post of the Armed Forces Movement. Are you, or are you not, willing to surrender? I warn you, you don't have much time.'

'But, comrade, I want to know who I'm speaking to.'

'Firstly, don't call me comrade. We are at this moment on opposite sides, and I don't consider you one. And I'm telling you for the final time, this is the command post of the MFA.'

'But there's been a mistake. The president of the Council isn't here. Almost certainly. You are misinformed.'

'You're lying,' Otelo growls. 'I'm telling you that's unnecessary. We have guarantees that Marcelo is there. For the last time, do you surrender or not? It's your last chance. If your answer is no, I'll order them to open fire, which is worse for everyone.'

'Look, I repeat, you're wrong. The president of the Council isn't here. But hang on a moment while I go and check.'

Otelo hangs up the phone, rather than risk his call being traced. Ferrari was just stalling – everyone's stalling – and it's time to take action. Otelo makes radio contact with Salgueiro Maia, but there's a bad connection – he can't get through to the young captain. He sends a runner to Captain António Rosado da Luz, in the field as his contact, with a written message for Maia:

Salgueiro Maia,
We've tried giving an ultimatum to the GNR for the hand-
over of the president of the Council, to no great effect. The

*guys hang up the phone or delay the call, saying they're going
to see if the people are in.*

*With your megaphone, try and communicate with them
and lay down an ultimatum for their surrender. I've threat-
ened Colonel Ferrari, but he doesn't seem to believe me.
With machine guns shoot open the locks on the door so they
know we're serious. I don't think they'll shoot back. Cheers.*

A hug,

Otelo

By the time the letter arrives at Carmo, the nerves have got to
Salgueiro Maia and he's paralysed by the task ahead. Not being
able to get through to Otelo, his commanding officer, puts the
young captain in a difficult position. If he was back in Guinea he'd
know what to do – he'd be able to take control, improvise if necessary. But this isn't Guinea, this is his home, and he knows the next
steps involve potentially ordering his men to open fire. The fear of
ricocheting bullets flying into the crowd is still high on his list of
concerns. Rosado da Luz presents Maia with Otelo's letter, urging
him on: 'You've got to, man! A lot of things get decided here...'

'I don't have the moral courage...' Maia says quietly, 'I don't
have the moral courage...'

'You have to take that building!'[5]

Maia needs one last nudge to take action. 'Put me in contact
with Otelo; I don't have a connection. I can't contact him.'

Luz darts off looking for a telephone, thinking he might be
able to call the command post directly. The captain is dressed in a
half-uniform – a civilian outfit to easily navigate the crowds, and
a blazer bearing his rank epaulettes, for situations where he needs
the authority. He dons the blazer now, rushes to the closest apartment door and tries to shoulder-barge it open. An elderly couple,
terrified, open the door. They fall to their knees in front of the
captain. 'Please! Please! We don't want to be involved in this!'

Luz runs instead to a closed café and hammers at the window. The manager comes to meet him, and after a quick exchange he has a phone, and Otelo on the line. In the time it's taken him to find a telephone, Maia and Otelo had re-established radio contact. Looking behind him into the square, Luz sees Maia's hesitation has faded away – the captain has his mission, and he climbs to a standing position on a tank facing the GNR building with a mega-phone in his hand. The crowd reverberates with another sustained cheer, and the captain's amplified voice cuts through – he gives the GNR forces in their headquarters ten minutes to surrender.

A few tense minutes pass. Then a solitary figure walks out through the main doors of the building. Major Fernando Velasco is not, however, there to wave the white flag of surrender. He has exited the quarters of his own initiative, and moves to stand next to Maia and his tank. Meanwhile, Rosado da Luz, keeping an eye on the action from the outer edges of the square, has his attention drawn to the roofs of the buildings. Whereas before the roofs had been taken up by a scattering of MFA soldiers, their weapons trained on the GNR building, some new figures have emerged. Peering into the crowd from above, shifty and grim-faced, he assumes they're agents of PIDE/DGS. As if by divine providence, a solution to this new prob-lem arrives almost immediately. A young woman approaches him from the crowd. 'There are almost two hundred of us,' she declares, 'we are armed and willing to help you. Make use of us.' Her assured demeanour gives him the impression she's part of some communist group. 'The rooftops', he replies, pointing up at the sinister figures. She nods and disappears back into the crowd. Soon, the rooftops above Carmo Square begin to clatter, as the forces assembled by the mysterious young rebel collide with the PIDE agents.[6]

Fifteen minutes have passed since Maia's ultimatum, and apart from the appearance of the solitary major, the GNR headquarters are silent. Maia orders a *Chaimite* unit to open fire on the upper level of windows, to avoid any bullets or shrapnel ricocheting into the crowd. The sudden rap of gunfire echoes around the square, briefly silencing the crowd, who cover their ears, and the top floor of the building blooms with dust and shattered glass. There's no return fire, no response at all. Maia calls over Colonel Abrantes da Silva, who stands observing the operation from the sidelines, and asks the colonel to enter the building and start a dialogue. Once again, his own rank is allowing doubts to bleed into his mission – he sends Abrantes da Silva in 'so those in there don't think this war is being waged by a lowly captain'. The colonel makes his way inside, and another fifteen minutes pass. It's now 15:45 – nearly thirteen hours since H Hour, and over three hours since the siege of the GNR building began. Maia barks into the megaphone again: 'Attention, Carmo headquarters! The conversations are taking too long! They're taking too long!' He orders another spray of gunfire at the windows. The last hours of the siege have allowed the captain to build up the courage to take what he believes is the next, necessary step. Maia orders one of the heavy tanks to position itself in front of the building, training its cannon at the door. If need be, he'll raze the whole building to the ground. He raises his megaphone to his mouth again: 'I'm going to count to three. You need to come out, unarmed, with your hands in the air, or I'll destroy the building.'

'One.'

The crowd's mood has shifted to a sudden panic, and those gathered around Maia and the armoured units begin to push back, away from the square and into the side streets. Some hide behind trees, others dive underneath benches and cup their hands over their ears, pressed into the ground. The cacophony of songs and cheers has been suddenly cut into a pregnant silence. The MFA, having come this far without firing anything more than warning shots, is about to commit an act of spectacular violence on Portuguese soil.

'Two.'

Maia doesn't get to three. Lieutenant Assunção runs up to the captain with two civilians in tow, who introduce themselves: Dr

Pedro Feytor Pinto, director of information services for the State Secretariat of Information and Tourism, and his secretary, Dr Nuno Távora. They have an urgent message from General Spínola, which they have to deliver to Dr Marcelo Caetano. Unbeknownst to the MFA, Feytor Pinto had, two hours previously, sent Távora to contact Spínola and offer his services as an intermediary between the general and the president of the Council. Spínola had maintained his story of not being associated with the Movement or any of the actions of the day, but had left Távora with a loaded message: 'I was not, am not and will not be someone to raise arms against his government. We risk a bloodbath. If the government has the good sense of finding an immediate solution that avoids one, I'm ready to try and take care of the situation.' It's with this vague promise that the two regime wonks arrive at Carmo, hoping to defuse the stand-off and arrange a handover of power between Caetano and Spínola. Salgueiro Maia is unconvinced, but the alternative is turning the building into rubble, so he lets the men enter the GNR headquarters.

Inside the building, Maia's sporadic gunfire has generated an atmosphere of total panic. Feytor Pinto and Távora are ushered into a back room, where Caetano sits behind an office desk, looking dejected. They present the president of the Council with a summary of their conversation with Spínola, and Caetano immediately assents – he's willing to hand control over to the general, which at the very least means power doesn't fall 'onto the streets'. Fifteen minutes later, the two intermediaries make their way back out of the building and request a vehicle from Maia to take them back to Spínola's residence. He grants them a jeep driven by Lieutenant Assunção, and the three men drive off, away from the square. The whole interaction with these supposed intermediaries leaves a bad taste in Maia's mouth. The Movement, from the beginning, had put its support behind Costa Gomes, and he's concerned that this recent development is some sort of delaying tactic to allow reinforcements to arrive. Around him, the civilians have restarted their cacophony of raised voices, and now a new chant has gripped the crowd. They understand that something is happening, something life-changing.

ESTÁ NA HORA
ESTÁ NA HORA
ESTÁ NA HORA

The time has come. The time has come. The time has come. As this phrase echoes in the background, mingled with the hoarse notes of the national anthem, Salgueiro Maia steps off his tank and walks towards the entrance of the GNR headquarters, to see what's going on for himself. He's left instructions with his men that if he doesn't come out within fifteen minutes, they are to destroy the building with him in it. The crowd seem to cheer him on as he walks, until he pushes through the double doors into the building. As the wooden doors swing closed, the roar deadens behind him. It's replaced by the sound of dripping water – his gunfire has pierced the pipes that run around the top of the building, and the walls are damp. There to meet him is General Adriano Pires, who vexes the captain. The general is incapable of surrendering because he's not in charge, and the brief back and forth between the two men accomplishes nothing – he declares that if the general isn't in charge, he should take him to someone who is. By this point, his fifteen-minute timeline is nearly up. The captain steps back outside, but calmer. Nobody in there seems keen to put up any resistance; it's only a matter of time now. He cancels the order to fire on the building, and steps back into the belly of the beast.

Meanwhile, the two messengers have arrived at General Spínola's house, and the general is professing more doubts. What they've brought him isn't a letter from Marcelo Caetano directly, but rather a scrawled summary of a verbal statement that the president of the Council made, and Spínola is hesitant to accept it. The phone rings. It's Caetano.

'General, I have to recognise that I'm beaten. I can hear a wailing crowd outside, and they tell me the square is full of combat cars under the command of a captain. If the government has to capitulate, let it be to someone who can take responsibility for public order and who can calm the country. I'm asking you to come here as soon as you can.'

'But sir,' Spínola replies, stunned, 'I'm not part of the conspiracy.'

'Doesn't matter. If you're not in the conspiracy you can still follow one of my orders. I know they'll respect you.'

'Well, I'll see what I can do.' The general hangs up the phone. That's all the evidence he needs. 'Put me in touch with Major Saraiva de Carvalho.'

Back in Carmo, Maia is led through the GNR building, passing a side room where he hears sobbing. Inside he spots the minister for the interior, César Moreira Baptista, clutching the foreign affairs minister, Rui Patrício, the latter weeping 'like a child' and staring off into the middle distance, distraught. Further ahead, Maia enters the room that Caetano has turned into his temporary office, the curtains drawn, the man himself rising to meet him. Caetano looks pale, unshaven, his tie pulled loose around his collar, but he stands up in a forced dignity, facing his fate head-on. Salgueiro Maia gives the man a salute, almost out of habit. The sounds of the crowd outside filter in, quieter but present, like a reminder. The time has come. The time has come. The time has come.

'Go ahead, captain. Can you tell me what you intend to do here?' says Caetano.

'I have orders from the command post of the Movement to put together an ultimatum. Either your excellency surrenders or I have to raze the building with heavy weapons fire. The command post thinks I've been too lenient so far.'

Caetano leans forward. 'Who commands the revolution?'

Maia thinks. 'General Spínola.'

'What? You received those orders from General Spínola?'

Maia hesitates. He didn't – but given the events of the last hour, he assumes Spínola must have been in the command post, at least during part of the operation. He answers truthfully. 'No, sir. The orders were transmitted to me by the command point, code name OSCAR.'

'So, is General Spínola behind this "Oscar"?'

'No, sir. The command is collective. In addition to General Spínola there are more generals, perhaps eight in total,* one of whom I know is our General Costa Gomes.'

'Who are the others?'

'That I don't know. All I know is I have to follow orders. That is why I'm demanding your excellency's surrender. Otherwise I'll be forced to raze the building.'

'Well, I'm conscious that I don't govern any more. But I hope you treat me with the dignity I have always lived with. I've given the country the best I knew and could, and my conscience is clear. I know I no longer have the forces to resist. But I don't intend to leave here alive leaving the country in the hands of a mask named Oscar, not knowing the face it covers. And I tell you this because General Spínola, with whom I just spoke on the phone, is in his house and denies being connected to the conspiracy.'

This admission surprises Maia, but he's not really here to debate the finer points of who holds power. He has a mission to complete, which he reiterates calmly.

'I have orders to follow and I have to receive your surrender. I'll take every measure to avoid you coming to any physical harm. Your excellency will, along with all the other members of the government, in a closed armoured vehicle, be taken to a place as yet unknown to me, where you will be placed under command of

---

* Referring here to the Junta of National Salvation.

the Movement. If your excellency does not accept,' Maia insists, 'I'll have to raze this building.'

'I'm asking you not to do that, and not to make any rash decisions. I've asked General Spínola to come here and he should be arriving soon. I will hand power to him. Well, I haven't even got power. I'll hand *myself* to him. I ask you now to go back to the square, calm that crowd down, and wait.'

The men look at each other for a beat. Maia turns to go.

'One more question,' Caetano calls out. 'What are your political ideas?'

'I can't specify them,' Maia replies, 'but someone will, later today.'

'And your position on the Overseas Territories?'

'Regarding that, I can tell you with certainty that it will be to avoid the Overseas Territories becoming another India.'

'I don't think it's with a coup that we resolve the problems of the Overseas,' says Caetano. He glances away. The conversation is over. Maia steps back out, composed, knowing his mission is being taken out of his hands.

Shortly after 16:30, one of the many phones rings in Pontinha. It's Lieutenant Colonel Dias de Lima, Spínola's aide and someone with a direct line to the command post. The room goes quiet as Otelo cups the receiver to his chest and waves his comrades over. 'Its Spínola, he wants to talk.'

The Old One's voice chimes in on the other end of the line. 'Saraiva de Carvalho? Are you well? Listen, I've just received a phone call from Professor Marcelo Caetano, from Carmo. He's willing to surrender and asked me to go there; he wants to hand himself in. But I told him I wasn't mandated by the Movement. So I wanted to let you know and get your opinion.'

'One moment, General.' Otelo blocks the receiver again and relays the information to his team. 'What do you guys think?' The response is quick – nods around the room, particularly from Vítor Alves, the MFA's political lead in this situation. It looks like the

Spínolista faction within the MFA are about to have their wishes granted. Otelo brings the receiver up to his ear.

'General? Consider yourself mandated by the Armed Forces Movement to receive the surrender of the president of the Council, and of power.'

'All right, I'll head over then,' Spínola replies. Otelo gives the general instructions to hand the politicians to Salgueiro Maia, who knows what to do with them. There is a DC-6 standing by at Portela airport to fly them to Madeira, in the short term.

In Carmo Square, what had started as a confrontation on the rooftops between PIDE agents and assorted armed communists has spread onto the streets, and the MFA units are busy pulling apart the occasional skirmish as the crowd, emboldened, begin to pick out the regime sympathisers among them and deal out mob justice. Still inside the GNR compound, Maia makes his way to the window to try and calm it all down and give some verbal aid to his men. The sun is edging its way down now, shadows drawing over the fountain and the armoured cars, the last slivers of dappled sunshine glancing off the metal frames and catching on the vibrant red and white of the carnations that appear like punctuation among the people, in rifles, on the ground. The crowd has not dissipated – if anything it's grown bigger as the day has gone on – a vast sea of people and voices united in a shared clamour. Soon that clamour intensifies as a Mercedes gently nudges its way through, shepherded by Salgueiro Maia's men who have to form a physical barricade, arms entwined in a long line, to let Spínola arrive. The masses in the square don't know who's in the car but many have a good guess, and launch themselves at it, arms outstretched as though they might be able to grab him and pull him out, to speed up the run of history that now seems inevitable before someone can take it all away again. The MFA has spent the last nine months in a silent conspiracy – their chief organisers, the day's instigators, are faceless, but António de Spínola is a name and face the crowd recognises, and his arrival is a harbinger of the finale everyone is waiting for. They are a crowd at a rock concert and this is the show-stopper. They are a crowd at a football final and this is the miracle goal in extra time. They are a crowd in a revolution, and the time has finally come for the soft-spoken men in suits with blood in their smiles to meet justice. This is what they've all come here to see. The Old One exits the car in his full regalia – monocle, gloves, cane – to another reverberating roar, the very image of dignified power, patrician and sombre, and enters the building.

It's over in a few minutes. Salgueiro Maia executes a salute which Spínola ignores. The general arrives bemused, almost as if he resents being here to resolve this problem. Their brief conversation is prac-tical – how can they guarantee Marcelo Caetano's safety? Maia replies – by putting him in a *Chaimite*. 'Then I'll go in the same *Chaimite*', is Spínola's reply, before marching into the professor's makeshift office. Caetano is sitting on the couch, relaxed. Gesturing behind him, almost as if to lighten the mood, Spínola says: 'Look at the state these guys have let this get to.' The two men have, in their own ways, been bested by the gaggle of upstart young captains who seem to have control of the country. They also, despite coming from different wings of the Portuguese state bureaucracy, feel it's impor-tant that the adults take command of the situation. After a brief exchange Spínola exits the office. Caetano follows behind soon after. Maia has pulled his men to the front of the building and rolled an armoured car into position – the *Chaimite* 'Bula'. Spínola's arrival has shaken up the expectant audience outside to the point that Maia is concerned about getting Caetano out safely. He grabs his megaphone and speaks out of the window, his voice swallowed by the clamour.

'Gentlemen! We are here in the name of liberty. It is in the name of liberty that we will not deal out justice by our own hands. The people you are waiting for must leave this place in total safety, so they can be judged.'

His words don't make a dent in the clamour. The megaphone is passed over to the lawyer Francisco Sousa Tavares, known regime opponent, who had made his way to the heart of the action. The bespectacled man climbs onto one of the guard booths that frame the entrance of the building and tries his own appeal.

'A regime has ended, one we know well. The miserable PIDE assassinations have ended. But now we have to fulfil our duty to the Armed Forces that have freed us. These men haven't eaten and drunk for eighteen hours. They want to conclude their operations. We should help them in this.'

Rather than disperse the masses, the effect of Sousa Tavares' words is a renewed outpouring of offerings at the feet of the soldiers: more bread, cheese, meats, wine. Nobody is leaving if they can help it. They demand Spínola makes an appearance at the window.

'You'll have plenty of opportunity to celebrate our general!' shouts Salgueiro Maia.

Before the crowd can surge again, the president of the Council of Ministers, now an empty title, is bundled into a car, and the door is shut. Despite his words to Maia earlier, Spínola slides into his Mercedes to follow behind. Slowly and gently, pressing up against the jubilant if frustrated crowd, Maia's convoy exits the square, carrying the most important payload. The coup, in practical terms, is over. What comes next is paperwork.

The day's action teetered on a tightrope – just one or two missteps and a largely peaceful transfer of power could have tumbled into brutal, thoughtless bloodshed. But Otelo's plan, as precise and effective as it was, ultimately has some crucial strategic gaps. And it is as a result of one of these gaps that, throughout the siege of Carmo Square, the sound of unexpected gunfire was heard to echo in the distance – and the goal of a pristine, bloodless operation was suddenly tarnished by the worst elements of the state apparatus.

An officer removes the portrait of António Salazar from the PIDE/
DGS headquarters on Rua António Maria Cardoso, 26 April 1974.

CHAPTER ELEVEN

HUNTING FASCISTS AND DISCUSSING THE PRICE OF COD

For almost five decades, the name of Rua António Maria Cardoso was synonymous with unspeakable horror. From the early 1930s to 1974, the building at number 20 is occupied by the various incarnations of the secret police – first the PVDE, then PIDE, and finally DGS, all institutional rebrands that belied the brutal ideological continuity of the ever-expanding organisation. Like the Aljube, the building – often simply referred to by the name of the street it occupies – towers at the centre of PIDE's sphere of influence. Much of the interrogation and torture PIDE metes out to its prisoners takes place here. On 31 July 1958, a 44-year-old welder named Raúl Alves is tossed from the third floor of the PIDE building, falling to his death. Alves' murder is witnessed by the wife of the Brazilian ambassador, who raises a direct complaint with the patriarch of Lisbon. The response, from the interior minister, is: 'There is no cause for such concern. It is merely an unimportant communist.' As is the standard for those deaths under PIDE custody, PIDE claims Alves' case as a suicide. After the Aljube's closure in 1965, the 'handling' of political prisoners is concentrated here, feeding into the prisons in the forts of Caxias and Peniche.

Now, the PIDE building is luxury housing, down a steep Lisbon street with much less of the centre's typical footfall. The black, anonymous double doors that made up the lower level have been replaced with a slick glass front, but the shape of the building is the same as it's been for a century. On its right edge, a marble plaque reads:

HERE, ON THE AFTERNOON OF
APRIL 25 1974
PIDE OPENED FIRE ON
THE PEOPLE OF LISBON AND KILLED
FERNANDO C. GESTEIRA
JOSÉ J. BARNETO
FERNANDO BARREIRO DOS REIS
JOSÉ GUILHERME R. ARRUDA
HOMAGE FROM A GROUP OF CITIZENS
25-4-1980

This plaque hasn't always occupied pride of place. When the building was renovated, it was removed, and reinstated only through public pressure – but in a much less visible position. Even then it was hoped it could be obscured by parked cars. Now, like it was six years after the revolution, the plaque is on full view at the front of the building – after pressure was put on Lisbon City Council. It's an important rejoinder to the myth of a bloodless revolution.

On the morning of 25 April, Carlos Almada Contreiras, in his bunker underneath the Navy Ministry and hooked into the entirety of its communications network, manages to send a unit of marines to try and take the PIDE/DGS headquarters – a task he and Vítor Crespo have been focused on since the early hours. The marine detachment, on arriving, decide that the building is too well fortified to take with the force available to them, and withdraw. It's in the aftermath of Salgueiro Maia's occupation of Terreiro do Paço, however, that a segment of the newly formed crowd assembled on the streets of Lisbon first turn their attention to the secret police. The politically minded among them lead the march, voices raised in another round of the slogans 'down with fascism', 'down with PIDE'. Now, as the civilian detachment reaches the end of the short walk from Cais do Sodré to António Maria Cardoso, a new chant blends into the repertoire:

ASSASSINOS!
ASSASSINOS!
A SSA SSINOS!
A SSA SSINOS!
A SSA SSINOS!

The small crowd, now riled up by the prospect of meting out justice to the snarling dogs of the *Estado Novo*, have mistimed their arrival. At around 13:00 the marines are gone, there is no military presence on the street, and despite Salgueiro Maia's success in controlling the situation in Terreiro do Paço, the regime hasn't tapped out yet. So when an upstart crowd of civilians arrives to shout abuse underneath the balcony of PIDE headquarters, the response is the one PIDE is accustomed to dishing out: a hail of bullets, fired with no regard for safety or targets, sprayed across the street, sending the crowd running and screaming to safety, and causing the first five civilian injuries of the day – though, thankfully, no deaths. Those civilians scatter, some to seek medical help – others to reconnect with the MFA and Maia's convoy, hoping to convince the Army to help them raid the building.

At around 18:00, PIDE/DGS observers in Carmo, witnessing the imminent surrender of power to the MFA, make a call to António Maria Cardoso. 'It's over, nothing to be done now. Our president is going to hand himself over to General Spínola, who is even on his way.' The news causes a flurry of activity within the building – the shredding and burning of sensitive documents, namely PIDE's list of informants and any compromising photo-graphs. A document is pulled from a safe that details an emer-gency plan to burn the whole building to the ground – should that be necessary. The agents decide it's not – at that stage, despite the regime's collapse, there is still a notion within PIDE/DGS that the changing of the guard might simply put the political police under new management. DGS director Fernando Silva Pais' position, in front of his closest collaborators, is 'if the govern-ment has fallen, then so has our obedience to that government, and we should place ourselves under the orders of the new Power.' That notion is swiftly dispelled by subsequent events.

The unfolding of the coup is cause for immediate reaction among the communist youth, whose political slogans have been carried by the crowds around the city. Early on in the day, in flur-ried phone calls between the secret hideouts of the Communist Party and in response to the radio missives of the MFA, a priority emerges: freeing the political prisoners, from António Maria Cardoso, Caxias and Peniche. During the siege of Carmo, Salgueiro Maia is at various points approached by anxious civilians, urging him to send some forces to take the PIDE/DGS building – but the young captain is so focused on his mission that he can't make the spur of the moment decision to deviate from the plan of oper-ations. But it's only in the late afternoon, once the government surrender is all but certain and the crowd's restlessness has taken on a tinge of violence towards the few PIDE observers among them, that the target is once again vocalised. Francisco Sousa Tavares' megaphone appeal had called on the gathered crowds at Carmo to make their way to Terreiro do Paço, an instruction that, eventually, many carry out. But some aren't content to simply stand and cheer in a spontaneous demonstration-cum-street party. 'What's happen-ing?' a voice chimes out. 'What are we doing standing around here for? Let's go down to António Maria Cardoso; those guys are in there...'[1] The suggestion gathers support, until there's a surge of young voices – 'Let's go to PIDE, let's go to PIDE', and a mass of people begins to break away, pushing up Calçada de São Francisco.[2] The make-up of the day's crowds has been young, but this one is particularly so, a mix of fresh, determined faces, some with an understanding of whom they're marching towards, others swept along by the excitement and there for the ride.

In the chaos of the day, the exact timeline of events is murky. There are conflicting reports on exactly when the population surged on the PIDE headquarters, and reports of gunfire through-out the day and of emergency cars driving wounded civilians away from the action in the mid-afternoon, likely the result of various failed popular incursions on the building, pushed away by the violent response. It's generally accepted, however, that at around 20:00, a group of around six hundred civilians from Terreiro do Paço congregate once again in front of number 20 António Maria Cardoso, baying for the heads of those inside, with shouts of 'Assassins!' and 'Death to PIDE'. PIDE's first response is to set loose an attack dog, which the crowd manages to scare off with sticks and rocks. Then, paving stones are prised from the ground, the mob putting their hands to anything they can hurl at the building, lashing out in hatred. And then – at around 20:10 – agents of the political police open fire from the upper windows and balconies, into the centre of the crowd, following a direct order from Fernando Silva Pais. The bullets meet bodies, dozens of them, as the civilians scatter and dive. They kill Fernando Carvalho Guesteira, seventeen years old, a waiter. They kill José James Hartley Barneto, thirty-eight, father of four, a clerk at the National Confectioners' Guild. They kill João Guilherme Rego Arruda,* twenty, a second-year philosophy

---

* Keen-eyed readers will note that the name listed here is different to the one presented on the plaque affixed to the side of the building. The name on the plaque is an error dating back to its initial placement in 1980.

student. And they kill Fernando Luís Barreiros dos Reis, a 23-year-old off-duty soldier who happened to be taking a holiday in Lisbon on the day of the coup, and who, joining his voice with the civilians around him, becomes the first and only military death of 25 April. The hail of PIDE bullets doesn't discriminate – the lucky ones are the men and women who dive behind parked cars or into alleys, taking grazes or even a few bullets in the back or even coming out unscathed altogether. In addition to the four dead, the PIDE bullets injure upwards of forty-five more – the vast majority in their late teens and early twenties.

PIDE/DGS's later reports indicate that the agents who opened fire on the civilian demonstration were firing into the air, warning shots to disperse the crowd out of concern for, among other things, the safety of the civilians, citing the presence of a gas pump inside that could explode should the building be set on fire. Meanwhile, smoke flows out of the windows as the pile of burning evidence grows bigger inside. Whether or not the PIDE/DGS agents were told to fire into the air, they didn't – the sheer number of injuries puts that lie to bed. The gunfire from the building carries on sporadically into the evening as the scattered crowd rushes to adjacent streets and brings in help from the armed forces, and soon there is a tense stand-off between PIDE/DGS and a squadron of soldiers, as the nearby cavalry units pull vehicles into both ends of the street and train their turrets at the headquarters. There is more gunfire from within – desperate shots followed by screams on the street, and a jostle between the military and the braver civilians who, despite the danger, seem intent on surging and taking the building. The soldiers stationed out front do not return fire, lest the situation escalate even further, preferring instead to maintain a steady siege – even as the civilians around them demand their weapons, demand the right to take the building themselves. It's

248

raining now – in the dim street lights, the tumult in front of the building is further shrouded by the plumes of smoke pouring out of the windows, as more and more paperwork is set alight inside. Men begin to emerge from the headquarters with their arms raised, early surrenders, met with screams of rage and abuse as the military has to step in and prevent the civilians from dealing out mob justice – though a few thrown rocks and fists find their mark. One of these men is a low-ranking DGS employee named António Lage. As Lage comes out he's pressed against a wall by a soldier and searched. Around him, voices are raised calling for his death. Terrified, seeing an opportunity in the bustling chaos, Lage makes a dash up the street, aiming for a gap in the crowd, hoping to make a break for it. A single rifle report reverberates between the buildings and Lage stumbles, falls, a soldier's bullet in his back. Blood pools around his lifeless body. And among the furore, even though the street is now surrounded by Red Cross ambulance cars, firefighters and taxis pulled in to drive the injured away to safety, the crowd places itself between the first aiders and Lage's corpse, shouting: 'PIDE dies in the street!'

The popular crowd that leads the assault on António Maria Cardoso is arguably the first action of the day not carried out by the military. Targeting the headquarters had been on an early draft of Otelo's plan of operations, assigned to Jaime Neves and his commando units before Neves balked at the concept, leaving the Navy elements integrated into the MFA to scramble for units, too little, too late. A similar story plays out with Caxias prison – despite the very real concern that the revolution might lead PIDE/DGS to start executing political prisoners out of desperation. The concern over Caxias had even led Otelo to seek out a detailed map of the inside of the prison, provided, through a convoluted string of contacts in the opposition movements, by the lawyer and activist Jorge Sampaio.* A last-minute withdrawal by the unit he would assign to the task, however, means Caxias also remains off the final plan – Otelo simply doesn't have enough units to try it. Charging António Maria Cardoso as a purely civilian crowd is the first moment in which the coup, until then an exclusively military action, begins to transform into a popular revolution. And, in a scene that will repeat itself in the next several months and years, for the first time in decades the will of the people overrules the machinations of the state.

After Marcelo Caetano's surrender to Spínola in Carmo, Maia's convoy escorts the general and his captive to the command post in Pontinha. Otelo is there to greet them.

'Otelo!' cries Spínola, 'Give me a hug, man! This was an extraordinary thing!' The two men – for the first and final time – embrace, their years of cautious animosity towards each other washed away by the emotion of the moment. Otelo introduces the general to the remaining men in the room, a gaggle of exhausted faces that, despite the long shift, glow with enthusiasm. The general doesn't miss a beat, stepping immediately into his practised role as a gracious orator.

'You gentlemen have just carried out, and brought to fruition, in exemplary fashion, an act of transcendent importance to the history of our country. From this point on we can construct a different society in a new country. The Nation thanks you. On a personal note I'd like to express my admiration and thanks, as a Portuguese, to all the men of the Armed Forces Movement.'

It's in the middle of the general's victory lap around the command post that Pontinha receives word of the incidents outside the PIDE/DGS headquarters. Otelo asks Spínola to order the now ex-interior minister Moreira Baptista to place a

---

* Jorge Sampaio will go on to be mayor of Lisbon in 1990, and Portugal's eighteenth president, from 1996 to 2006.

call to DGS and order their surrender. It's agreed – provided the military can be mobilised to protect the agents from the baying mob outside. It's in part due to the population's presence outside the building that the siege of António Maria Cardoso lasts until the afternoon of the next day. Captain Luís Andrade Moura, exhausted by the day's events and left in charge of the siege, has the unenviable task of handling the crowd, ultimately calming things down with the promise not to let the agents get away. MFA units, including more marines mobilised by Vítor Crespo, trickle in to join the siege.

In Pontinha, the next vital step for the MFA is assembling the Junta of National Salvation – until a provisional government can be established, the order of operations agreed among the political wing of the MFA dictates that the Junta takes power, and it's imperative that it presents its face to the nation as soon as possible. The Junta carries representatives of all three wings of the armed forces, with a bias towards the Army given both their proportion within the Portuguese armed forces and their overwhelming contribution, numbers-wise, to the outcome of the coup. It's one of the Army officers on the list for the Junta who causes a moment of awkwardness for the new state in bloom: Brigadier General Jaime Silvério Marques, tipped by Spínola to be part of the Junta, had been captured by the MFA in the early morning and is being held at the 5th Cavalry Regiment (RC5). Vítor Alves urges Otelo to summon Silvério Marques so the Junta can have their first meeting before making a television declaration to the nation. In RC5, Silvério Marques kicks off at the suggestion he be taken to Pontinha – he feels safe in RC5 and isn't sure what's waiting for him at the command post, and it takes some convincing to put him into a car. Little does he know he's about to be handed joint control of the nation.

Over the next several hours the members of the MFA's Junta arrive in Pontinha. General Costa Gomes joins Spínola first, followed by Frigate Captain António Rosa Coutinho (Navy), Captain José Baptista Pinheiro de Azevedo (Navy), Colonel Carlos Galvão de Melo (Air Force) and finally Silvério Marques. The only member of the Junta not present is the second representative from the Air Force, General Manuel Diogo Neto, still based in Mozambique. Whereas the military coup has been planned and carried out by junior officers, the vast majority of whom are in their late twenties to early thirties, the ages of the Junta range from Rosa Coutinho's comparatively sprightly forty-eight to Spínola's sixty-four. The MFA has come a long way since Vasco Lourenço's flippant declaration that all they need to form a junta are captains, and the make-up of this one is another sign of the Movement's unshakeable urge to place themselves under a proper military hierarchy. The Junta members are ushered into a room with the political wing of the MFA's coordinating group – Vítor Alves, Manuel Franco Charais, Vítor Crespo and Costa Martins, the latter freshly returned from coordinating things at Portela airport and keen to get involved.

It doesn't take long at all for things to get tense. When Charais informs the gathered senior officers that he's about to circulate the MFA programme to the press, Spínola intervenes straight away – 'It's now necessary to review the political programme we will present to the country.' The MFA is almost expecting this, and the Coordinating Committee jumps in ready for the fight. 'I don't understand,' says Charais. 'The general knows the MFA programme very well, as it was finished a few days ago and modified at various points according to the general's will. It was to carry out this programme that the Revolution was done.'[3] The programme is laid out on the table, and Charais begins to read it out, line by line. It's soon apparent what the key points of divergence are – Spínola wants to completely remove section 8c, which contains the phrase '...Clear recognition of the rights of the peoples to self-determination, and the adoption of accelerated means leading to the administrative and political autonomy of the overseas territories with effective and widespread participation of the indigenous peoples.' He also objects to the framing of point 6a, which refers to a 'necessarily anti-monopolist economic and political strategy'. Costa Gomes also chimes in during the discussion – he doesn't object in principle to the passages covering the immediate extinction of PIDE/DGS within Portugal, but has concerns about immediately getting rid of the political police in the colonies, where they provide (in his view) a necessary service while military operations continue. Silvério Marques only chimes in to agree with Spínola – the Old One knew what he was doing by placing the brigadier general on the Junta, and already has a steadfast political ally. The other members of the Junta remain silent, saying only that they already agree with the programme as drafted. The debate escalates – Spínola is intransigent, thinking he can bend the young officers to his will straight away. Vítor Crespo's tetchy response causes the general to backtrack: 'Our armoured cars and troops are still all out on the streets. If it needs to, this coup will carry on.'[4] As the night wears on, the need to get the Junta in front of cameras and the nation grows, and they agree to postpone the discussion until after the address. The Junta are bundled into cars and driven to the RTP station in northern Lisbon, just south-west of the airport.

To an MFA officer watching the broadcast in the early hours of the morning on 26 April, doing so, much like the rest of the population, with bated breath, the make-up of the new holders of power might come as a surprise. Not only is former regime loyalist Jaime Silvério Marques present, but when the cameras zoom out it's General Spínola, grim-faced and adjusting the half-moon glasses that have temporarily replaced his monocle, who addresses the country. General Costa Gomes has always been at the top of any Movement list for the role of leader, and was the MFA's choice for president, but before leaving Pontinha the six members of the Junta had a brief private meeting in which they agreed that Spínola should take on that role. He is undeniably the most senior among them, but is also the one with the most assertive personality, one that Costa Gomes could never match. Thus it's Spínola, in his full military uniform, who reads out the Junta's proclamation to the nation, framed by the still, blinking faces of his compatriots – a turn that takes even the MFA Coordinating Committee by surprise. The full address takes just under three minutes, and with the general's assertion in front of the cameras that the Junta's role is to include 'Guarantee[ing] the survival of the sovereign Nation in its Pluricontinental totality', Spínola has already pulled a coup within the coup. When the Junta return to Pontinha after their sojourn at the RTP station, the negotiations carry on until past dawn on the 26th, and in the early morning exhaustion the Junta reaches a compromise with the MFA: the lines about self-determination are removed from the final programme, and a caveat is added to the section referring to the DGS in the overseas territories, restructuring it as Military Information Police while conflicts are ongoing.

When the Portuguese people wake up on 26 April 1974, they do so to a new country, one brimming with possibilities few could have imagined two nights before. But when journalist Fernando Balsinha stations himself at the bottom of Avenida da Liberdade in Lisbon in his coiffed hair and dark suit, speaking to the RTP cameras, one of his first remarks is about how the traffic seems the same as it always is on a weekday morning. The change to the city is subcutaneous, for now – Balsinha retraces the MFA's steps of the previous day, asking the city's residents how they're feeling, trying to get a sense of the mood. The flower sellers of Rossio and the café waiters smile at the journalist, but remark that the morning crowd seems no different to before, that everyone is calm. Two things seem immediately different – the crowds that congregate on street corners, peeking over each other's shoulders into the pages of open newspapers, all of which carry variations on the same headline – 'The Armed Forces Have Taken Power'. 'Let's hope this changes things for the better,' says a middle-aged man puffing away at a cigarette. 'Cod is too expensive these days.' But the fishmongers claim they've received fewer complaints – and there's enough cod to go around today. Another congregation assembles in front of an open door through which a television can be heard, a press conference led by General Spínola. A man raises his fist and shouts, 'All hail our General António de Spínola,' and the call is met along the street, faces breaking out into smiles. And among this, constantly, the timid footsteps of Lisbon's citizens wandering through the city's centre with simple curiosity, here to catch glimpses of the soldiers and armoured vehicles that still dot the streets and squares, reassuringly, as if to say yes, it really happened. That morning is also when Américo Tomás is finally arrested. In the chaos and excitement of securing Marcelo Caetano, the president had somewhat been forgotten – not least because his exact location was unknown. Tomás had, however, simply spent the day of the coup in his own home – and that's where a detachment from the Army finds him on the morning of 26 April and politely escorts him to the same DC-6 aeroplane set to take Caetano to Madeira.

Even by the afternoon of 25 April, the afternoon issues of the newspaper *República* had, plastered along the bottom of the front page, the line 'THIS NEWSPAPER WAS NOT TARGETED BY ANY CENSORSHIP COMMISSION'. On the morning of 26 April, the top floor of *República*'s head office on Rua da Misericórdia is an excellent vantage point from which to witness the continuation of last night's events at Rua António Maria Cardoso and even before that at Carmo Square, an activity that will grow to become known as *caça-PIDE*, PIDE-hunting. Number 95 Rua da Misericórdia is the headquarters of the newspaper *A Época*, the unambiguously pro-regime rag that was formerly the equally partisan *Diário da Manhã*. A few doors down, the state censor had notoriously occupied number 125 since 1969, with the steady influx of documents for approval making their way into the building through the back entrance on Rua das Gáveas. In an expression of decisive intent, crowds of people occupy the front of these two buildings in the early hours and begin, stones in hand, to destroy the facades, breaking into the *Época* offices and scattering the offending papers until the streets are carpeted in a crumpled, damp layer of white pulp, gleefully trampled underfoot. The news that a DGS agent is hiding out in the *Época* building summons military vehicles and kicks off another siege, another expression of popular rebellion against the regime's butchers. If last night's Junta meeting brought into question the dissolution of PIDE/DGS in the colonies, those doubts don't exist in the minds of the Portuguese population, and the regime collaborators are chased mercilessly through the streets by crowds allowed to run riot until the violence is stopped here and there by armed police and soldiers.

That friction between the will of the people, the MFA and the Junta's more vocal figures rises to the surface around the occupation of Caxias prison. Commander José Júlio Abrantes Serra arrives at the entrance of the fort at 07:30 in the morning, leading a force of marines, having been sent there to release the political prisoners by Carlos Almada Contreiras. He finds PIDE/DGS waiting in front of the hill fort, prepared to surrender. Abrantes Serra orders the prison's gates open, and places the PIDE agents under arrest. After some back and forth with the chief prison guard, the cells are opened, and the roughly two hundred men and women held in Caxias gather in the prison courtyard, many suddenly set free from long periods of total isolation. Outside, friends, well-wishers and family members can be heard congregating, cheering for the immediate release of their comrades. To some in the prison, news of the coup has already trickled in, through comrades on the outside driving past and honking out messages in Morse code. But releasing everyone isn't straightforward – despite the MFA's clear stance on freedom for political prisoners, the Junta (and particularly Spínola) have imposed a ruling that only prisoners incarcerated for political reasons are to be freed.

This poses an immediate, headache-inducing problem for the officers in Caxias: one of PIDE's obfuscation strategies was to append some sort of common crime to most of the prisoners' accusations, to be able to hold, publicly, on to the fiction that the Portuguese state didn't imprison people for political crimes. Thus, certainly on paper, out of the hundreds held in Caxias, only around twenty are eligible for release under the Junta's restriction. The PIDE/DGS agents brought in to help Abrantes Serra sort through the files insist that the vast majority are violent criminals who shouldn't be released – advice which the commander is minded to ignore. As the day stretches on, the sudden, new limbo the prisoners find themselves in builds tension both within the prison and outside, where the gathering crowd's chants grow in frustration and intensity. Abrantes Serra finds, by the northern entrance, a group of lawyers waiting anxiously, each with a well-known track record of defending opposition figures and with multiple clients in the prison. The commander invites the lawyers in to help resolve the situation, and it becomes rapidly clear that the Junta's directive is impossible to follow. It's only by late evening, when Major Menino Vargas places a phone call to Manuel Franco Charais in Pontinha, that something gives – Charais orders the immediate release of all of the prisoners, taking personal responsibility for the decision. Shortly afterwards, Spínola's man Dias de Lima arrives with the same instruction from the Junta – they should all be let go. It's shortly after midnight when the crowd of around a thousand people, having kept a day's vigil, greet the beaming prisoners with chants of 'the people united will never be defeated'. Out pour the last victims of the *Estado Novo*'s political repression, swallowed up by the mass of waiting, cheering bodies, the decades spent shouldering the weight of democratic and anti-fascist struggles imprinted on their drawn faces. Among them is Hermínio Palma Inácio, who is raised onto shoulders, his face frozen in a smile of pure ecstasy. This freeing of prisoners is both a symbolic and a very real act – a complete rupture with the past regime. One of many that need to happen in order to to forge the new Portugal. They won't all be so straightforward.

President António de Spínola makes a public address, 1974.

PART THREE

ONGOING REVOLUTIONARY PROCESS

The MFA was something that, right from the beginning and 25 April, had officers who knew what socialism was and many who didn't know what it was. There were many that had an idea, an image, of what socialism was, they had done some reading, and they thought that socialism wouldn't demand some sacrifices, that it wouldn't demand the abdication of some privileges. That's why some of them have reached their 'Peter Principle', as they say, they've reached their revolutionary incompetence. This cannot be.

Manuel Duran Clemente, 1975

Crowds in Lisbon on 1 May 1974.

CHAPTER TWELVE

THE DECLINE AND FALL OF ANTÓNIO DE SPÍNOLA

Just south of Lisbon's airport, near the intersection of Avenida de Roma and Avenida Estados Unidos da América, stands a modest football stadium. This is the Estádio 1 de Maio – but prior to the first of May 1974, the stadium was simply known as the FNAT Stadium. FNAT *Fundação Nacional Para a Alegria no Trabalho* (National Foundation for Joy in Work) is another glimpse into the cynical, patriarchal control *Estado Novo* institutions exercised over Portuguese society. FNAT was founded in 1935 with the specific purpose of providing cultural and recreational activities for workers, aimed at 'physical and moral development'. As the FNAT directorship stated in 1936, 'physical culture is seen as essential for us, not only with the goal of bettering the physical condition of Portuguese workers, but above all to discipline, and hold true and effective control over them'. Salazar may have started with God, Family and Homeland, but the regime's dissidents put it more bluntly: a state hegemony built on Fado, Football and Fátima*. Salazar himself makes an appearance at the FNAT Stadium's inauguration in 1959, a nod to the idea that the stadium wouldn't be used for such vulgar

---

* Fátima, the town where the Virgin Mary is said to have appeared and delivered prophecies to three shepherds, is the epicentre of Portuguese Catholicism.

activities as professional sport. It served a much greater purpose than that.

There is no football on the pitch at the FNAT Stadium on 1 May 1974 – only a vast sea of people, arms raised, shouting, singing and cheering, carnations clutched in hands and hundreds of banners bearing dozens of political slogans. 1 May's international status as workers' day had always made it the annual holiday of dissent, each year marked by labour demonstrations and protests inevitably beaten back viciously by the police and GNR. PIDE/DGS's focus on rounding up likely troublemakers for this event no doubt played a part in keeping the state's eye away from the MFA during the crucial months in the run-up to Otelo's operation. Now, for the first time in forty-eight years, almost everyone is out on the streets in every corner of the country – the largest popular mobilisation anyone can remember, even including the rare, stage-managed mass gatherings occasionally orchestrated by the regime. In Lisbon alone it's around one million, some five hundred thousand of whom have followed a procession from the park in Alameda to the FNAT Stadium, instantly rechristened the First of May Stadium, to witness the new Portugal being presented to the world. There are dozens of members of the national and international press here, snapping photos and recording video of the crowd – but the main attraction is the speeches. The days immediately following 25 April saw an influx of former exiles to Portugal, returned to popular acclaim. Among them is Mário Soares, who pulled into Santa Apolónia train station on the 28th from Paris after four years in exile, to be greeted by an expectant audience that mirrored the acclamation of Humberto Delgado in that same location in 1958. Álvaro Cunhal landed at Portela airport on the 30th, having led the Portuguese Communist Party from Moscow and Prague for the last thirteen years. The two men are the celebrities of this march and gathering, the faces of the most prominent banned political parties, returned to a nation transformed. They share the stage overlooking the packed stadium with a host of trade unionists, representatives of the different facets of a labour movement, primed to reshape the country in their own name.

In the very first days after the coup, the signs of a new land-scape for the working class begin to emerge. Workers in the Mague metallurgical plant in Alverca, the only workers on strike at the time of the coup, calling for a monthly minimum of 6,000 escudos, have their demands met at once by a management suddenly terrified of their workforce. A few days later on the 28th, families occupy vacant properties in the Lisbon neighbour-hood of Boavista and refuse to leave – an action that springboards the occupation of thousands of empty, government-owned prop-erties over the next few weeks and mobilises the creation of resi-dents' commissions, particularly within the large shanty towns (*bairros de lata*, literally 'tin neighbourhoods') in urban centres such as Lisbon and Porto.[1] Within workplaces the word of the day is *saneamento* – a word with connotations of purification and cleanliness; the removal of (primarily) managers who were closely tied to the *Estado Novo*, carried out by the spontaneously gener-ated workers' councils beginning to emerge both in the industrial colossuses but also among smaller workplaces. The sudden vacuum left by the repressive state coincides perfectly with the mounting unrest among the workers. These workers' councils are in many cases completely unaffiliated to official trade unions – they appear within individual workplaces and are coordinated and led democratically, debate and organisation spurred by grass-roots activism. Already a fertile ground for dissent and activism, student councils emerge throughout educational institutions and carry out their own purges within academia, adding kindling to the flames of student unrest that had started in the early 1960s and never really died out. Within the upper levels of the state, another *saneamento* is taking place – as per the deal struck with the MFA, General Spínola dismisses vast swathes of the senior military and political hierarchy, replacing them with his allies within the armed forces – beginning, slowly but steadily, to consolidate his own power. Or at least, to believe he is. The very nature of the coup should have been an indication that having control of the senior members of the armed forces is no guarantee of actual power *over* the armed forces. The various structures put together by the MFA have not disappeared overnight.

Along with the return of the Socialist and Communist parties, from within the so-called Liberal Wing of the former regime and the tolerated democratic opposition, new parties emerge that populate the new political landscape. Francisco Pereira de Moura, economist and university professor, who had participated in the occupation of Rato Chapel the year before, had been on the MFA's list for potential prime minister, and emerges as the de facto leader of the Portuguese Democratic Movement (*Movimento Democrático Português*, MDP), which had contested the 1969 election against the regime. From within the former regime, Liberal Wing deputies Francisco Pinto Balsemão, Francisco Sá Carneiro and Joaquim Magalhães Mota form the Popular Democratic Party (*Partido Popular Democrático*, PPD) on 6 May. Spínola's First Provisional Government is a deliberate amalgam of these various political forces – including, to the surprise of the more moderate members of the MFA, the Communists. On his arrival back in Portugal, Ávalro Cunhal is personally offered a position in the new government in his first meeting with Spínola, which, despite the decades-old PCP line against participation in bourgeois governments, Cunhal accepts. Mário Soares had also called for Cunhal and the PCP's inclusion in the new political framework. It's a canny move by Spínola – aware that the transitional period will see an unprecedented upsurge of workers' struggles, placing Álvaro Cunhal in government as minister without portfolio and fellow PCP militant Avelino Gonçalves in the role

266

of labour minister will, he hopes, lead to a tempering of those struggles by the self-proclaimed torchbearers of the workers' movement.[2] The First Provisional Government thus contains two representatives from the PCP, two from the PPD, one from the MDP and three from the Socialists, with Mário Soares as the foreign affairs minister, among a remaining cohort of independent or unaligned ministers. For the role of prime minister the MFA had suggested the above-mentioned Pereira de Moura or the journalist Raul Rego, another of the Socialist Party's founders, given his track record of critical articles in the newspaper *República*. Spínola opts instead for the liberal lawyer Adelino da Palma Carlos, former director of the Faculty of Law at the University of Lisbon and linked to big business[3] – a choice, in part, intended to avoid rocking the boat of the Portuguese capital too severely. The new government takes power on 16 May with Spínola as president, still bound (on paper) by the Junta and the MFA programme.

The MFA had never intended to take political power after the revolution – the intention of the programme was always to hand over democratic control to the will of the Portuguese people. But the first days of a Spínola-led government show the clear need for the Movement's continued existence, to guarantee the execution of the key aspects of the programme. Vasco Lourenço returns to Lisbon on the evening of 28 April – to much less fanfare than Cunhal and Soares. He's met with an emotional embrace from Otelo, who fills him in on everything that's happened since his exile to the Azores. The captains find their capacity to intervene suddenly diluted – not only are there no MFA representatives in the First Provisional Government, but the newly created State Council (formed as part of the MFA's programme) is created in such a way as to sideline the MFA. The State Council contains twenty-one members: the seven members of the Junta (none officially in the MFA, though the Junta itself has split sympathies), seven from the eight-member Political Committee of the MFA and seven more assigned personally by the president. Spínola thus has an overall majority of support within the official organs of government. Within the armed forces, especially the Army and the colonies, however, the MFA is still active and influential. This relationship between the junior officers and the rest of their units leads to an uneasy hierarchical dynamic, as often the MFA members who had taken active roles in the conspiracy are subordinated to officers who did not. Salgueiro Maia, for instance, returns to the Practical Cavalry School in Santarém as the man who was responsible for Marcelo Caetano's surrender – yet he's not the unit commander. The MFA thus has a nebulous status within the armed forces – a separate structure, developed in conspiracy, that now has to find a way to sit alongside the edifices of military bureaucracy. Otelo carries on his coordination functions in the MFA command post, initially in Pontinha and then Cova da Moura, following the Junta's headquarters with the renamed Operational Control and Coordination Centre (*Centro de Coordenação e Controle Operacional*, CCCO), the 'armed wing' of the MFA. Even before May, Spínola attempts to integrate this bureaucratically into the armed forces, but his attempts are rebuffed by the captains – the MFA will continue to operate independently.

Already in the first days of May, the roots of a budding Spínola-MFA confrontation begin to spread. João Varela Gomes, the notorious anti-fascist ex-officer with a history of involvement in the 'See Coup' and the assault on Beja, spent the '60s and early '70s languishing in PIDE prisons and became integrated into the underground opposition. After 25 April he had been brought back into the military and promoted to the rank of colonel, tasked, given his history, with dismantling the PIDE/DGS infrastructure. Varela Gomes takes to the job with enthusiasm and an eye for detail, and soon begins making connections between PIDE/

DGS and the heads of large Portuguese corporations (outside of his remit), spooking Spínola and Jaime Silvério Marques. Soon MFA units hear that Varela Gomes has been arrested and transported to the military prison in Trafaria, on Silvério Marques' orders. Captain Dinis de Almeida, at the 1st Light Artillery Regiment, contacts the MFA leadership and declares himself ready for action if needed, to release their comrade – he already has some batteries pointed at the presidential palace! Otelo and Vasco Lourenço tell him to calm down, but contact Spínola directly demanding Varela Gomes be released. They travel to Trafaria themselves and personally oversee the release of the colonel – but not before wounding the president's pride with their open defiance of his, and his allies', overreach. The colonel is moved away from his role dealing with PIDE/DGS, however, and in June is placed at the head of the 5th Division of the Armed Forces – a branch set up as a public relations and civilian liaison unit during the transition to democracy.

On 20 May, after a rapid negotiation with the Junta, Marcelo Caetano and Américo Tomás are put on a plane and flown to Brazil, thrown into a life of exile. It's a decision that the MFA doesn't hear about until it's too late, and one that leaves them sour – sending Caetano away means Salazar's successor cannot undergo a trial or receive the judgment that Salgueiro Maia promised the crowds at Carmo. They don't have time to object – the revolution is advancing apace, as are the conflicts between the MFA and the new president. The main point of friction between Spínola and the captains is the issue of decolonisation, something that's been apparent from the very first meeting of the Junta and his mealy-mouthed statement in front of the cameras in the Junta's first address. As the month of May rolls on, the new president drags his feet on the issue, refusing the call for outright independence even as the demands for the immediate end of the war echo louder on the streets of Portugal, and from within the armed forces stationed abroad. On 5 May, members of the MRPP had physically prevented a new batch of soldiers from being sent overseas. Spínola still clings to a notion of a Pluricontinental Portugal – a Commonwealth of sorts – and his stalling tactics are aimed in part to muddy the waters of who the 'legitimate' negotiators are in the overseas territories. Over the course of the war, various factions had emerged in Angola, Mozambique and to a lesser extent Guinea, often conservative, at times supportive of the Portuguese forces, and openly hostile to the main independence movements represented by MPLA, FRELIMO and PAIGC. There is also a real concern about the wellbeing of both the Portuguese colonists and the locals who were integrated into Portuguese militias, should independence be established. Across the Portuguese fronts in Africa, however, the change in regime means the loss of the will to fight – and even without government approval, soldiers begin to refuse mobilisation orders and stop participating in actions beyond routine patrols. In early May in Guinea, MFA-aligned officers enter into contact with the PAIGC and broker a de facto ceasefire. In Angola and Mozambique, however, without a clear commitment to independence from Lisbon, the guerrillas carry on the war – and the deaths carry on also. When Mário Soares is sent to London on 25 May to negotiate with the PAIGC, his hands are tied politically, and the talks founder. Spínola wants the colonies to undertake popular referendums on independence, something none of the liberation movements are willing to countenance. After the talks with FRELIMO fall flat in Lusaka in early June, FRELIMO's president Samora Machel remarks: 'You don't ask a slave if he wants to be free, particularly when he is already in revolt, and much less if you happen to be a slave owner.' Otelo Carvalho is sent along on Soares' trip to Lusaka, and unlike the beleaguered foreign affairs minister, the major has no qualms about making the MFA's position – self-determination and independence – as clear as possible.

As Spínola collides head-on with the MFA over decolonisation, the workers' struggles that had started immediately after the
collapse of the *ancien régime* accelerate. Throughout May and
June, strikes take over the country and bring important sections
of the economy to a standstill, with demands that range from
significant pay increases, shorter working weeks and sick pay to
explicit political statements such as support for the MFA and,
always, an end to the colonial war. The strike wave spans the
breadth of Portuguese society – from workers at the state airline
TAP, the transportation company Carris, the Lisbon Metro and
the Timex factory to the postal service. On 24 May the PCP-led
Ministry of Labour passes a minimum monthly wage of 3,300
escudos (£55), which falls short of the majority of the workers'
demands[4] and sparks even more strike action and protest. Much
as Spínola had predicted, the PCP in government is forced to
collaborate in quelling the unrest, putting out calls against strike
action and occasionally sending in the Army to quell disputes,
which sends many of the Party's card-carrying members into the
arms of the more militant far-left organisations such as the
MRPP, the Revolutionary Brigades and the Movement of Left
Socialists (*Movimento de Esquerda Socialista*, MES), all of whom,
through workplace activity, pick up members and influence
among the workers. And despite the PCP's complicity in his own
government's opposition to the strike wave, Spínola decries the
communist influence and the economic ruin the unfettered
left will wreak on the country. And even on the streets, albeit
small, a popular movement begins to emerge that seems to back
Spínola's ambitions. 10 June has historically been celebrated as
Portugal and Camões Day, a day which Salazar, in 1944, declared
was also a celebration of the Portuguese Race. Under the *Estado
Novo*, 10 June was therefore an opportunity for nationalistic and
jingoistic parades in Terreiro do Paço, and it's under this banner
that on 10 June 1974 a demonstration numbering a few thousand

marches from the top of Avenida da Liberdade to Camões Square, cheering Spínola and twisting a popular workers' slogan into 'Portugal, united, shall never be defeated'. A revolutionary statement flipped into an imperialist one. The collapse of the *Estado Novo* has left a void that is being filled by the workers' movement. But it's also an opportunity for Portugal's most reactionary elements to regroup. They have not disappeared.

On 13 June, Spínola attempts to settle the issue with the MFA by calling a meeting in the vast Military Maintenance building, on the south-eastern edge of the river in the Beato neighbourhood of Lisbon. As well as the Coordinating and Political Committees, the room is packed with roughly two hundred of the Movement's delegates. Spínola intends to gain a personal mandate from the young officers to solve the colonial problem and be the true interpreter of the MFA's programme, and he brings with him the economic minister, Vasco Vieira de Almeida, and the chief PPD minister, Francisco Sá Carneiro. Both of Spínola's ministers paint a dire economic picture, claiming that there is only enough money in the country's coffers for the next few weeks, and that after that 'the MFA will be responsible for the hunger.'[5] Sá Carneiro's proposed solution is to call a state of emergency and place the military into temporary control, granting Spínola full decision-making capabilities, to quell the social unrest. Major José Cardoso Fontão, one of the officers who had led the siege on Vilalva Palace, asks if they mean to start another military dictatorship, but Sá Carneiro dodges the question. Colonel Vasco Gonçalves, key member of the Political Committee, declares that if there's not enough money they should take it from where it's concentrated – out of the hands of capitalists. Gonçalves' outburst sends the stage into a flurry of personal insults against the colonel, and a break for lunch is called where the disgruntled MFA men discuss how to respond to Spínola's power grab. When the session resumes, Vasco Lourenço, sitting in the front row, stands to speak.

'General, you were appointed president of the Junta, and are president of the Republic, because the MFA had faith in you. The fact that you are still the president means the MFA still has faith in you. But—'

Hearing the 'but', Spínola jumps in before Lourenço can go any further. 'I knew it!' cries the general, 'I knew I had your trust and your support!'[6] Spínola stands and exits the stage tailed by his coterie, ignoring Lourenço's dour face and crossed arms as the room bursts into applause, leaving the officers alone and startled. Lourenço jumps onto the stage and addresses the room. 'Now, the general didn't let me finish. And I want to know if you support me in what I was going to say! Which is that Spínola keeps our trust as long as he remains faithful to the MFA programme! Do you agree with that or not?' The room once again bursts into rapturous applause, which just makes Lourenço mad. 'Why did you clap the general just then?' he barks. 'Why did you let him leave on that note? You're like a bunch of meek lambs!'[7] Lourenço takes a mandate from the room for the Coordinating Committee to confront the general, and state in clear terms that they haven't granted him any of the powers he demanded, least of all the freedom to declare a state of emergency. And the general, despite his outward bravado, sulks. Spínola travels to his usual holiday haunt of Luso, in northern Portugal, and threatens to resign. It's only after the MFA threatens to accept the president's resignation that Costa Gomes, unwilling to take on the role of president himself, takes a helicopter to Luso to convince Spínola to return to his office in the presidential palace in Belém.

Spínola meets with Richard Nixon in the Azores on 19 June, at the height of the Watergate scandal and a mere two months before Nixon's eventual resignation. Nixon makes noises of open support for the new Portuguese democratic process and quiet nods towards Spínola's own domestic and colonial strategies, with particular emphasis on fighting the communist surge. The US has a vested interest in the rise of the National Liberation Front of Angola, which had received CIA support as the main anti-communist alternative to the MPLA. Spínola returns to Lisbon with a renewed fervour for consolidation of power. He backs a constitutional proposal from Prime Minister Palma Carlos which aims to delay the upcoming Assembly elections to late 1976, but also to bring forward a presidential election to October of 1974. The goal, certainly on paper, would be to grant a degree of popular legitimacy and power to a transitional government, whose powers would be split between the president and the prime minister, under a transitional constitution. It also flies in the face of the terms of the MFA programme, which lays out a timeline for elections to the Constitutional Assembly that should take place within a year of the coup. On 7 July, the MFA hold a meeting in the building formerly occupied by the Portuguese Legion, at the top of the hill in Penha de França and now given over to a unit commanded by Captain Dinis de Almeida. The meeting, though fractious, agrees to reject Palma Carlos' proposal – it's understood that the political paralysis the new proposals intend to resolve have their roots in Spínola's own neocolonial policies – the general wants the freedom to more closely control the decolonisation process, aided in that by his appointed prime minister. And with that rejection they manage to find enough allies within the State Council to, just barely, tip the votes for a majority against the proposals. With this balance of power, Spínola makes a volte-face and opts to oppose the proposals, falling in line with the will of the State Council. Palma Carlos' proposals had arrived as a sort of ultimatum, and with their rejection the prime minister, and the ministers who had backed him, opt to resign. Thus, on 11 July, less than two months after its original creation, the First Provisional Government dissolves itself.

Meanwhile, during the run-up to what would later become known as the Palma Carlos crisis, the Operational Control and

Coordination Centre that had started as the command post in Pontinha further establishes itself. The new structure is the Operational Command of the Continent (*Comando Operacional do Continente*, COPCON), which Spínola formalises on 8 July. COPCON is its own beast – made up of special military units and taking on roles traditionally assigned to the police and the GNR while these go through *saneamento*, it sits outside the main military command structure as a machine for guaranteeing the success of the revolution.[8] After failing to gain his MFA mandate on 13 June, Spínola had declared to the MFA that they needed 'chiefs'[9] – their response had been to put forward Otelo Saraiva de Carvalho for the role of COPCON's commander, a role that he takes on alongside his other, new responsibility as the commander of the Lisbon Region Military. The new titles come with a promotion, and on 13 July Otelo is given his new stripes as a brigadier general. Otelo doesn't miss the opportunity to take a dig at Jaime Silvério Marques who, through gritted teeth, has the task of presenting him with the honours. After Silvério Marques makes a barbed comment about Otelo's youth and the youth of the captains who carried out the events of 25 April, Otelo replies: 'Youth here was really a matter of age, because we were between twenty-five and forty and we took the immense weight of responsibility upon us to topple a government that we all deplored, but which our generals, despite all of their youth, probably in spirit, didn't have the courage to topple. On 25 April we therefore took on the future of the Nation.'[10] As much as Otelo's wry statement further insults the military establishment, there's little they can now do – the MFA has been granted a parallel military hierarchy, now with the strategic mind of the revolution at its head. And Otelo is quick to clarify that he's not in that position through the will of the president, but by a vote of his own comrades. The Movement isn't going to let the fall of the First Provisional Government pass them by.

Palma Carlos' resignation takes a few ministers with him, particularly Sá Carneiro. Although the MFA were initially willing to leave the appointed politicians in charge of the transitional period, the conflict with Spínola and the spectre of a turn to reactionary neocolonialism causes them to impose themselves on the make-up of the new government.[11] Rejecting all of Spínola's proposals, the Coordinating Committee puts forward Major Ernesto Melo Antunes for prime minister – which Spínola rejects out of hand. Melo Antunes had been the author of the original political programme that Spínola had eviscerated, and the general considers him an unrepentant communist. It's all the more ironic that Spínola accepts Colonel Vasco Gonçalves, one of the main voices in the Political Committee, into the role. In the next year he will become Spínola's bête noire. The cabinet reshuffle brings in a swathe of other officers, including José da Costa Martins into the role of labour minister, replacing the PCP's man. Melo Antunes and Vítor Alves join Álvaro Cunhal and the remaining PPD member in government, Magalhães Mota, as ministers without portfolio. And Major Sanches Osório takes on the role of social communication minister – albeit representing the newly formed Christian Democratic Party (*Partido da Democracia Cristã*, PDC). Sanches Osório's own political leanings are little known to the Movement – for now, he's a trusted officer of the MFA. All told the MFA presence in the Second Provisional Government, unveiled on 18 July, tallies in at eight out of seventeen, enough to push forward a real agenda and push back against Spínola's own plans, along the terms of the original programme. But the MFA as an entity is not in any way homogenous, certainly politically. Even before 25 April, and especially after the publication of *Portugal e o Futuro*, the most organised faction within the Movement has been made up of those directly aligned with Spínola (particularly in the Army), which over the last few months has created an active confrontation within the organisation. The *Spinolistas* in the MFA are, however, a minority

– in the broad meeting of the Army section, held after the formation of the Second Provisional Government to replace the members
of the Coordinating Committee now holding ministerial posts, the
officers elected are Nuno Pinto Soares, Manuel Franco Charais and
Vasco Lourenço – each strong critics of Spínola, and what might be
referred to as 'continuity MFA'. However, among the officers still
married to the principles of strict military hierarchy, the very existence of the MFA Coordinating Committee is unacceptable – and
there are attempts, always rebuffed or dismantled, to dissolve the
MFA leadership into the existing armed forces structure.*

It takes less than ten days from the induction of the Second
Provisional Government for Spínola, now on the retreat, to suffer
his biggest defeat yet. In the context of the collapse of government control in Angola and Mozambique, catalysed by a wave of
terrorist activity perpetrated by disgruntled white colonists, and
the perpetual presence of street movements in Portugal calling
for the immediate end of the war, the number one priority for the
new government is to draw the colonial issue to a rapid conclusion. Through pressure from the MFA in the new government,
Spínola finally breaks – in a press conference on 27 July, the
general states: 'The moment has come for the President of the
Republic to solemnly reiterate the recognition of the rights of the
peoples of the Portuguese Overseas Territories to self-determination, including the *immediate recognition of their right to independence.*'The members of the Coordinating Committee gather
with their comrades in government in the National Assembly

---

* The culmination of these efforts is a document, drafted by Lieutenant
Colonel Manuel Engrácia Antunes and circulated in August, which manages
to generate a good number of signatures (many through underhand methods
suggesting it is supported by the MFA leadership). The fallout as a result of the
document places General Costa Gomes unambiguously on the side of the
MFA in the conflict between the Coordinating Committee and the president.

building in São Bento, and watch the address on television. When it's over, Vasco Gonçalves shares out some bottles of champagne to toast the victory, and Vasco Lourenço suggests they go and see Spínola directly. Three members of the Committee drive to the presidential palace in Belém. When the Old One receives them, he looks dejected, beaten in a way Lourenço has never seen before. But the MFA is there to offer an olive branch – Lourenço tells the president that he has the MFA's support provided he continues on the path his press conference has laid out. 'I knew it,' Spínola replies, 'I knew that's what you wanted me to do.' And as if finding a renewed strength, he leaves the officers startled with his next statement – 'Now, leave Angola to me.'[12] Spínola had declared the *right* for the colonial peoples to seek independence, but the terms of *how* is still murky. In Guinea the ceasefire has been in place for months, and PAIGC's hegemony means the transition is straightforward – they had unilaterally declared independence in September of 1973, and there's little Spínola can do to change that. FRELIMO's dominance over Mozambique means the situation there is similar – a ceasefire is requested on 8 August, and negotiations begin in earnest on the 16th, amidst a wave of unrest and protest from white colonists. Cape Verde, however, had never been the site of any armed conflict – neither had São Tomé and Timor – and so the president still has some leeway to manage the independence of those colonies without the threat of prolonging a conflict. Angola is a different story entirely – the size and international support of the different political factions means the negotiations are less straightforward, and Spínola hopes to take advantage of that to avoid giving the crown jewel of the Portuguese Empire away without a fight.

For Spínola, the political bogeyman is and has always been the Communist Party, and the factional divides begin to move beyond the ones developed purely within the armed forces, to ones represented by the political parties. The MFA is not a party political organisation – its main proponents have maintained the *cordon sanitaire* with the civilian politicians. However, the Communist Party's policies, particularly in the push for rapid decolonisation and the *saneamento* of institutions, have meant the development of a tacit alliance between the PCP and the MFA. On the other side of the divide is Spínola, who aligns himself with a nascent (or rather, reassembled) political right that sees the general as the best chance of representing their interests and the interests of capital – namely the Liberal Party (*Partido Liberal*, PL) and the Progress Party (*Partido do Progresso*, PP), the latter of which started as the Portuguese Federalist Movement. The more overtly fascist elements within Portuguese society that didn't flee the country or go into hiding after 25 April flow into these legitimate political parties, gathered around what has always been the clarion call of Portuguese reaction: holding on to the colonies. And as much as in early June Sá Carneiro's bloviating about the economic dire straits of the country was an attempt to scare the MFA into falling in line, Portugal seems close to spiralling into a serious economic crisis, exacerbated by the strike waves, capital flight and an international investment boycott that emerged shortly after the coup. The fall of the First Provisional Government makes things even more uncertain – there go the 'steady hands' brought in to avoid spooking the capitalists, and in enter a group of military officers with little to no political experience but seemingly operating on a parallel trajectory to the Communist Party. Vasco Gonçalves' government, with support from the Communists, attempts to curb the strike wave, repudiating the industrial action and continuing the tactic of sending the Army and COPCON in to repress the workers in more extreme cases (with mixed results). There are numerous cases of soldiers and officers being sent to break strikes and demonstrations and, after being cheered by striking workers, simply refusing to act or even crossing over to join workers.[13] The government even goes as far as to bring in new legislation regulating strike action on 27 August, labelled an 'anti-strike' law by the progressive press. The new legislation, apart from forbidding strike action among military, firefighter and police services, also forbids workplace occupations and solidarity strikes, and enshrines employer lock-outs into law.[14] All the while, both the Communists and the amalgamation of official trade unions known as the Intersindical denounce 'strikes for the sake of strikes' as 'adventurist' and 'acts of sabotage' to the revolution, as potential agents of fascism and reaction.[15] This disconnect between the left on the streets and the left in government leaves ample space for the right to surge, attacking both.

The acceleration of the decolonisation process leads, also, to a strong backlash from the white colonial populations, with reverberations in Portugal. Given their united interests, the reactionary right form an alliance across the collapsing Empire with the right-wing factions desperate to avoid independence. In Angola, the far right threatens to declare unilateral independence against the MPLA. There are spurts of violence across northern Mozambique after the FRELIMO ceasefire is announced on 8 August, and in Lourenço Marques when the terms of independence are agreed in early September (the Lusaka Accord). The culmination of these disturbances is the occupation of Rádio Clube de Moçambique by colonists, taking over airwaves with missives declaring the Lusaka Accord null and void. Samora Machel sees the occupation as a direct attempt to subvert the independence process, and demands Spínola denounce the unrest – Spínola delegates the task to Costa Gomes, and after a few days of a tense stand-off the takeover of the radio station is lifted by commando units in Lourenço Marques. Both at home and in the colonies, Spínola is seen as the man to rally around, and the general leans into the role by employing a phrase borrowed from Richard Nixon – the 'silent majority' – already part of his lexicon since the Palma Carlos crisis and now making regular appearances in his speeches. On 10 September, as part of a speech finally recognising Guinean independence, Spínola raises the spectre of authoritarian communism:

> The silent majority of the Portuguese people has to awaken, and actively defend itself from the extremist authoritarians that fight in the shadows. [...] The moment has come for the Country to wake up.

It's a call that the authoritarian right heeds straight away. Already on 9 September elements within the Liberal Party decide to call a mass demonstration in support of the general, throwing themselves into a leafleting and postering campaign across the country, thinking they can coax hundreds of thousands, if not a million, disgruntled reactionaries from hiding; the unveiling of a new facet of the post-revolutionary political edifice. On the evening of 18 September, posters appear all over Lisbon, bearing the symbol of this new movement – a drawing of a male face with enormous pinched-oval eyes, *maioria silenciosa* (silent majority) stylised over the mouth, framed by the call: 'Demonstration in support of General Spínola: NO to extremisms, YES to firmness and faithfulness to the MFA programme.' That same evening squads of PCP and MDP activists make their way around Lisbon tearing up the posters in response. Predictably, the demonstration is opposed by the MFA, the Communists and the MDP, and backed by Sanches Osório's Christian Democrats, the Liberal and Progress parties and the new Democratic and Social Centre Party (*Centro Democrático e Social*, CDS), which emerged in mid-July with the bold claim of occupying the political centre. Spínola wants an excuse to implement a state of emergency and take on broad powers, a project he's had since June – the MFA and COPCON in particular are concerned that the demonstration, set for 28 September, intends to create a level of disturbance that could give him that excuse. COPCON receives a tip-off from an informant within the right-wing movements that there might be a large shipment of weapons being brought into Lisbon for the demonstration, and on 24 September it sets up a cordon of military units in a 100-kilometre radius around the capital to stop and search vehicles coming into the city, looking for weapons.* On the 26th, the right pulls another stunt – Spínola and Vasco Gonçalves are set to attend an event in the majestic bullfighting ring in Campo Pequeno, organised by the League of Combatants. The organisers of the Silent Majority demonstration had booked out the arena, and take the opportunity to cheer Spínola and boo the prime minister, with chants of 'Portugal! Portugal! Portugal!' and, tellingly, '*Ultramar! Ultramar! Ultramar!*' A poster bearing the details of the proposed mass demonstration is tossed into the centre of the arena and bandied about by the bullfighter José João Zoio,** to rapturous applause. Outside, a counter-demonstration representing a broad stretch of the left, held back by the police, jeers the *Spinolistas*.

28 September fast becomes a focal point for political tensions, from street confrontations between PCP members and right-wing organisers to heated arguments in government halls. Vasco Gonçalves refuses to declare outright that the demonstration is allowed to go ahead, which sends Spínola into a petulant fury. On the evening of the 27th, a new development further antagonises the general's supporters in government: seemingly copying COPCON's initiative from a few days before, groups of civilians, organised by the Communist Party and the MDP in a temporary alliance with

---

* Nothing close to the rumoured arsenal is ever found, only an array of hunting rifles and small arms. However, as Otelo points out in an interview with *Cadernos Portugália* later (Carvalho, 1975), 'people don't come from the countryside to hunt pheasants in Lisbon'.
** An action that results in a sanction from the bullfighters' union and eventual forced exile to Spain.

other left factions, have set up barricades along the motorways and ingress routes into Lisbon, undertaking their own searches for weaponry and generally heightening the sense that the population have taken matters into their own hands. Rádio Clube Português and Rádio Renascença put out calls for the public to join those barricades – seeing the 'silent majority' for what it is, the Lisbon population surges to support the MFA and stop what feels like a brewing coup. Noting the radio stations as potential targets, some COPCON units are sent in to provide armed support, and the popular barricades are also joined by COPCON detachments, who begin arresting people 'on suspicion of participation in a counter-revolutionary coup'.[16] That same evening, Vasco Gonçalves is summoned to the presidential palace, where a group of Spínola's allies have gathered to try and push the prime minister to resign. It's vicious: high-ranking officers, members of the National Salvation Junta, spit insults at the MFA man. Colonel Galvão de Melo calls him a 'son of a whore' and General Diogo Neto calls him a 'shit' and accuses him of being 'a vulgar communist who wants to take the country to a civil war', threatening 'if you open your mouth I'll break your face!' Throughout, the various senior officers scream at Gonçalves to resign. Spínola watches the whole exchange in silence. And Vasco Gonçalves doesn't budge; he takes the onslaught, and merely replies: 'I'm not here for me, but because there's something much more powerful than any of you, that chose me and put me forward: the Armed Forces Movement. I'm here purely through the will of the Movement, that trusts me, and I'm not resigning in any way, shape or form.'[17]

Otelo arrives at the presidential palace at two in the morning, ostensibly under the auspices of discussing a lifting of the barricades. 'So, those are your barricades? Now the communist barricades are replaced by Armed Forces barricades?' Spínola barks.

Otelo fires back, 'You want us to shoot? You want us to go there and fire off machine guns, kill all those people? Is that it?'

'If needs be, yes, sir! Shoot them!'[18]

Otelo doesn't know it yet, but by coming to Belém he's effectively been detained by the president – Spínola withdraws Otelo's control of COPCON and hands it over to General Costa Gomes (who is in no real position to take it). The general also orders that RCP and Rádio Renascença be shut down immediately, ordering GNR units to occupy the buildings – replacing the COPCON units that are already there. Vasco Gonçalves has at this point acquiesced to calling for the barricades to be lifted, in the name of 'peace among the Portuguese people', a call that is eventually read out through the Lisbon Associated Broadcasters. But this isn't a de-escalation: COPCON's activity has alarmed the president, and the 7th Cavalry Regiment is called to a defensive position around the presidential palace.* With Otelo absent, the MFA mobilises its own units and prepares the ground for a counter-offensive if necessary. The 5th Chasseurs Regiment sets itself up by Lisbon penitentiary and prepares to dislodge the GNR unit in RCP, and the 1st Light Artillery Regiment (*Regimento de Artilharia Ligeira 1*, RAL1) dispatches heavy armaments to defend the RTP television stations in Lumiar. Otelo, not physically detained but under orders to remain at the palace, eventually receives a phone call from Vasco Lourenço at the COPCON headquarters, declaring that the MFA has units ready to descend on Belém to force Otelo's release, if necessary. Rather than risk

---

* A small detail that's worth highlighting is that RC7 was one of the few units to mobilise *against* the revolution and is responsible for some of the more tense moments of 25 April. It's therefore one of the units with the fewest ties to the MFA. Even still, after RC7's defensive positioning, Vasco Lourenço receives a visit from a young officer promising to turn the unit's turrets 180 degrees towards the palace, should the MFA give the word. Even among the more 'loyal' units, the MFA presence is unmistakeable.

a messy confrontation, Otelo is allowed to make the ten-minute drive to São Duque fort, at the top of the hill to the west of Belém palace, an old police building now used as COPCON's base of operations. Across the city, operating from lists of known organised fascists, COPCON sees dawn with around two hundred prisoners – and the MFA Coordinating Committee, having been forced to mobilise units for the first time since April, finds the balance of forces is decidedly in their favour.

That balance of forces is also clear to Spínola, and he's been backed into another corner. At noon on the 28th, the general puts out a statement thanking the 'silent majority' but announcing the demonstration would be inconvenient – a statement that is followed by an official banning order over the radio. The 'silent majority' is now effectively silenced. The MFA arrives on the 29th with a new set of demands aimed at finding a compromise with the president, through a *saneamento* of their own: the dismissal of Galvão de Melo, Diogo Neto and Silvério Marques from the Junta, Sanches Osório from the government, and a restriction of Spínola's roles to the purely presidential, not interfering in the actions of the provisional government or the armed forces, which Spínola refuses. A meeting of the State Council is called where the president again tries to gain permission to declare a state of emergency – and this time even his allies in the room refuse to back the demand. And finally, that afternoon, Spínola announces his intention to resign as president. What the State Council isn't expecting, however, is how he does it. When the Council meets again in the presidential palace the following morning, they're surprised to find the room full of video cameras and recording equipment. Spínola intends to go out with a bang, and he does – sitting at the head of a long table and surrounded by the rest of the State Council, the speech he gives, broadcast live to the population, is unapologetically vicious, calling out the 'general climate of anarchy' the country is plunged into under the current government.

...My sense of loyalty inhibits me from betraying the People to whom I belong and for whom, under the flag of a false liberty, new forms of slavery are being prepared. I have dedicated my whole life to the service of the Homeland and I do not wish to have the weight on my conscience of ever having betrayed my fellow citizens. Under these conditions, and facing the utter impossibility of building an authentic democracy in service of peace and progress in the current climate, I renounce my position as president of the Republic...

Vasco Gonçalves and those loyal to the prime minister watch the resignation on TV, with Melo Antunes occasionally interjecting with profanity at Spínola's barefaced stunt. But despite the bombastic exit, there is widespread relief – the internal contradictions within the government, and particularly around the decolonisation process, have always been driven by the president's personal politics and the support of his allies. Now he's gone, and so are the three most volatile members of the Junta. Five months after he was originally meant to, General Francisco da Costa Gomes takes on the role of president of the Republic, in the Third Provisional Government. Besides the further removal of Sanches Osório in Communication and the resignation of General Mário Firmino Miguel from Defence (both posts taken by Vítor Alves in the interim), the cabinet remains fundamentally the same. But the restructure seems to give the government a new lease of life, a feeling that appears echoed in the streets across the country, where spontaneous demonstrations take place with chants of 'the People are with the MFA'. On 3 October Vasco Gonçalves appears on television declaring the following Sunday a day of voluntary work – asking the population to work on their traditional day of rest as a symbolic gesture of their willingness to propel the country forward into a new period of progress and stability. Within the MFA, the decision is taken to broaden the Coordination Committee to a new Council of Twenty – made up of the original seven in the Committee, the newly reconstituted seven-member Junta (which is now fully made up of senior military officers trusted by the MFA), and the MFA-aligned ministers in government, along with Otelo Carvalho in his role as commander of COPCON.

Unsurprisingly, unshackled from Spínola, the decolonisation process accelerates apace, with efforts to resolve the tripartite impasse in Angola resulting in a deal reached between the three main liberation movements, MPLA, FNLA and UNITA (National Union for the Total Independence of Angola; *União Nacional para a Independência Total de Angola*) to be negotiated with Portugal by the end of the year. And on 5 October, tasked with leading a commemoration celebrating the 1910 Republican revolution, an improvisational flourish on the part of Colonel João Varela Gomes forever cements the carnation revolution into the toponymy of the capital. The imposing red suspension bridge that spans the Tagus, modelled on the Golden Gate Bridge in San Francisco and still bearing the name Ponte Salazar is rechristened Ponte 25 de Abril.

One of the main points of the MFA programme, from the very beginning, is to hold elections for a Constitutional Assembly within a year. The purpose of that Assembly is to draft a constitution that will replace the *Estado Novo*'s 1933 constitution, with a mandate of one year before legislative elections determine the make-up of the actual government. And with the government's guarantee that elections will take place in that stated timeline, the new crop of political parties begins to hold national congresses and present their vision of Portugal to an eager population, as well as putting themselves forward for legalisation. Gone are the days of a severely limited suffrage – new electoral legislation,

published in November, extends the vote to anyone over the age
of eighteen, and for the first time includes the illiterate and some
of the diaspora. Among the key ideals shared by the captains who
made the revolution was a government that truly reflected the
will of the people, and part of that process means bringing as
many of the population on board as possible. As a result of the
patriarchal and elitist nature of the *Estado Novo*, large swathes of
Portugal's rural population have been deliberately kept unedu-
cated. For instance, in 1974 the illiteracy rate is 21% for those
aged over fifteen, skewing higher outside of the cities. To establish a bond between the people and the armed forces in the hope
of the latter becoming a true expression of the former, in October
the MFA launches the Cultural Promotion Campaigns
(*Campanhas de Dinamização Cultural*). Inspired in part by the
educational and propaganda campaigns carried out among local
communities during the colonial war, the campaigns involve
sending young MFA officers to host large meetings in rural
communities, holding discussions on 'the anti-fascist struggle,
the MFA programme, support for the Armed Forces' and a
broader discussion of national problems. The first of these initiatives takes place in November, with cadets from the Military
Academy sent to the northern city of Guarda and its surrounding
area, and with other regions targeted in early 1975. Architect and
artist João Abel Manta represents the ideals of this initiative in a
striking sketch: captioned 'a pleasure to meet your excellencies', a
military officer is depicted as the intermediary between a family
dressed in traditional rural Portuguese garb and a crowd of
assembled figures from Portuguese and global history, meeting in
a handshake. The MFA looks to pull Portugal out of forty-eight
years of isolation, to finally meet the world. That introduction to
the global stage also takes place in October, when President Costa
Gomes addresses an Extraordinary Session of the United Nations,
becoming the first Portuguese head of state to do so.

THE DECLINE AND FALL OF ANTÓNIO DE SPÍNOLA

On the decolonisation front, between 10 and 15 January 1975, the Portuguese government meets with the three main Angolan liberation groups to sign the Alvor Agreement, which grants Angolan independence from 11 November of that year, following a transitional period under Portuguese supervision. The fragile peace between MPLA, UNITA and FNLA doesn't last long – Angola is a crucial pressure point in the Cold War, and partly due to international pressures, the war of independence soon turns into a brutal and protracted civil war – one that the Portuguese government fails to contain. In Portugal, one of the key outcomes of that civil war – and the decolonisation process as a whole – is a mass influx of citizens from the former colonies into the Portuguese mainland. These people are given the name *retornados*, a title, often seen as pejorative, that is not entirely accurate – many of the 'returning' population were not born and never lived in Portugal proper. Born in a globe-spanning Empire, they are now forced to return to a 'home' hostile and foreign to them in equal measure. The arrival of hundreds of thousands of *retornados* needing homes and jobs puts additional strain on the resources of the state, among a population that views them with suspicion at best and, at worst, as the very people against whom the revolution was directed: colonisers and exploiters. The *retornados* are effectively refugees, but ones to whom the international refugee conventions don't apply. They have crossed continents but not borders; their frosty reception is the price they pay to be citizens of a crumbling empire. Over the next several years hundreds of thousands of people will migrate from the colonies and into Portugal, representing a population surge of between 5% and 15% for the now much smaller Portugal. It's another beat in the constant rhythm of change.

The first weeks and months of 1975 see a whirlwind of political activity. One of the key points of friction, particularly between the Socialist Party and the Communist Party, is the issue of trade union unity. The Communists, along with the Intersindical, the de facto

289

umbrella group representing the emerging trade unions in the country, rally around the concept of *unicidade sindical* – uniting all the existing trade unions under the umbrella of the General Confederation of Portuguese Workers (*Confederação Geral dos Trabalhadores Portugueses*, CGTP). It's a strategy that makes sense for them – the Communists and the Intersindical are closely linked, and significant tranches of the existing trade union leaderships are taken up by PCP activists. The Socialist Party stands against this notion, arguing instead for a system of trade union 'unity' whereby multiple trade union federations can coexist and collaborate in joint struggle, without being bound to a single monolith. The structure and power of the trade unions is a crucial issue for the future of Portugal. The question of workers' control, self-management and organisation, given the overwhelming upsurge in labour movement activity in the aftermath of 25 April, needs to be addressed by the state. After months of public consultations and assemblies, there is a broad majority in support of *unicidade* – a position that is also taken by the Council of Twenty and announced on television by Captain Vasco Lourenço, spokesperson of the Council and thus the MFA. Despite this, the Socialist Party continues to oppose the legislation, and the division will come to set the groundwork for confrontation between the two main left parties.

Also at the top of the agenda is the institutionalisation of the MFA. 28 September reinforced the need for the MFA's continued existence to preserve the goals of the revolution, but its relationship to the government is still relatively murky. In early 1975 plans begin to emerge within the Council of Twenty to present the legalised political parties with an MFA-Party Pact – essentially establishing a set of objectives to achieve, collectively, in order to meet the goals of social and economic development set out in the MFA programme. At the same time, Ernesto Melo Antunes is developing a detailed economic package for 1975, the framework of which is intended to drive the country through the next important period of constitutional work following the elections. Within the different levels of political influence in the Council of Twenty, Melo Antunes' plan sits decidedly in the social democratic camp. There is an ongoing debate, primarily between him and the more revolutionary Vasco Gonçalves, over how much emphasis to place on class struggle, and how much sway the middle classes and big capital should have in the economic situation. There is broad agreement, however, within the Council, the MFA and the government, that Portugal is deliberately steering towards socialism. But what kind of socialism? They don't have time to fully answer that question. In March, all timetables for the next year of Portuguese democracy are thrown out of the window. General António de Spínola emerges from the shadows and lashes out one final time.

Captain Dinís de Almeida (*second from left*) parlays with Captain
Sebastião Martins (*right*) following the attack on the 1st Artillery
Regiment, 11 March 1975.

CHAPTER THIRTEEN

CRISIS

Just north-east of Lisbon airport, past where the dense loop of the A1 motorway divides the airport from the residential neighbourhood of Portela proper, a squat cluster of white buildings with angled orange roofs sits in front of a wide open courtyard, ringed by a green fence. It's a decidedly military place – an austere site nobody visits without a very good reason. The short concrete building by the main gate hints at its purpose with a narrow white bunker that peeks out menacingly overhead, a defensive position in case of a head-on attack. This is now the Portuguese Army's Transport Regiment, but like most places in an old city the local toponymy hints at its past; the road that traces the south-east edge of the complex in Avenida do Ralis – RALIS stands for *Regimento de Artilharia de Lisboa* (Lisbon Artillery Regiment). On 11 March 1975, the regiment is still a few months away from being given that name – this is still the headquarters of the 1st Light Artillery Regiment (*Regimento de Artilharia Ligeira*, RAL1). And at around 11:45, a squadron of T6 Harvard single-engine jet aircraft, Fiat G.91 bombers and several helicopters armed with cannons, all bearing the distinctive cross of the Portuguese Air Force, zoom above RAL1 and begin dropping bombs and strafing the buildings and cars with bullet fire and grenades.

If there's such a thing as a unit purely loyal to the MFA, it's RAL1. Since COPCON's inception in 1974, RAL1 has been the repository of a big chunk of the unit's firepower, and it's where Captain Eduardo Dinis de Almeida has been based, almost since the moment his detachment from Figueira da Foz captured the regiment on 25 April. The aerial bombardment takes the unit by surprise, but these officers have been to war, and the recent political tensions give them reason to be on high alert. Dinis de Almeida, unshaven and tired from a sleepless night, is so seemingly unfazed by the sound of the explosions that it calms the wide-eyed soldiers who come to him for orders. 'This must be the coup, then,'[1] Almeida mumbles to himself, surrounded by the sounds of shattering glass. A closer explosion sends him and his men diving to the ground. Getting up moments later he quips to a soldier, grinning, 'I didn't order you to do push-ups!' Within minutes, men armed with rifles and machine guns flood into the streets adjacent to the regiment complex, rushing to the tall residential tower blocks in the surrounding area and taking positions inside doorways, in windows and on the rooftops. These buildings are largely occupied by military families, and the soldiers find no issues with making their way in, even as some civilians stand on the street bemusedly watching the planes fly overhead, some screaming, some praying, some nervously smoking. As the helicopters bank and swerve overhead, they're met by a rat-tat-tat of gunfire that sends them scattering, the regiment's anti-aircraft batteries now wheeled out into the courtyard and presenting a defensive front against the aerial attackers.

Suddenly, there's more boots on the ground – the bob of green berets as squads of paratroopers appear around RAL1, clustered in strategic formations and levelling their weapons. But the defensive situation is already stacked against them: they've lost the higher ground advantage, and the helicopters and planes can't continue bombarding the area without risking doing collateral damage to their own men on the ground. The gunfire stops – now there's just a face-off between the RAL1 men in the tower blocks and the squadrons of beret-wearing paratroopers skulking through the area, neither side willing to open fire, and often flitting within conversational distance of each other. Dinis de Almeida, now stationed on a fifth floor, peeking over a balcony, gets a bead on a lone paratrooper making his way between the buildings. Almeida has fallen right back into habits he built up in the war in Africa, and he's removed his cap and all signs of rank from his uniform, including his shoulder stripes, almost by instinct. He has a clear shot. The captain considers it, briefly.

'Hey!' shouts Dinis de Almeida to the ground below.

The paratrooper turns and looks up, right into the barrel of Almeida's gun above him. He freezes, suddenly terrified.

'Beat it!' shouts Almeida.[2] The paratrooper dashes away to safer ground. And soon, the small scattering of civilians that started with local residents swells as people from the surrounding area rush in, joined by journalists and airport workers, until the prospect of an armed engagement becomes impossible without descending into utter carnage. But by this point the paratroopers seem to have lost the will to fight – and some seem confused as to why they're there at all. Among the paratroopers there seems to be a dearth of actual officers, or anyone with a sense of their mission.

It's the civilian intervention that first brings the RAL1 officers and the commanders of the parachute units together to parlay, in an open field that becomes a strange no-man's land between the buildings. They huddle together, journalists' microphones hovering near them to catch the interaction. A short paratrooper, noticing the cameras and microphones, makes an appeal for nobody to make statements to the press until they know what's going on. He gestures to Dinis de Almeida. 'If even the captain doesn't know what's going on...'

'I do know what's going on,' Almeida interjects. 'They bombed my quarters, injured my men; there's betrayal here. Not betrayal, well, surprise, evidently.'

'Best not to say anything, still,' the paratrooper continues. Captain Sebastião Martins, commanding one of the paratrooper units, eventually comes face to face with Dinis de Almeida.

'We're here to avoid spilling blood…'

'You've already spilled it,' Almeida replies.

'…and restore the spirit of 25 April.'

'Where were you on 25 April? I didn't see you,' Dinis de Almeida fires back quickly, his calm demeanour betrayed by his words. 'You and the paratroopers and the fucking Air Force…'

'I received orders to occupy this unit.'

'From whom?'

'From my commander.'

'Well as you might imagine we have orders from my commander not to let ourselves be occupied. Orders from Brigadier General Otelo Saraiva de Carvalho and Chief of Staff of the Armed Forces Carlos Fabião.'

'Precisely why I've opted to, in this stage of the occupation, have a dialogue to avoid deaths. So I've received these orders, you have other orders, so to avoid deaths on either side or among the civilians, there will come a point where you either surrender…'

Dinis de Almeida shakes his head emphatically at this.

'…or otherwise we start shooting at each other.'

'Look,' Almeida replies, 'we have to establish motives here. We have to have reasons to fight. Now you and your men have to establish whether you're committing a betrayal, whether you're disobeying established orders, or not.'

Martins reaches into his uniform and pulls out a paper. 'These pamphlets must have been disseminated among you,' he says, handing it to Almeida. It's a one-page document, alleging that 'subversive forces' are planning a 'terrorist coup' that will 'shackle the country under the so-called dictatorship of the proletariat'. It calls for arms to be taken up, to guarantee that elections go ahead. Almeida gives it a scan. 'I confess we didn't get these.' He looks up at Martins. 'Hang on. Have you come to occupy our unit because of a pamphlet?'

'No, no, no, no,' replies Martins quickly. 'Behind this, look, there's a certain number of high-status individuals who aren't happy with the way democracy is being carried out in this country.'

'So this is a coup?'

'It's not a coup—'

'Like in Chile.'

'It's not a coup like in Chile. Much to the contrary. It's to guarantee that the elections set for 12 April go ahead as intended.'

'My dear friend, the people who give orders in this country are the President, the Prime Minister, Otelo Saraiva de Carvalho and the Chief of Staff of the Armed Forces. Or, shall we say, the established hierarchy.'

'The Chief of Staff didn't give us any orders.'

'He gave us orders. To defend the unit in case of attack.'

'Defend it then.' Martins looks set to back away from the conversation when a man in civilian garb who had been standing nearby interjects.

'Listen, I'm Costa Correia. I led the unit that occupied the DGS headquarters. I didn't do that to witness fratricide. We have to put the interests of the country above these spats.'*

While the conversation is taking place, the cluster of officers is surrounded by a wider huddle of RAL1 soldiers and officers, mingling with paratroopers and civilians, all engaged in heated dialogue. Before the parlay with the paratroopers, in a foray back in the barracks, Dinis de Almeida had stumbled across some

---

* This dialogue is taken verbatim from the RTP television footage shot on the day, by a team led by Adelino Gomes. Dinis de Almeida also transcribes the conversation in his report, with some differences in the dialogue (though the fundamental thrust is the same).

young Academy graduates who had arrived in civilian clothes and were in the process of getting ready for the fray. He had sent them out into the crowd, still as civilians but armed with pistols, and their conversations with the paratroopers had encouraged the real civilians to do the same, all making the case that the paratroopers had been tricked, that they were making a mistake. Now even if Captain Sebastião Martins or any of his fellow officers had wanted to take up arms again, the moment is gone – their soldiers are shaking their heads, babbling, some are weeping. One young paratrooper speaks to a camera, repeating: 'I'm not a reactionary, we're not reactionaries. This isn't our fault.' Another raises himself up to an elevated position on the side of an armoured vehicle and, his face a mask of despair, speaks out to the crowd, saying they were sent there without understanding their orders. The population breaks out in chants, cheers and applause as the paratroopers lower their weapons and walk to meet the men of RAL1 in embraces and muttered apologies, making their exit from the area and effectively ending the confrontation by their own initiative. The attack, from the initial bombardment to the lifting of the siege, has taken just under three hours. The effects are a cratered RAL1 headquarters left worse for wear, fifteen RAL1 men left injured (plus two soldiers in the helicopters, victims of the return fire), and one death: Joaquim Carvalho Luís, a soldier who had been asleep in his bunk, unfortunately within lethal radius of one of the bombs.

What happened on 11 March? It's a question laden with multiple layers of historic fog, with various interpretations and rumours, leaving questions unanswered even years after the fact. What seems clear, however, is that after 28 September, despite largely retreating out of the public eye, Spínola had not given up his political ambitions. Even before being ousted as president, the general had made a point of taking a tour of military units around the country – often followed on his trips by Vasco

Lourenço, who saw his role as keeping the president in check. In a sense, Spínola's tour was a form of 'counting rifles', gauging which sections of the armed forces were on his side and trying to swing the officer class of others to his way of thinking about the future of the country – and his interpretation of the MFA programme. The wing of the armed forces opposed to the ascendant left within the Army didn't go away on 28 September – the *Spinolistas* are definitely still distributed among the ranks of the Army, officers who have always remained loyal to the general, as well as some branches of the Air Force and, in particular, the parachute regiments. Over the course of the early months of 1975, this group of Spínola-aligned agents have begun a conspiracy of their own. The blueprints of a coup begin to form – with the aid of several trusted military units, including the Parachute Regiment in Tancos (*Regimento de Caçadores Paraquedistas*, RCP), the Amadora Commando Battalion and the Practical Cavalry School in Santarém, the goal is to neutralise the 'communist and communist-aligned' elements of the Council of Twenty, re-establish a strict military hierarchy within the armed forces and place Spínola back in the presidential seat. One of the driving notions behind the revolt is straightforward anti-communist paranoia, the fear that the promised elections will not take place after all, or will in some way be rigged to install a Soviet-style authoritarian dictatorship. The coup operation is initially planned for 20 February, but when the timeline of the elections is confirmed, setting them for 12 April, some of Spínola's allies get cold feet and the conspiracy is put on hold. On 17 February, a meeting of the MFA Assembly, made up of the Council and two hundred MFA officers, learns of the creation of the Portuguese Liberation Army (*Exército de Libertação de Portugal*, ELP), a hard-right militia group based in Spain with links to exiled PIDE agents. In late February, information comes through to the MFA and COPCON of the Spínola conspiracy, and of links between that conspiracy and the ELP. It's a confluence of interests, ranging from officers concerned about guaranteeing the elections, to active fascists intending to restore the pre-revolutionary regime. Allegedly, the US ambassador in Portugal had also been contacted in the hope of gaining support for the operation.

The catalyst comes on 8 March when, through contacts in the French secret service, Spínola's co-conspirators get hold of a document alleging that the Portuguese left, including the Communist Party, COPCON and LUAR, intend to undertake a mass purge of right-wing elements in Portugal. There is an alleged list of over fifteen hundred names, five hundred of whom are in the military, set to be eliminated in a brutal operation on 12 March, referred to as the Easter Slaughter. The actual origin of the Easter Slaughter document is unclear,* but whatever its provenance, the fear and perceived escalation of the situation ignites the operational fuse. And with the rumour of an imminent leftist purge, the conspirators have the perfect reason to justify mobilising against RAL1 to their subordinates. On the night of 10 March, General Spínola, wearing a fake beard, makes his way by car to Air Base 6 in Tancos, roughly 125 kilometres north-east of Lisbon. When he arrives, he's informed by Colonel Moura dos Santos that there's not yet a guarantee of support from any units besides the ones based in Tancos – the paratroopers and the Air Force. This proves to be the downfall of the operation – while the jets and helicopters are being scrambled over Lisbon, a meeting goes ahead at the Practical Cavalry School in which the colonel in command of the unit tries to convince his officers to lead the

---

* Speculation has ranged from the CIA or the KGB all the way to the MFA itself, the latter supposedly disseminating the document in order to bring the brewing coup out of hiding. It should be noted that no such document existed, nor was there any large-scale plan for mass executions.

reserve charge to Lisbon, bringing up the imminent Easter Slaughter. He receives pushback from Captain Salgueiro Maia, who ultimately convinces a majority of his fellow officers not to go ahead with the mobilisation until they have more information. The commando units led by Major Jaime Neves also back out of their mission when they hear the EPC isn't on the move. Only some other parts of Spínola's plan succeed. In Carmo, the captain in charge of the GNR force arrests General Pinto Ferreira and his staff, and sends a squadron of armoured motorbikes to take the RTP station – an effort ultimately blocked by COPCON forces. And a group of conspirators make their way to Rádio Clube Português' generators and antennae, damaging them and taking the station off the air.

Much as with both 25 April and 28 September, the power of radio proves decisive in shaping the day. As the details of the coup attempt become known, Rádio Renascença – a station whose workers had been on strike for twenty-two days – breaks its silence and opens up its frequencies to Rádio Clube Português – and there is an immediate appeal to the population to mobilise. Colonel João Varela Gomes, through his role at the head of the 5th Division, breaks protocol and also begins calling for mass mobilisations through the radio. It's partly due to this that by the time the paratroopers surrender to RAL1, the area outside the artillery compound is surrounded by vocal members of the population, chanting 'The people are not with you' and convincing the soldiers that they're on the wrong side. And just like the last coup attempt, barricades go up on the outskirts of Lisbon, set up by civilians hoping to stop any units that might be on their way to the capital. In Tancos, Spínola realises, as late afternoon rolls around, that his knowledge of what forces he had on the ground was mistaken – his coup has failed. The general, defeated, bundles his family and numerous officers into helicopters and makes a swift escape to Spain. Other conspirators make their way to the

Spanish border by car, or are otherwise detained by COPCON forces, or hand themselves in. In the latter case, Major Mensurado, commander of the paratrooper units that laid siege to RAL1, leaves his men licking their wounds after their surrender and travels to COPCON. It's abundantly clear that the paratrooper regiments were tricked – they had been sent to RAL1 on the false information that the unit was involved in a vast conspiracy of left-wing slaughter, and did so believing the orders were being sent through the proper channels, through the chiefs of staff and even General Costa Gomes himself.*

Mensurado walks into Otelo's office, where the brigadier general is conferring with Vasco Lourenço and Rosado da Luz, and admits his mistake. The major removes the stripes from his shoulders and places them on the table, intending to hand himself in. Otelo looks at the defeated man in front of him. 'Mensurado, your men need you now more than ever. Come on. Go back to them and command your company.' Otelo and Vasco Lourenço take the major's stripes and place them back on his shoulders, letting the major leave with a hug and a pat on the back.³ In Carmo, in a strange mirror image to the events of 25 April, the occupied GNR headquarters is surrounded by a braying population that eventually leads the revolting forces to surrender. The civilian action of the day leads Otelo, in the aftermath, to truly acknowledge the nature of the implicit People-MFA Pact that has developed organically over the course of the revolution:

> The popular masses must remain vigilant, but calm, and not sign up to extremist movements. In any moment

---

* Though perhaps not the kindest comment, it should be noted that in the 1970s, paratroopers have a reputation in the Portuguese military as being blunt instruments – 'more given to action than thought' (Vasco Lourenço). The colloquial term for them in military circles is 'stones with eyes'.

where the Armed Forces don't control the situation, I will not hesitate to call in the precious aid of the popular masses. [Our] democracy is still very young and we must fight with gritted teeth against all of these attacks.

That late afternoon, Spínola's house in Lisbon is attacked by a mob, and his documents, including copies of *Portugal and the Future*, are burned on the streets, as a mass mobilisation addressed by the main parties of the left marches through the city cheering the MFA. The 11th of March is the second large-scale assault on the revolution from reactionary forces, which is repelled once again. And in the wake of the failed coup, Vasco Gonçalves' government, up until now taking a relatively slow, consultative approach to the country's direction, remove their kid gloves. Even as the government scrambles to put out a statement on the day's events, the MFA Assembly decides to hold an urgent meeting. They meet already close to midnight in the National Defence Institute, next to Necessidades Park to the west of central Lisbon, between Santos and Alcântara. The meeting room is the lecture theatre where the Assembly has met before – a curved bank of tan leather chairs, facing inwards to a long table where the leading members of the Junta and the Coordinating Committee take their seats. It's a meeting that will become notorious under the name the 'Savage Assembly'. After officers are asked for their reports on the day, the question turns to what the next steps should be. That's when Captain Dinis de Almeida stands to read a statement on behalf of RAL1, which takes the meeting in a perhaps unexpected direction.

The officers of RAL1, the sergeants of RAL1, the soldiers of RAL1, having given me the role and responsibility that I don't reject in any way, of relaying the following: we cannot use moderation in this process.

We go to the point – I relay this opinion – of putting
against the wall, in other words immediately shoot, the
officers that participated in this attack.*

The question of executions will come up repeatedly over the
course of the meeting, and Dinis de Almeida isn't the only
one calling for them. The room is clearly split on the issue, but it's
one the senior officers don't take lightly. When it seems the mood
of the Assembly is set to bring about capital punishment for traitors of the revolution, two interventions stand out as changing
the tide. First, from engineering captain Cabral e Silva, the young
military adjunct to the prime minister:

> I should say in relation to RAL1 that my kid, who is
> six, has had nine mortar attacks done against him.** And
> I'm not going to Mozambique to go after the terrorists
> who hit him with those. So let's have a certain amount
> of calm because this reaction after a first attack, every-
> one has it, it's not new. We are not the best in the world.
> We don't play with people's lives. An attack on a barracks
> is substantially different, however reactionary it might
> be, to shooting people in cold blood like you gentlemen
> are demanding here. I feel like today I had a change of

* The recording of the 'Savage Assembly' only came to light relatively
recently, and through a concerted effort on the part of (primarily) Carlos
Almada Contreiras and Vasco Lourenço, the full transcript has been published
into a book. Dinis de Almeida, after the fact, repeatedly denied calling for
executions. The recording seems to suggest otherwise.
** During the colonial war, it was not uncommon for even junior officers to
have their families with them on deployments. Otelo, for instance, had his wife
and children with him for almost the entire time he was at war.

heart, I don't know, it seems I'm being reactionary, which is out of the ordinary.[4]

Cabral e Silva's intervention gets a tumultuous round of applause from the Assembly. Colonel João Varela Gomes, however, remains a steadfast advocate for executing the traitors. Captain José da Costa Neves raises his voice to address the colonel.

'I ask Colonel Varela Gomes if he's alive, or if he's dead.' The colonel, straightening himself up in his seat, replies that he's alive. But the question, in context, is laden with historical nuance: even under the brutality of the *Estado Novo*, even after having perpetrated notorious revolutionary actions against the old regime, Varela Gomes was never executed by a firing squad. The officers, seeking to hold themselves to a higher standard than the system they replaced, vote ultimately against imposing the death penalty on the perpetrators of the attempted coup. But revolutionary justice, though a significant portion of the 'Savage Assembly's' agenda, isn't the most important decision to make it out of the room. The meeting lasts until around 08:45 in the morning on 12 March, and when the officers emerge blinking into the dawn light, they do so having amalgamated the MFA Coordinating Committee, the Council of Twenty, the Junta and the State Council into one unit: the Revolutionary Council (*Conselho da Revolução*, CR). If the name isn't enough of a hint, the CR asserts its intention to take Portugal on to 'the socialist option of the Portuguese revolution started on 25 April 1974'. And with that lofty goal on the horizon, the Council sets off immediately with a wave of nationalisations, convinced that they need to act quickly before the right can regroup and strike again. Announced on 14 March, as the country is still reeling from the aftershocks of Spínola's attack, is the nationalisation of the banks – an action that's aided measurably by the fact that organised bank workers across the country had sequestered their workplaces in the immediate aftermath of 11 March. Twenty-four banks and credit institutions are brought into public ownership, soon after followed by thirty-six insurance companies. Then the nationalisations spread, to electricity, petrol, mineral and chemical companies, transport, fishing and agriculture, the wide expanse of Portuguese production placed into the hands of the state. It's a radical act, but one that's hailed by almost all of the main political parties, with the centre-right CDS's feeble objections barely heard above the general roar of acclamation. It's a process that slots hand in hand with the spontaneous examples of workers' self-management that had cropped up across the country, either by force, or situations as simple as bosses emptying their safes and fleeing the country, leaving their workers to discover that they didn't need managers after all. Almost as if the government had given them a surreptitious nod and wink, agricultural workers, particularly across the rural south, occupy vast stretches of land, beginning, organically and with the support of the PCP, a process of agrarian reform that Álvaro Cunhal had been urging the state to organise for months. In the urban centres, the occupation of empty houses that had started within a week of 25 April accelerates and spreads beyond the purely residential, with residents taking up larger buildings to set up self-managed nurseries and social centres, reimagining their living spaces for themselves. The MFA's Cultural Promotion Campaigns begin to take on an added layer of Civic Action – not only educating and widening the cultural horizons of the masses, but also using military units to build needed infrastructure such as roads in remote rural communities. So the Ongoing Revolutionary Process (*Processo Revolucionário Em Curso*, PREC), as the revolutionary period after 25 April and particularly after 11 March comes to be known, advances.

25 April didn't just get rid of the spectre of Salazar or the *Estado Novo* – it had begun the steady process of whittling away the repressive and punitive arms of the state. And over time, as

the roles of the police and the GNR are handed over more and more to COPCON, those arms have almost ceased to operate altogether, certainly when it comes to revolutionary action. Throughout the revolutionary period, COPCON had been called in at various points to mediate in workers' or citizens' disputes – after 11 March, the unit begins decisively taking one side – that of the working class. In the case of housing occupations, for example, this means COPCON taking a position of open support for the 'revolutionary action' of the occupying residents, going as far as trying to create a legal framework for the occupations. COPCON itself, however, is bursting at the seams – the unit is under-resourced and overwhelmed, with the logistical framework it was handed at the start of the revolutionary period not really updated since occupying São Duque fort. There is an attempt from within the MFA to give COPCON more resources, given their importance as the 'armed wing' of the MFA, but ultimately only one of the recommendations is followed:[5] after 11 March, Otelo is promoted to three star general. The deep shifts towards democratic control spread even to within the armed forces, a direct result of RAL1's actions on 11 March. The strict military hierarchy that had been one of the defining features of the Portuguese armed forces, certainly during the colonial war, gives way to an attitude that asserts the right to question orders, to make democratic decisions within units, and which blurs the command structure in a way that panics senior NATO officers. When Jean-Paul Sartre visits Portugal shortly after 11 March, he has a beer in an open-plan canteen at RAL1, sitting at a table with men from a whole range of ranks – the separate officers' messes have been abolished, and there is open fraternisation all the way down the hierarchy. The visual representation of this change is the soldiers themselves – many bearded, with long hair, their looks flying in the face of what an army is supposed to look like. In the more revolutionary or radical units, the military hierarchy has been replaced with inter-soldier plenary sessions, in which discussions take place on whether to follow certain orders. Spínola's nightmare made manifest. The *ancien régime* is being exorcised, by force, from every section of society. Which is not to say that its presence has disappeared entirely. It has merely slunk back into the shadows.

One thing that hasn't changed with the attempted coup is the CR's commitment to holding elections in the promised timeline. Due to the logistics involved in registering, for the first time, over six million people, on 19 March the date of the elections is pushed back to 25 April – a decision as practical as it is symbolic. Despite the commitment to an open and pluralist election, three parties are banned in the run-up: the Christian Democrats, due to their members' involvement in 11 March, and the MRPP and the Worker-Peasant Alliance (*Aliança Operária-Camponesa*, AOC), explicitly for 'use or incitement of violence and disturbance of public order'. And taking another action that had been firmed up in the 'Savage Assembly', the MFA completes the process of its institutionalisation through the MFA-Party Pact (officially known as the Platform for Constitutional Accord). The Pact, in discussion with the main parties since mid-February, is now reintroduced in a period where the MFA has a certain amount of momentum, which enables it to impose itself. It guarantees the right of the MFA, through its sovereign bodies the Revolutionary Council and Assembly, to have a direct say in the next three to five years of Portuguese politics. It imposes the constitutional enshrinement of the 'principles of the MFA programme', namely the 'legitimately obtained conquests throughout the process, as well as the updates to the Programme imposed by the revolutionary dynamic that openly and irreversibly pushed the country on to the original path to a Portuguese Socialism'. The Pact is agreed several weeks before the election with the PS, PCP, PPD, CDS and the People's Socialist Front (*Frente Socialista Popular*, FSP, a split from the Socialist Party headed by Manuel Serra). And on 26 March, after some minor ministerial reshuffles, Vasco Gonçalves unveils the Fourth Provisional Government, ready to take Portugal into the election and a period of constitutional deliberation.

The electoral campaign, despite national and international concern, goes ahead without any major conflict. The Communist Party, and the various political parties to its left, blanket the walls of cities with posters of all stripes bearing the hammer and sickle. It's a period of rallies, marches and intense political debate in lecture halls and on street corners. From a certain subset of the MFA, as well as some of the more radical revolutionary organisations such as LUAR and the Revolutionary Brigades, comes an appeal for a spoilt ballot, or simply an empty one – suggested as a demonstration of faith in the revolutionary process, or an actual vote for the MFA given their absence from the electoral lists. On the day before the election, President Costa Gomes makes an appeal for a choice for parties that don't block 'the Socialist path, and that promise pluralism in the exercise of liberty'. It's perhaps also in part due to this particular choice of phrasing that when the results come out, the Socialist Party receives the highest number of votes, 37.87% of the 5.7 million-strong electorate, in what amounts to a turnout of 91.66%. Second is Sá Carneiro's PPD with 26.39%, the Communists with 12.46%, CDS with 7.61% and the MDP with a surprisingly low 4.14%. The total number of blank votes tallies in at 6.95%, which would have placed 'none' or 'the MFA' as the fifth largest party under some interpretations. There is no party majority in the 250-strong Assembly, but at first glance the constitutional process seems set on the path upon which the MFA has explicitly put it: socialism. Finding unity on the left, however, is easier said than done.

1 May 1975 mirrors the mass popular mobilisations of the year before, but with an edge. Whereas 1974 felt like an awakening, a

re-emergence of people and ideas that had lain dormant for decades, one year later the lines have been drawn between the left and workers' movements, and that hopeful, prelapsarian enthusiasm has been replaced with sectarian bickering. The Intersindical's rally once again takes place at 1 May Stadium – now officially renamed. It's here that the main parties of the left are gathered (even the PPD), along with the more senior government figures like Vasco Gonçalves and Costa Gomes – but the proposed presence of MES and FSP causes the Socialist Party to boycott the main march and organise their own, separate rally, starting at Praça de Chile. The two marches meet on the way to the stadium, and it's clear that the show of unity from Mário Soares and Álvaro Cunhal a year ago is, literally and metaphorically, a thing of the past. The question of trade union *unicidade* is still bubbling over from the start of the year and adding to the broader strategic political disagreements between the two parties. When the PS march arrives at the stadium the speeches have already begun, and Vasco Gonçalves' address is met with audible boos and whistles from the PS contingent streaming in. The same happens during Costa Gomes' speech, during which Mário Soares tries to approach the platform and is refused entry by an Intersindical organiser, allegedly for 'stoking divisions'. The PS draws a line in the sand on 1 May, one that divides it clearly from the PCP. And within the Revolutionary Council and the MFA, three factions begin to emerge that align roughly with the political lines of the left: adjacent to the Communist Party and the MDP, like Vasco Gonçalves and his allies; the PS line, to which officers like Melo Antunes are more closely drawn; and a third line further on the revolutionary left (such as, for instance, the Revolutionary Brigades), to which Otelo/COPCON have drifted over the last few months. It is the various attempts at resolving these internal contradictions that will determine the next six months of Portuguese politics – and ultimately the decline and end of the PREC.

Outside of those lines there's another, perhaps more important, division between those who believe partisan decisions should
be made on the basis of the electoral results (the closest thing
anyone has to a census of the will of the population), and those
who believe organic, revolutionary activity is the ultimate deciding factor. One clear example of this division happens in mid-
May, when the long-time anti-fascist paper *República* is taken
over by its workforce, forcing the expulsion of its leadership on
the basis that the paper has become too much an organ of the
Socialist Party. Even as the PS protests the workplace takeover,
Vasco Gonçalves and Otelo are split between handing the newspaper back to its administration (ousted by the workers) or allowing the takeover to stand, following the will of the employees. It's
almost the exact same dynamic that leads to a split between Otelo
and Gonçalves when workers at Rádio Renascença occupy the
station in May, continuing a long-standing dispute with the
station's owners, the Catholic Church. Divisions such as these
within the upper levels of the 'forces of order', i.e. the government
and COPCON, are reflected more widely in the atmosphere of
social and political turmoil the country experiences in the months
after the elections. In mid-May, militants in the MRPP capture
and torture two military officers, on the accusation of reactionary
activity and involvement with the far-right militia group ELP.
The MRPP further accuses Jaime Neves and Salgueiro Maia of
belonging to a broader far-right conspiracy – a culmination
of factors that leads Otelo to send commando units to raid
MRPP headquarters across the country and arrest over four
hundred members of the Maoist organisation. It's a step up in
action on the part of COPCON as the military unit becomes
increasingly politicised.

In an attempt to amalgamate the various political tendencies
within the MFA, in mid-June Captain Vasco Lourenço presents
the Assembly with the Plan for Political Action (*Plano de Acção*

Política, PAP), a sort of second, updated pass at the MFA programme drafted by four CR members, among them Melo Antunes. It affirms the MFA's intention of constructing a 'socialist society', defined as a 'society without classes, obtained through the collectivisation of the means of production' – but also makes an affirmation that the route towards that socialist society is democratic and pluralist, repudiating the 'implementation of socialism through violent or dictatorial means'. It defends, to adopt a more British terminology, a parliamentary road to socialism, or certainly a route to socialism achieved through conventional representative democracy. It is, much like the original MFA programme, a rough guideline – but one that uses some choice phrasing (namely around pluralism) chosen to curb what Melo Antunes, Lourenço and their allies feel is the danger of a 'vanguardist' turn on the part of Vasco Gonçalves and those more closely aligned to the Communist Party in government. Despite the election results, the Communists, and other left groups like MES that didn't have a good showing in the polls, are still hugely active and militant on the streets, in the official trade union bureaucracies and in the rural areas where agrarian reform is taking off at full speed. The worry is that with that balance of power, the *Gonçalvistas* intend to continue consolidating that power throughout the revolutionary period, turning the MFA into the vanguard party of the revolution and leaving the Constitutional Assembly behind as Portugal turns into an Eastern-bloc-style socialist state. The PAP is passed by a majority in the MFA Assembly and announced to the country on 21 June – with, unsurprisingly, support from the PS, which sees it as aligning with its own ambitions in the constitutional process. A few weeks later, however, on 8 July, Vasco Gonçalves presents the MFA Assembly with the Guiding Document for the People-MFA Alliance Project (*Documento Guia do Projecto Aliança Povo-MFA*). Despite his claim that it doesn't contradict or supersede the PAP,

312

the People-MFA Alliance aims to 'mobilise the People for the Revolution' through the creation of 'unitary groups', a pyramid of popular structures building up from Local Assemblies to a Popular National Assembly, with the Revolutionary Council as the sovereign body. It's a structure of popular power that places emphasis on workers' and residents' commissions, claiming to be independent of 'party ties', translated into a People-MFA structure that ultimately runs the country. As suspected, however, the People-MFA Alliance by default does away with the established constitutional and parliamentary structure the original MFA programme had set out to pursue – something Vasco Lourenço points out in the Assembly meeting, accusing Gonçalves of being a liar when he supported the PAP. Despite these objections, the general plan of the Alliance is also voted through in the 280-strong Assembly, with Lourenço's being the one notable vote against it. The MFA body have essentially passed two mutually contradictory plans for the future of the country in quick succession – a decision that will inevitably lead to rupture.

It's in mid-July that events in the north of Portugal kick off what will forever be known as 1975's 'Hot Summer'. The publication of both MFA documents leads to mass demonstrations in the urban centres, with the People-MFA Alliance in particular giving voice to a section of the militant left and to the call to dissolve the Constitutional Assembly and move directly to the proposed construction of popular power. The Alliance is also a harbinger, however, of a period of true violent unrest and backlash against the Communist Party, and other left parties such as the FSP and MES, and even trade unions, particularly in the rural centre and north. In the municipality of Rio Maior on 13 July, a mob attacks the local headquarters of the PCP and the FSP, burning propaganda and documents and leaving the buildings destroyed. It's the start of a campaign of terror that sweeps the centre and north of Portugal – an area in which COPCON,

313

already stretched in its resources, can barely mobilise. The actions – around two hundred attacks, bombings and sieges of left head-quarters over the course of the months of July and August – are the culmination of a build-up of anti-communist sentiment among certain communities, particularly ones where the influence of the Catholic Church is strongest. The Church had been one of the more open critics of the socialist and communist turn of the revolutionary process, in a confrontation with the government that came to a head particularly around the occupation of Rádio Renascença. Fomenting this anti-communism are militant far-right organisations – as well as the ELP, active since the start of the year, the 11 March coup attempt had led to the creation of the Democratic Movement of Portuguese Liberation (*Movimento Democrático de Libertação de Portugal*, MDLP), a terrorist group based in Madrid and led from Brazil by the exiled António de Spínola. Within Portugal, the Maria da Fonte Movement* declares itself as the 'armed wing of the northern Church against the forces of the left', taking direct funding and aid from Church networks for its activity. Bouncing off the conservative tendencies of some northern Portuguese communities, enhanced by the perceived oversteps of Gonçalves' government, these three far-right organisations launch a brutal wave of terror on the left in the north and centre of Portugal – a level of political violence that the revolution had until now avoided. The government finds it difficult to quell the level of violence – the coercive arm of the state, whittled away as it is, led by a government unwilling to engage in a pitched battle with the population, can for the most part only respond with feeble denunciations. In mid-July the PS leaves the government in protest, soon after followed by the PPD. Marches and mass gatherings are almost daily occurrences – on

---

* Named after an 1846 rebellion based in the northern Minho region.

CRISIS

the one hand the revolutionary left, including some RALIS*
armoured vehicles, cheering the dictatorship of, the proletariat
and calling for the constitutional process to be halted; on the
other hand, Mário Soares and the PS host rallies one hundred
thousand strong in Lisbon and Porto, taking a platform in front
of Fonte Luminosa (the 'Luminous Fountain' at the edge of
Alameda Park) declaring Vasco Gonçalves too partisan to form a
new government.

As July advances, so too do Vasco Gonçalves' attempts to sideline his critics, and the critics of his 'vanguardist' strategy. At the
MFA Assembly meeting on 25 July, Gonçalves brings a proposal
for the creation of a Directorate of the Revolutionary Council –
placing himself, President Costa Gomes and Otelo (as head of
COPCON) as the triumvirate (or 'troika') of sovereign decision-
makers, with the Assembly and the rest of the Revolutionary
Council reduced to advisory roles. This is proposed out of a need
for rapid decision-making, as the speed of unfolding events
makes consulting the CR cumbersome. Vasco Lourenço loudly
opposes the proposal, once again taking on the role of spokesperson for the 'moderate' faction within the MFA – but with the
balance of power within the Assembly, the motion is passed and
the 'moderate' faction loses its ability to intervene in the func-
tioning of the state. Vasco Gonçalves sets out on the task of
putting together a new government – a process which is delayed
due to the fact that Otelo is on a visit to Cuba, and the newly
established troika can't appoint a new government without him.
The moderate faction, following the establishment of the
Directorate, formalises itself: nine officers – Vasco Lourenço,
Ernesto Melo Antunes, Canto e Castro, Vítor Crespo, José da
Costa Neves, Vítor Alves, Manuel Franco Charais, Pedro

* RAL1 has, in the meantime, been renamed as the Lisbon Artillery
Regiment.

Pezarant Correia and Rodrigo Sousa e Castro – begin drafting a document laying out a clear political line in opposition to the extreme-left positions held by the prime minister and the government. The group – taking on the title Group of Nine – circulate the document among military units before its publication in the newspapers on 7 August, one day before Vasco Gonçalves' thinned out* Fifth Provisional Government is set to come to power. The Document of the Nine – referenced in the first edition of the *Jornal Novo* as the Melo Antunes document, is a reformulation of the main theses of the PAP – a rejection of both 'Eastern-type socialism' built on a 'narrow vanguard' and the 'social-democratic model of society present in many Western European countries', believing that 'the great problems of Portuguese society cannot be overcome by the reproduction of classical capitalist schemes in our country'. Instead, as before, the document argues for 'the formation of an ample and solid social block that supports a national project for the transition to socialism', inseparable from 'political democracy [...] and pluralism'. As the *Jornal Novo* flies off the shelves, leading to a new printing of the document the very next day, Vasco Gonçalves and his government reel from the document's release. It feels like a betrayal – these nine officers, many long-time members of the MFA Coordinating Committee from the very beginning of the captains' conspiracy, have undermined the democratic structures of the MFA in a direct frontal assault against the government and the Revolutionary Council, and have circulated that document of their own initiative among military units, seeking signatures. And those they get – over the course of the following days, the Group of Nine receive what suddenly feels like overwhelming support from fellow officers stationed around the country; hundreds of signatures to the

---

* The only party that makes an appearance among the independent ministers is the MDP.

316

document. The Group of Nine are suspended, shortly afterwards, from the Revolutionary Council.*

The first proper response to the Group of Nine's document, however, doesn't come from the Fifth Provisional Government, but from Otelo and a drafting committee of COPCON officers. This includes members of the revolutionary left such as Carlos Antunes and Isabel do Carmo in the Revolutionary Brigades.[6] Otelo's personal politics had evolved over the course of the revolutionary period, and in August of 1975 his own position is a bit of a jumble – an amalgam of views with a focus on popular power, brought over from his time in Cuba, mixed in with a distrust of the Communist Party that he acquires from his advisors in the PRP-BR (*Partido Revolucionário do Proletariado-Brigadas Revolucionárias*, Revolutionary Party of the Proletariat-Revolutionary Brigades, the political/party wing of the BR). Otelo approaches the Group of Nine document critically but not necessarily with hostility – he takes on some of the document's criticism of the revolutionary process, but sees it as not programmatic or revolutionary enough. The result of the weekend-long drafting process in COPCON is the COPCON Document – a pages-long text that doesn't push the Gonçalves, 'vanguardist' political strategy but still rejects the primacy of bourgeois parties and governments, and places its emphasis on popular and workplace power as the necessary heart of any future political settlement. The COPCON document is also much more detailed than the Nine document in terms of clear and concrete tasks that should be undertaken during the transitional period. The Group of Nine, and particularly Melo Antunes, show themselves willing to engage with COPCON in finding a middle ground between the two documents – and to that end Melo Antunes is given the

---

* Vasco Lourenço claims after the fact that they were in fact expelled – simply told to return to their military posts.

task of drafting a proposed consolidation. On the streets, the tenor of the popular divisions shifts from a conflict between the Fifth Provisional Government and the Group of Nine to one between the COPCON document and the Nine document – isolating Vasco Gonçalves, who begins to see that his position in government has its days numbered. It's an isolation that's also clear from the outside – in mid-August, Otelo sends the prime minister a letter (later published from Gonçalves' own office) in which the general asks Gonçalves to 'rest, relax, meditate and read'– a not so subtle suggestion to resign from government.

The Group of Nine meet with the core officers of COPCON on the evening of 22 August, hoping to find common ground in a shared document. By the time they meet, at least one of the COPCON contingent is already on board – Otelo had been convinced by Vasco Lourenço of the viability of the Nine-COPCON draft, but he does so on the condition that the rest of the COPCON officers also back it. Those officers, however, are less than enthusiastic – not least because, unlike Otelo and the Nine, this meeting is the first time they have seen the paper. The meeting drags on into the evening, and then into the early morning, over an atmosphere of increased entrenchment. Various lines in the new document are denounced as reactionary by the COPCON contingent – it's clear that the draft leans much more heavily towards the Nine than towards COPCON. At one point in the early morning, Otelo throws a strop at his own men for their refusal to find a compromise and storms out, followed by Vasco Lourenço who tries, unsuccessfully, to bring the general back into the room. Finally, at around six in the morning, Rosado da Luz issues an ultimatum – either the Group of Nine accept the COPCON document as it was originally drafted, or the COPCON officers walk out. Vasco Lourenço sighs, looks at his watch, and replies, 'I wish you'd said that nine hours ago.' The much sought-after accord between the two factions, ultimately, doesn't get resolved. Two days later, a large section of left organisations including the PCP, FSP, MDP, MES, and even LUAR and PRP-BR hold a series of meetings with the end goal of forming the United Revolutionary Front (*Frente de Unidade Revolucionária*, FUR), with the intention of mobilising all of their collective resources in favour of the COPCON document – and the notion of popular power. That mobilisation happens on 26 August – but the fragile edifice of left cooperation that brief show of unity seems to harbour crumbles almost immediately when the march reaches the presidential palace in Belém. The chants for 'Vasco! Vasco!' are denounced as PCP divisionism, causing the various groups present to split.

At the end of August the Group of Nine have undeniable momentum. The number of signatures of support they've received from within the military shows that the balance of power within the MFA Assembly is in their favour. With the Fifth Provisional Government floundering and the prime minister having lost the support of Otelo and COPCON, President Costa Gomes looks ahead to the next government – one where Vasco Gonçalves is no longer the prime minister. Even during the initial MFA rupture with the Group of Nine there had been internal conversations with the president and various MFA officers about putting General Carlos Fabião (chief of staff of the Army) in the role – but Fabião ends up declining the position. With support from the Navy, Admiral José Pinheiro de Azevedo, member of the Junta since the first day of the revolution, is broadly accepted as Gonçalves' replacement. Costa Gomes intends to put Gonçalves in the role of chief of staff of the Armed Forces instead, but this proves controversial – the Group of Nine want Gonçalves distanced entirely from the Assembly, and from power. A meeting of the MFA Assembly is set for 5 September, at the Practical Engineering School (*Escola Prática de Engenharia*, EPE) in Tancos – which will become one of the most important Assembly meetings of the revolutionary period. This particular Assembly is held after various smaller meetings of the different branches of the MFA in the Army, Navy and Air Force. The Army meeting, on 2 September, is particularly tense, and marked by verbal confrontations between Melo Antunes and Vasco Gonçalves. It takes so long that it needs to be continued on the morning of the 5th, delaying the start of the general Assembly. After a preamble on the status of the decolonisation process, the meat of the Assembly is arrived at: a vote to reject Vasco Gonçalves from the post of chief of staff of the Armed Forces passes, with 180 votes in favour and 47 against. This is followed by the crucial one: a vote to restructure the Revolutionary Council (under threat of the Army walking out of the Council, should this be rejected) passes 176 to 47. That CR restructure is brutal for the *Gonçalvistas* – it removes not only Gonçalves himself, but nine of his allies, replacing them with the majority of the Group of Nine. With that Tancos Assembly, the power play that started with the publication of Melo Antunes' document is complete – the MFA moderates have pulled the government's reins away from the 'revolutionary vanguard' and back towards the sovereignty of the Constitutional Assembly.

On the day after the Tancos Assembly,* the newly reconstituted Revolutionary Council passes legislation forbidding journalists from publishing any news related to military matters. It's significant for two reasons – firstly because it shows the new and increasingly authoritarian turn of the CR and secondly because it's a law that never takes effect, as all the organs of the press simply refuse to follow it. And with COPCON's internal policy of always backing the workers, the state's ability to enforce legislation such as what would become known immediately as the 'military

---

* Sometimes referred to as the Tancos Proclamation, given the ultimatum-like pressure the Army branch of the MFA imposed on the proceedings.

censorship law' is severely hampered. The Sixth Provisional Government takes power on 19 September under Pinheiro de Azevedo, and a newly formed ministerial bench is packed with representatives from all of the main parties – once again ready to play ball with the government now that their own power is seen as guaranteed. The day after, before leaving on a trip to Sweden, Otelo leaves the new government with a warning: if they start drifting rightwards he, and COPCON, will move to the opposition. In a revolutionary period already marked by mass popular upheaval and (in the latter months) serious violence, the period of September to October brings about a level of social agitation never seen before. The country lives in a perpetual state of paranoia – there are constant rumours in the press and on the streets of impending coups, from both the right and the left. Mass demonstrations, protests, workplace sieges and occupations have become part of the daily thrum of life – especially in Lisbon, the heart of political power and also the site of some of the more radical upheavals. Within the military, the more radical soldiers amalgamate into a new unit, Soldiers United Will Win (*Soldados Unidos Vencerão*, SUV), linked to the PRP-BR and forming a split with the MFA and its 'counter-revolutionary' tendencies. At the end of September, Pinheiro de Azevedo (in the role of interim president, due to Costa Gomes' absence on an international visit) orders the military occupation of television and radio stations 'to avoid declaring a state of emergency' – which leads to renewed protests against the government. When Otelo and COPCON follow the order, he too comes under attack from the population, and is called a reactionary and a fascist – something the beleaguered general takes to heart. By the end of October, Otelo, and COPCON, have once again withdrawn their willingness to crack down on popular protests – and they lift the military occupations at the radio and television stations, sending Rádio Renascença back on the airwaves with its incisive broadcasts as the voice of the revolutionary left.

The 6 November meeting of the Revolutionary Council is the flame that ignites the tinderbox the country seems set atop. Prime Minister Pinheiro de Azevedo demands action that allows him to govern under the current state of anarchy that prevails in Lisbon. One of the decisions taken that evening, then, is to silence the bombastic and provocative Rádio Renascença once and for all. At 04:30 on 7 November, under orders of the chief of staff of the Air Force, Morais da Silva, a squad of paratroopers and police sets off a bomb against the antennae of the occupied radio station, taking it off the air. The action sets off a wave of protests among the increasingly politicised and radicalised paratroopers who, since their involvement in 11 March, have veered progressively more to the left, and feel once again as though they are being tricked, used as fodder for reactionary aims. On 8 November, General Morais da Silva and Vasco Lourenço visit Tancos to try and justify the action and calm the paratrooper regiment, but the meeting is disastrous – a soldier takes the microphone and calls the general 'bourgeois', and there is a mass walkout to a parallel meeting. It's an embarrassing display of insubordination that leads Vasco Lourenço to turn to his colleague and state, 'I'm never coming anywhere with you again.'[7] That very day, in protest at the level of discipline in the lower ranks, 123 officers walk out of the Tancos Paratrooper School and leave it under the command of sergeants and privates. Soon after, the occupants of the school pass a motion repudiating the bombing of Renascença. On 11 November, two of those sergeants arrive at the COPCON headquarters and offer their units to Otelo, in exchange for COPCON's support in the paratroopers' struggle. Otelo agrees; soon after, there is a confrontation between the COPCON commander and the Air Force chief of staff, when Morais e Selva begins the process of dissolving the paratrooper units altogether.

'They don't respect me,' laments Morais da Silva.

'They don't respect you because you give them orders that don't make any sense!' replies Otelo.

Meanwhile in Lisbon, a mass demonstration in support of the Sixth Provisional Government is called for 9 November in Terreiro do Paço, backed by the PS and the PPD. When Pinheiro de Azevedo takes to the microphone on the balcony of the old ministerial buildings, a smoke bomb goes off in the crowd, setting off mass panic and causing the police to disperse the population with warning shots into the air. 'It's only smoke,' the prime minister calls from the balcony as the demonstration descends into chaos, 'it's only smoke! The people are serene! The people are serene!' Three days later, several thousand public sector construction workers surround São Bento Palace, where Pinheiro de Azevedo, the ministers and the Constitutional Assembly (along with various observers and staff) are in the middle of a session. It turns into an effective siege – the workers drive a cement mixer to the building's main entrance and force the doors shut, demanding the prime minister give in to a series of pay demands. Nobody is allowed to leave the palace until the workers' demands are met. After the prime minister refuses to engage with the protestors, the main hall of the Assembly is taken over with loudspeakers, beginning what will turn into a thirty-six-hour siege of the government. Otelo and COPCON, stalwart in their position of not opposing the workers' struggle, refuse to send in troops to lift the siege. Azevedo eventually agrees to sign a compromise document on 13 November, breaking the siege – but the situation in Lisbon has become untenable.

In the balance of power within the country, over the last two months of social upheaval, one thing has become clear: the forces of the hard left are primarily concentrated in Lisbon, and apart from the rebellious paratroopers in Tancos, the most revolutionary sections of the military are based in the capital. Lisbon has become the Red Commune, ungoverned and ungovernable, while more moderate and right-wing forces are scattered throughout the rest of the country but representing a more sizeable military force. The country is splitting itself into two – the leaders and many ministers from the PS and PPD relocate themselves and their families to Porto, where the environment is decidedly less anarchic. In a meeting of the Group of Nine there's a vocal debate about taking the same position and moving away from the Lisbon Commune to set up somewhere in the north – a position that Melo Antunes eventually agrees to, provided Vasco Lourenço, the Group's de facto leader, is on board. Lourenço is adamantly against the idea, however – moving the Revolutionary Council away from Lisbon will undeniably lead to civil war, with the lines drawn through the middle of the country. What needs to be prepared is a response to any potential coup. Since August the moderate MFA faction have been 'counting rifles' – translating the signatures in support of their document into a concrete account of boots on the ground. It's a process that COPCON has also gone through, intending to oppose a repeat of 11 March and a counter-revolutionary incursion from the right. General António Ramalho Eanes is tasked with coordinating the moderates' military capability, standing by for any potential overstep – but on a purely defensive basis.[*] They know that in this tense staring contest between their faction and the revolutionary left, whoever blinks first, loses. On 15 November, the Group of Nine have a meeting on the stairwell outside Laranjeiras Palace, in northern Lisbon. Jaime Neves is there, representing his commandos regiment, one of the key forces the Nine have at their disposal – and he makes the case once again for the move north. 'If we do it, we have to do it now,' he says, 'because now I can guarantee that two hundred men will come with me. In one or two weeks I don't know how many will be left.'

---

[*] This notion of a purely defensive response is not entirely followed by Eanes and his fellow officers – an offensive plan is also drafted.

Vasco Lourenço isn't having it. 'What kind of a shit commander are you?' the captain shouts. 'You're a bluff! You go to your unit and you hold on hard to your men, and in fifteen days you'll have all two hundred with you. Because as I've already said, I veto fleeing north.'[8]

The key issue for the Nine is Otelo, and COPCON. That same meeting makes the decision to remove Otelo from his position as commander of the Lisbon Military Region, a post he's held almost since 25 April. The longer-term goal is the dissolution of COPCON altogether. But the issue of government, in the interim, needs to be resolved. It's in this Laranjeiras meeting that the idea emerges for the government to suspend itself, refusing to continue performing its duties until the president can guarantee the conditions in which to do them. In a country paralysed by a year and a half of strike action, the government follow suit, and begins a strike of their own. On 20 November, Pinheiro de Azevedo makes his way to the presidential palace to announce the decision to Costa Gomes. A crowd of journalists meets the prime minister outside the building.

'I'm tired of playing games… I've been sequestered twice. I'm tired of being sequestered. That's enough. I don't like it. It annoys me. I'm sick of it. So we're on strike.'

In the next meeting of the Revolutionary Council on the 18th, Otelo is told of the decision to remove him from command of the Lisbon Military Region. It's a tough conversation – but it's important for the Nine, and especially Otelo's old friend Vasco Lourenço, that the COPCON commander agrees to the shift in role. After some heated argument where Otelo is backed by the Navy, but still outnumbered, he eventually relents. The government want to put Vasco Lourenço in the post, but Lourenço again only agrees to take the position if Otelo concurs – which again, he does. Returning to COPCON, however, Otelo meets a problem – his men, the officers of the Lisbon Military Region, refuse the appointment of

Vasco Lourenço as their commander. Otelo returns to the president and the Revolutionary Council with the news, having been convinced by his men not to accept the changing of the guard – and the decision on the RML appointment gets pushed back to the 24th. Meanwhile the two sides of what feels like an impending confrontation begin to flex their muscles. At RALIS, under the eye of the chief of staff of the Army, Carlos Fabião, the soldiers are seen performing a revolutionary salute to the Portuguese flag – arms raised forward in a fist – while pledging allegiance to the working class. In the northern region of Rio Maior – site of the first large-scale attack from the far right – conservative agricultural workers begin building barricades and blocking access to Lisbon, demanding an end to the anarchy in the capital – barricades that the Revolutionary Council quickly request be dismantled.

It's on the evening of 24 November that President Costa Gomes once again insists that Vasco Lourenço take on the role of commander of the Lisbon Military Region. It's put to a vote of the Revolutionary Council, after Lourenço – speaking, mainly, to Otelo – registers his objections. The vote passes. On returning to COPCON in the early hours of 25 November, Otelo relays the information to his fellow officers. Costa Martins, from the Air Force, is there. 'The paratroopers aren't going to stand for this,' he says. 'They're going to occupy the airbases.' This is news to the COPCON commander, but he's too tired to deal with it, and he receives reassurance from his officers that they can handle the situation. 'You guys put a stop to that crap, if anything happens,' he says, and goes home for the evening. Costa Martins' prediction turns out to be prophetic. Shortly after the CR transmits the announcement of the RML's change in command, the paratrooper regiments in Tancos, made up primarily of sergeants and soldiers, trigger an operation that will bring Portugal to the very brink of civil war.

*

CRISIS

The situation at the Paratrooper School in Tancos has been dete-riorating rapidly – with orders from the Air Force chief of staff, the base has been starved of water and electricity, the paratroop-ers left without orders and living under the threat of losing their military identity, with Morais da Silva's dissolution of their vari-ous units. At around 04:30, the paratrooper units mobilise away from the school and occupy the airbases in Tanços, Monte Real and Montijo. By 07:00 they have captured the Air Force command building at the edge of Lisbon in Monsanto, holding General Pinho Freire hostage in his office. Meanwhile, parallel actions take place as RALIS set up positions along the main motorway entrances into Lisbon, and by the weapons storage warehouse in Beirolas troops from the Practical Military Administration School (*Escola Prática de Administração Militar*, EPAM) occupy the RTP station in Lumiar, and a military police unit occupies the National Broadcasters. It's General Pinho Freire, still with access to a telephone, who contacts Morais da Silva and reports the news: the 'coup' is on. The revolutionary left in the military appears to have blinked. As dawn breaks, several radio stations begin putting out the paratroopers' statements:

No longer willing to accept the positions of the Chief of Staff of the Air Force, contrary as they are to the interests of the Portuguese people, we have decided to prove our operational ability and revolutionary disci-pline, in a vast operation to neutralise the primary units of the Air Force, intending to openly contest a general [...] that distances himself through his decisions from the objectives of a democratic socialist revolution.

In Belém, President Costa Gomes and the military apparatus of the Nine jump into immediate action. An extraordinary meeting of the Revolutionary Council is called as the Nine and their allies race to the presidential palace. Belém is set up as a command post for the response operation, and Costa Gomes takes full operational control. At 09:00, the full situation on the ground is still a mystery – it's unknown whether the paratrooper/RALIS/EPAM actions are stand-alone, or whether they're part of a broader action that includes COPCON and other units likely to act against the Nine, like the military police and the marine regiments just south of the river. These latter units are, for Vasco Lourenço, the biggest concern – the marines have access to significant firepower, and if they decide to mobilise it's hard to imagine the situation not descending into a shooting war on the streets of Lisbon. Costa Gomes tries to get hold of Otelo on the phone, but he's unreachable – nobody knows where the COPCON commander is. At around 10:00, the president is presented with Ramalho Eanes' response plan. Costa Gomes is hesitant to pull the trigger on that just yet, without knowing exactly whom they're up against. There are several hours where the command post in Belém tries the diplomacy route, first sending messages to the parachute regiments demanding they stand down, then contacting the Intersindical and the PCP to get their help in restoring order. It's easy to forget, given his presence at the highest levels of government, that Francisco da Costa Gomes arrived at those levels through years of experience as a military officer in a colonial war. Having Costa Gomes onside is also the ace in the Nine's sleeve – the president holds the highest authority in the military, and despite the decline in military discipline over the last few months, the hope is that few units will have the courage to act directly against the president. Costa Gomes manages the command post in Belém masterfully – he pulls all the chiefs of staff into the war room, and as many unit commanders as he can get hold of, concentrating as much authority as he can into one space so he can avoid, at all costs, an exchange of gunfire or civil war. Among them is Naval Commander Manuel Martins

Guerreiro who, along with Admiral Rosa Coutinho, is in contact with the marine regiments, preventing them from doing anything rash. As the morning turns into the afternoon, large civilian crowds begin to congregate around key locations – RALIS, the commandos regiment in Amadora, the marines in Alfeite, and the COPCON quarters at Almada Fort – in many cases hoping the military will begin handing out weapons to them. Thankfully, that barely happens – it would turn what is currently only a tense military stand-off into a full shoot-out with civilians.

At around 15:00, having been out of radio and telephone contact for several hours, Otelo Saraiva de Carvalho arrives at the presidential palace in Belém. His appearance sends a wave of relief through the command post – it's a sign the COPCON commander isn't at large leading a secret revolutionary army about to take Lisbon. Without Otelo, the COPCON command structure is broken, and even if some units decide to mobilise without him, they're adrift. Otelo hands himself over to Costa Gomes' command, which is the last piece in the puzzle before the general can fully implement the response plan. At 16:30, Belém issues a statement establishing a state of emergency in the Lisbon military area. With that, the Amadora Commando regiment, led by Jaime Neves, begin setting off from their headquarters south of the river, heading to lay siege to the various bases that have been occupied by the paratroopers. Whereas the Belém operation is effectively coordinated from a central command post, the various rebellious military forces are disjointed, without clear leadership or a clear plan, operating independently. Despite this, the declaration of a state of emergency escalates things – Colonel Varela Gomes stations himself in COPCON and tries to mobilise units, with no success. Through a concerted effort on the part of the Navy elements in Belém, the marine regiments never leave their base – as much as many of their officers are keen to hop into the action on the side of the rebel factions. Captain António

Rosado da Luz, a COPCON officer based in Almada Fort, is contacted at one point by marine officers, claiming Martins Guerreiro and Rosa Coutinho are being soft, and offering to put their forces under his control to 'sort out the situation' in Lisbon. Rosado da Luz politely declines the offer of escalation, his hands already full dealing with the mass of civilians demanding weaponry outside his door. Martins Guerreiro and Rosa Coutinho eventually make their way personally to Alfeite to dissuade the marines, who had started threatening to march on Belém to 'release' Martins Guerreiro. Later, Rosado da Luz receives a phone call from an Air Force captain, informing him that the Air Force chief of staff has ordered a squadron of planes to be loaded up with 500lb bombs to bombard Almada Fort in order to neutralise the COPCON presence there. Rosado da Luz glances out of his window and replies, almost jokingly: 'Well I hope your boys have a really good aim, because there's about fifty of us in here, but ten thousand civilians outside, so if they miss there's going to be a bloodbath.'[9] Moments later, Ramalho Eanes informs the Air Force that if they scramble any units offensively, they'll be shot out of the air. The tightrope of civil war is being trodden carefully on all sides, with nobody yet willing to take the plunge into full armed conflict.

At around 18:00, viewers tuned in to RTP in Lisbon and the south witness one of the stranger events of the day. The presenter introduces Captain Duran Clemente, the spokesperson of the EPAM unit that has occupied the television station, to 'explain the current situation at the Portuguese Radio and Television station'. Clemente comes on the screen – a young officer in uniform, his face shrouded in a thick mane of dark beard and hair, carrying the scruffy look of the new young revolutionary officer class with a calm assurance. Clemente addresses the viewers in an eight-minute speech that seems off the cuff, exposing, in a measured way, what he and his comrades understand is the socialism they're fighting for, and gently denouncing the 'retreat' of the MFA away from the socialist objective. He seems just at the beginning of a longer talk when he suddenly stops, distracted by something happening off screen. 'They're giving me signals, I don't know if I can continue. Perhaps it would be better to explain to the viewers that I can't continue talking due to technical reasons, is that it?' There's an inaudible back and forth between Clemente and the RTP team. Then suddenly the broadcast cuts to the start of the 1963 Danny Kaye film *The Man from the Diners' Club*. Soon after, the RTP broadcast over the Lisbon region is taken over by the stations in Porto, a shift that also happens with the radio stations. Rádio Clube Português is shut off completely.

A little over an hour later, Jaime Neves' commandos have surrounded Air Force Command in Monsanto and quickly forced the paratroopers to surrender. It's the start of a clean sweep operation for the 'moderates'. Realising no one else is joining their fight, the paratrooper occupations begin withdrawing from the various airbases in the north and returning to Tancos. The civilian gatherings begin to disperse in the night. In the early hours of 26 November, the Revolutionary Council officially dissolves COPCON, and orders all of its officers to report to Belém where, on arrival, they are arrested, among them Dinis de Almeida. The commandos continue their operations, fumbling an assault on the military police headquarters in Ajuda (resulting in a brief shoot-out and three deaths), and, on the 27th, they surround COPCON and carry out further arrests. The victory solidifies over the next several days as the Lisbon forces are joined by reinforcements from the rest of the country, including a convoy from the Practical Cavalry School led by Salgueiro Maia, which stations itself five kilometres from the capital. As successive radio and television statements from the heads of government declare the situation is under control, one thing becomes clear: whether they wanted to or not, regardless of the paratroopers' intentions, the revolutionary left had forced a confrontation on the future of the country – and they'd lost.

COPCON – once the armed wing of the MFA, and later the armed wing of the 'military left' – hadn't mobilised directly against Ramalho Eanes' operation, and now it's gone altogether. Of the three members of the Troika that the international press claimed would plunge Portugal into Soviet chaos – Otelo, Lourenço and Costa Gomes – two have been removed from power in successive actions aided by the third. Power has been bluntly restored to the Sixth Provisional Government, and the political parties that back the parliamentary process. Like the electricity being cut during the crescendo of a nineteen-month rock concert, the thrumming vibrancy of the revolutionary left on the streets and in the government is suddenly and unceremoniously silenced. The Portuguese revolution is, in a very meaningful sense, over.

EPILOGUE

Number 95 looks different to the rest of the buildings on Rua da Misericórdia, even though it blends into the Lisbon skyline because of its third and fourth floors, complete with small pots of flowers – practically a requirement for buildings on this street. In this case, they're carnations. The lower facade, however, is two levels of beautiful floor-to-ceiling windows and doors that slope noticeably upwards with the steep angle of the street, framed in two mushroom-curve domes that give it a hint of Art Deco. At the turn of the century this was the headquarters of the newspaper *O Mundo*, where its front was taken up by a large stone globe. Later, it was the headquarters of the regime newspaper *Diário da Manhã*, before falling out of use in the late 1970s. In 2000 it was redeveloped, and the poster board on its front as well as the neon sign high above reveals its new occupants: the 25 April Association.

I meet Colonel Vasco Lourenço in May 2023. When I arrive for the 15:00 meeting, I'm told – kindly and apologetically – that the colonel is late, his other meeting has run over. 'He's a very busy man,' the receptionist tells me with a smile. I'm happy to wait – the large marble room on the ground floor of the building is a micro-museum in its own right, tall boards with information and photos of the revolution, abstract paintings hinting at carnations, a vase containing what look to be old MFA flags. In one corner there's a glass case with a scale model of a *Chaimite* armoured car. In another, a small brass sculpture of a soldier receiving a carnation from a child. When the colonel arrives a few minutes later, he shakes my hand energetically, out of breath from the heat outside. Vasco Lourenço is eighty-one years old, a stout man who still carries himself with the energy of the bombastic young officer he was fifty years ago. He asks me to wait a few minutes while he composes himself, and I sit in the foyer of the building, flicking through a copy of the Association's free quarterly magazine *O Referencial* – the 2021 issue, covering the death of Otelo Saraiva de Carvalho. I'm sent up a few moments later, and Lourenço meets me in his imposing office, which I barely have time to register. More MFA flags, walls lined with framed diplomas, a large display case seemingly full to the brim with medals and commemorative trinkets. In the run-up to the commemorations of the fiftieth anniversary of the Carnation Revolution, I imagine I'm one of thousands of people Vasco Lourenço has had knocking at the Association's door. He looks unfazed by the work. I recognise the same wry smile on his face that I've seen in countless black-and-white video clips, an almost impish twinkle in the eye, a man who was both a Captain of April and a Captain of November and without whom, undoubtedly, Portuguese history would have been very, very different. 'I have something here that will probably interest you,' he says in a booming voice that doesn't seem to have been softened by age, and pulls an enormous folder from a drawer, a pile of what look like hundreds of documents haphazardly stacked together in some arcane filing system. He spends a few minutes flicking through, before pulling one out and passing it to me. I recognise it immediately – a list of twelve names, Lisbon establishments, numbers and pen scrawls all around the edges. The corner of the document has had something spilled on it, and it has the look of something that's been folded dozens of times. It's the original list of cafés and restaurants the Captain's Movement met in before the Cascais meeting on 5 March 1974. It feels like something I shouldn't be allowed to touch with my bare hands. The colonel leans back in his chair. 'So,' he says, 'what would you like to know?'

25 November is generally considered to mark the 'end' of the Portuguese revolution. Some, like Captain Rodrigo Sousa e Castro, place the end even earlier, on 5 September and the Tancos proclamation – the date the Group of Nine, effectively, took (or retook) control of the state apparatus.[1] The country moved then from an Ongoing Revolutionary Process to an Ongoing Constitutional Process,[2] with the balance of power shifted over to those advocating for a pluralist democracy. 25 November can be seen, in that context, as the death spasm of a revolutionary process that was perhaps always destined to spit out a complicated and contradictory democracy. The months that follow November involve an internal dismantling of the 'military left' and a sidelining of the radical elements of the government, pushing the revolutionary left into their usual role of opposition movements. There is a concerted effort on the part of the nascent, democratic right to ban the Communist Party altogether, opportunistically blaming them for the unfolding of 25 November. The right accuse the Communists of trying to start a left-led coup – an accusation that will persist for decades. These attempts don't work, largely through interventions from moderates like Melo Antunes, adamant, as from the very beginning, that the transition to democratic socialism should be truly pluralist. The defeat of the revolutionary left does not mean that when the constitution is finally drafted and presented to the public in 1976, it's not radical – the 1976 Constitution, supported by all the political parties in the Assembly except for the CDS, enshrines key pieces of the MFA programme into law. For one, a version of the MFA-Party Pact is maintained: the Revolutionary Council remains part of the government structure as an advisory body with parallel powers, including the right to declare war, and to permit the

president to dissolve the Portuguese parliament. The new constitution is openly socialist in its framing, stating explicitly that the object of the Republic is to 'ensure the transition to socialism' and urging the state to 'socialise the means of production and abolish the exploitation of man by man'. It officially comes into force on 25 April 1976, the date of the legislative elections for the first actually representative government since 1926. As expected, the Socialist Party wins the highest number of seats – short of a majority, with the PPD once again in second place. Mário Soares becomes the first prime minister of the constitutional government. General António Ramalho Eanes – the officer who had coordinated the military operation on the Group of Nine's side on 25 November, is swept along on a wave of popular support from that military victory to win the presidential election with 61.59% of the vote. In second place, Otelo Saraiva de Carvalho, with a respectable 16.46%.

That ideal of a shining, democratic socialist constitution and country is short-lived. In 1978 Soares' Socialists enter into a coalition with the right-wing CDS, and the next two decades (and oscillations between centre-right and centre-left governments) revise the constitution to scrap the Revolutionary Council, remove its more explicit ideological content, and carry on the process of turning Portugal into a conventional, capitalist, European liberal democracy. Most of the nationalisations carried out after 11 March are reversed throughout the 1980s, the fears and warnings of the revolutionary left during the PREC made manifest as the Socialist and Social Democratic parties follow the European trend of drifting rightwards. With that rightwards drift comes a complicated relationship with the revolution, what it meant and what it means decades later. 25 April was a specific historic moment that led to an incredibly complex and turbulent period before resettling into 'conventional' politics – and like all historic processes it's a story that can be retold, partitioned and reinterpreted in all sorts of ways to generate a given narrative. The revolution has become another story we tell ourselves and each other – with all the editorialising that involves. To the main political parties of the centre that have held power since 1976 (PS and PPD, later PSD: Social Democratic Party, *Partido Social Democrata*), it's easy and more convenient to gloss over the genuine grassroots popular upheaval that characterised the PREC, sweeping past the uncomfortable reality that, for a while, true power didn't lie in their hands, but on the streets, and occasionally with some upstart captains. By doing that, they can frame themselves as the true harbingers of democracy, using the revolution as a backdrop to their own legitimacy. The Communist Party, on the other hand, directly link the radical grassroots movements of the PREC with the Party itself, claiming for themselves the positive 'gains of the revolution' while sidelining the multitude of left groups and unaligned individuals that also participated in those processes (many of them indifferent or openly hostile to the Party), effectively writing them out of history. One lasting consequence of the revolution is that actively right-wing parties, on the level of the British Conservatives or the American Republicans, have never held much power in the Portuguese Assembly. To them, the PREC is a bogeyman, a symbol of uncontrolled anarchy that the country will return to should the left be given any leeway in the government. Much like how British Conservatives talk about the 1970s as a Dark Ages of economic chaos before Margaret Thatcher steadied the ship with her iron grip, the PREC is a stick to beat the left with, and 25 November the date on which cooler heads prevailed to avoid a full descent into Soviet authoritarianism. In 2004, for the thirtieth anniversary of the 1974 coup, the government led by the centre-right PSD launch the commemorative campaign *Abril é Evolução* (April is Evolution) – an example of how, by omitting one letter, the state can attempt to sanitise and

337

compartmentalise one of the most radical moments in Portuguese history. The response from the left includes an open call to deface the campaign's posters and billboards by adding the missing R, alongside a sharp debate on the preservation of revolutionary memory.

But where are the captains in all this? The 25 November crisis effectively extinguished the MFA, and was followed by a steady reversion of the armed forces to the conventional military hierarchy – and its discipline. The officers arrested in the aftermath of 25 November were soon afterwards freed and amnestied without trial, and most of the Captains of April simply returned to their posts in the military and occasionally within political parties. In 1982, the same year that the Revolutionary Council is abolished, former members of the MFA found the 25 April Association, whose purpose is the 'consecration and dissemination, in the cultural sphere, of the spirit of the liberating movement of 25 April 1974'. Part of that role is the preservation of the historic memory of the revolution – and from the very start, the Association integrates 95% of the officers who played an active role in the coup. Despite at various times being factionally set against each other during the PREC, fifty years later the majority of the surviving 'protagonists' of 25 April are close friends. In 2016, as part of an initiative to educate the next generation of Portuguese schoolteachers on the details of the revolution, Vasco Lourenço appears alongside Manuel Martins Guerreiro and António Rosado da Luz for a module on the PREC, respectively representing the three main factions that emerged after 11 March. The deep bonds built up during war and conspiracy, it seems, can't be broken by something as pedestrian as being on opposite sides of a brewing civil war. But fifty years is a long time, and, one by one, the people who remember the revolution because they lived it or led it are dying. Among the first of the 'protagonists' to go is Salgueiro

Maia in 1992, after a three-year battle with cancer, leaving an enduring legacy as one of the most fiercely independent and heroic participants in 25 April, the platonic ideal of an MFA officer, untarnished by political ambitions beyond releasing his country from the clutches of fascism and war. His funeral is marked by the playing of '*Grândola, Vila Morena*', at his request. A plaque in his honour is unveiled in the year of his death, on the ground in front of the GNR headquarters in Carmo, where he made history.

Other participants leave more mixed legacies. Otelo Saraiva de Carvalho is held in prison for three months from January 1976, on 'suspicion of military involvement in the events of 25 November 1975' following the internal report on the crisis. His vote share in the 1976 presidential elections proves to be a high point in a long and fraught political career. Otelo becomes closely involved with the small revolutionary left party Popular Unity Promotion Groups (*Grupos Dinamizadores de Unidade Popular*, GDUP), becoming its leader – a level of political activity incompatible with his status as an on-duty military officer, which lands him in disciplinary prison for twenty days and eventually removal from active service. In the 1980 presidential election, backed by GDUP, Otelo receives only 1.45% of the vote. In 1984, after a vast counterterrorism operation named Operation Orion, Otelo is arrested on the charge of being one of the founders and leader of the terrorist group Popular Forces 25 April (*Forças Populares 25 de Abril*, FP25), a split from the Revolutionary Brigades that had carried out numerous bombings and targeted assassination attempts throughout the early 1980s, leading to multiple deaths including children. Through evidence gathered from detailed notebooks found at his home, in 1985 he's sentenced to fifteen years in prison, later extended to seventeen. An appeal to the Constitutional Court has him released in 1989 awaiting a further trial. Over the course of the next several years, partly through the involvement of Mário Soares and after international pressure, Otelo receives a pardon as part of a broader amnesty that covers 'infractions of a political nature committed between July 27 1976 and June 21 1991'. The perpetrators of the 'blood crimes' of FP25 are never found, and as a result Otelo goes free, declared innocent by the courts. He spends the next several years as an active commentator in Portuguese politics, his status as one of the most important figures in the revolution tainted by his links to terrorism. He dies in 2021, his funeral held in the chapel at the Military Academy in Lisbon.

Fifty years is a long time. If the memory of the revolution has been eroded, the same has happened to the memory of why the MFA launched it, and what came before. Portugal had maintained a tacit rejection of explicitly fascist political parties until the emergence of CHEGA (literally, 'ENOUGH') in 2019, an explicitly hard-right national-conservative unit that has as its slogan 'God, Homeland, Family, and Work' – adding a tellingly capitalist twist to Salazar's old motto. With twelve deputies in the Assembly at the time of writing, CHEGA is currently the third largest party in parliament, a development mirroring the rise of the far right across Europe and beyond. It would be inaccurate to see this as a total novelty in Portuguese politics – there have been far-right elements in parliament for years, but their activity has been covered by their presence in the parties of the right and centre-right, taking refuge in the respectability of tendencies like Christian Democracy. The collapse of CDS in the latest legislative elections is a gain for parties like the libertarians in the Liberal Initiative (*Iniciativa Liberal*, IL) and the vicious far-right thugs in CHEGA. Forty-five years is apparently how long it takes for the spectre of Salazar to make an open return to the Portuguese political stage. Apart from André Ventura, the first fascist elected to the Assembly since the revolution, CHEGA's cadre includes figures like Diogo Pacheco de Amorim, a former member of the MDLP political wing, who was active while the group was setting off bombs in the Hot Summer of 1975.

If there's a bitterness on the part of the 'protagonists' of the revolution, shared by all the former PREC factions of the left (which include the Group of Nine), it's twofold. Firstly it's a general lament on the direction the country has taken since 1975 – the slow descent into privatisations, inequality and austerity, everything the MFA programme explicitly hoped to avoid in the new democratic settlement. The 'victory' on 25 November for the Group of Nine necessarily meant a victory for the right in Portugal, which could exploit the democratic process to maintain the wheels of capital spinning in their favour. Secondly, it's that despite the captains' best efforts, the seeds of fascism were never truly eradicated from Portuguese society. Now those seeds of fascism are blooming again, their toxicity creeping into the halls of power and the pages of the press. There is still time to halt their advance again.

In the wake of the right's resurgence, and the revolution's contested legacy, it might be tempting to accuse the revolution of failing to live up to its own ideals. But this is a fatal mistake. The Portugal of 1976 was undoubtedly, in a million distinct ways, better than the Portugal of 1973. The revolution killed, decisively, two of the most vicious elements of Portuguese history – the centuries-long colonial project, and the vile carceral apparatus that kept the population under the regime's boot for nearly five decades. For women, for workers, for immigrants, for the poor, for the masses – things are better. If there's one thing historical memory is important for, it's to avoid repeating history's greatest mistakes. The *Estado Novo* was one of them, and we will never go back. As Salgueiro Maia confidently stated on the very first 25 April, the day, forever, now commemorates the revolution. These days, there are flower sellers on most street corners in Lisbon, who will sell you a carnation for a euro, and maybe a bottle of water if it's especially hot. The march down Avenida da Liberdade from Marquês de Pombal is vast and loud. We sing 'Grândola, Vila Morena'. We hold our carnations aloft. We wave to the elderly officers who drive in on the tops of the *Chaimites*, in full uniform. And perhaps most importantly, we remember.

ACKNOWLEDGEMENTS

When I decided to write this book, sometime in early 2022, I had no idea what a monumental task was ahead of me. I have been hugely fortunate to have been buoyed along the way by some deeply generous and supportive people, to whom I owe my undying gratitude, a phrase that even in its hyperbole seems inadequate. Firstly to my editor Rida, whose balanced mix of enthusiasm and clinical criticism has kept me motivated and scared enough to finish this. To Oneworld, for taking a punt on me. To Kate, Paul, Laura, Julian, Francesca and Anne at Oneworld for their fantastic work and boundless patience. To Steven for the good advice, support and book sourcing. To Urte, for providing an early critical eye. To Ed, Mark, Jo, Kelly, Michael, Augustina, Simon, Mercedes, Alex, Zack, Chris, Tom and Justine for being the enthusiastic participants in the revolutionary walking tour of Lisbon that first planted the seed for this, and my cheerleaders thereafter. To Dan for help sourcing books. To the 25 April Association and particularly to Colonel Vasco Lourenço for gifting me their time and resources. To Lara Pawson and Catherine Fletcher for providing early thoughts. To Miguel, Alexandra and Dina, for familial support. And finally to Ruth, for the idea, and without whose early support not a single word would have been put to paper.

Selected Locations, Lisbon

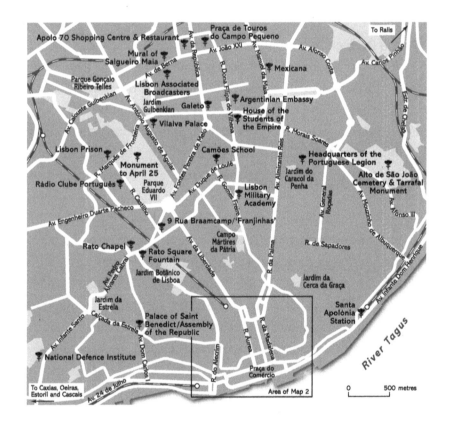

Selected Locations, Downtown Lisbon

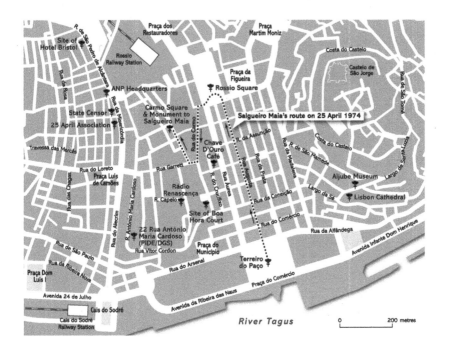

SELECT BIBLIOGRAPHY

BOOKS IN ENGLISH

Accornero, Guya. *The Revolution Before the Revolution*. Berghahn Books, 2016.

Hammond, John L. *Building Popular Power*. Monthly Review Press, 1988.

Ramos Pinto, Pedro. *Lisbon Rising*. Manchester University Press, 2015.

Sunday Times Insight Team. *Insight on Portugal*. André Deutsch, 1975.

Varela, Raquel et al. *A People's History of the Portuguese Revolution*. Pluto Press, 2019.

OFFICER ACCOUNTS

Contreiras, Carlos Almada. *Operação Viragem Histórica*. Edições Colibri, 2017.

Carvalho, Otelo Saraiva de. *Alvorada Em Abril*. Bertrand, 1977.

—. *Cinco Meses Mudaram Portugal*. Cadernos Portugália, 1975.

—. *O Dia Inicial: [25 de Abril, Hora a Hora]*. Editora Objectiva, 2011.

de Almeida, Dinis. *Ascensão, Apogeu E Queda Do M.F.A.* Edições Sociais, 1978.

—. *Origens E Evolução Do Movimento de Capitães*. Edições Sociais, 1977.

Lourenço, Vasco. May 2023. [Interview].

Lourenço, Vasco, and Maria Manuela Cruzeiro. *Do Interior Da Revolução*. Âncora Editora, 2009.

Maia, Salgueiro. *Capitão de Abril*. Âncora Editora, 2014.

Pontes, Joana et al. *A Hora Da Liberdade: O 25 de Abril, Pelos Protagonistas*. Bizâncio, 2012.

Sousa e Castro, Rodrigo. *Capitão de Abril, Capitão de Novembro*. Editora Guerra e Paz, 2010.

BEFORE THE REVOLUTION

Araújo António. *Matar O Salazar: O Atentado de Julho de 1937*. Tinta Da China, 2017.

Castro, Pedro Jorge. *O Inimigo No. 1 de Salazar*. A Esfera dos Livros, 2010.

Hipólito Santos, José. *A Revolta de Beja*. Âncora Editora, 2012.

Marques, Fernando Pereira. *Uma Nova Concepção de Luta: Materiais Para a História Da LUAR E Da Resistência Armada Em Portugal*. Tinta Da China, 2016.

Martins, Helder. *Casa Dos Estudantes Do Império*. Editorial Caminho, 2017.

Pimentel, Irene Flunser. *Inimigos de Salazar*. Clube do Autor, 2018.

Rosa, Frederico Delgado. *Humberto Delgado*. A Esfera dos Livros, 2008.

Rosas, Fernando. *Salazar E O Poder: A Arte de Saber Durar*. Tinta Da China, 2015.

Salazar, António de Oliveira. *Discursos E Notas Políticas*. Coimbra Editora, 2015.

Vaz, Luís. *Palma Inácio E O Desvio Do Avião (1961)*. Âncora Editora, 2012.

SELECT BIBLIOGRAPHY

THE REVOLUTION

Araújo, António. *'Morte À Pide!' – a Queda Da Polícia Política Do Estado Novo.* Tinta da China, 2019.

Contreiras, Carlos Almada. *A Noite Que Mudou a Revolução de Abril.* Edições Colibri, 2019.

Contreiras, Carlos Almada et al. *Antologia: O 25 de Abril de 1974: Testemunhos Da Luta Pela Democracia E Pela Liberdade.* Edições Colibri, 2020.

Cruzeiro, Maria Manuela, and Coimbra Maria Natércia. *O Pulsar Da Revolução: Cronologia Da Revolução de 25 de Abril (1973–1976).* Edições Afrontamento, 2000.

Cunha, Alfredo, and Adelino Gomes. *Os Rapazes Dos Tanques.* Porto Editora, 2014.

Fonseca, Ana Sofia. *Capitãs de Abril: A Revolução Dos Cravos Vivida Pelas Mulheres Dos Militares.* A Esfera Dos Livros, 2014.

Maia, Matos. *Aqui Emissora Da Liberdade.* Editorial Caminho, 1999.

Patriarca, Fátima. *Sindicatos Contra Salazar.* Imprensa de Ciências Sociais, 2000.

Rezola, Maria Inácia. *25 de Abril – Mitos de Uma Revolução.* Esfera dos Livros, 2008.

Rodrigues, Avelino et al. *O Movimento Dos Capitães E O 25 de Abril: 229 Dias Para Derrubar O Fascismo.* Moraes Editores, 1974.

—. *Portugal Depois de Abril.* Intervoz, 1976.

Varela, Raquel. *História Do Povo Na Revolução Portuguesa, 1974–1975.* Bertrand, 2014.

NOTES

CHAPTER 1: THE STORIES WE TELL OURSELVES

1   *Salazar e o Poder*, Rosas, 2012.
2   Galvão, Henrique. A Função colonial de Portugal. Razão de ser da nacionalidade. Conferência. Part of the 'Edições da 1a Exposição Colonial Portuguesa'. 1934.
3   de Almeida, João. A Cooperação dos nativos na expansão e na defesa do Império. Conferência. Part of the 'Edições da 1a Exposição Colonial Portuguesa.' 1934.
4   Biscaia, João, 'Luís Raposo: "O Estado Novo É O Autor Da Mais Vil Destruição Memorialista Em Belém"', *Setenta e Quatro*, 2023, https://setentaequatro.pt/entrevista/luis-raposo-o-estado-novo-e-o-autor-da-mais-vil-destruicao-memorialista-em-belem.
5   Galvão, 1934.

CHAPTER 2: FEARLESS

1   Pimentel, Irene Flunser. *Inimigos de Salazar*. Clube do Autor, 2018.
2   Farinha, Luís. 'A Revolta de "3 de Fevereiro de 1927"'. https://www.esquerda.net/artigo/revolta-de-3-de-fevereiro-de-1927/72617.
3   Pimentel, 2018.
4   Front page, *A Victoria*, 19 November 1927. http://2.bp.blogspot.com/_csva7PFVgLg/S9N41osqQVI/AAAAAAAADRg/EFQPirRc-CM/s1600/A-VICTORIA.JPG.
5   Salazar, António Oliveira. *Discursos e Notas Políticas 1928 a 1966*. Coimbra Editora, 2016.
6   Patriarca, Fátima, *Sindicatos Contra Salazar: A Revolta de 18 de Janeiro de 1934*. Imprensa de Ciências Sociais, 2000.
7   Pimentel, 2018.

8   Rosa, Frederico Delgado. *Humberto Delgado*, 1a ed. 2008.
9   Pimentel, Irene Flunser, in Duplas. *À Portuguesa – Henrique Galvão e Humberto Delgado* (RTP documentary).
10 Rosa, 2008.
11 Rodrigues, Avelino; Borga, Cesário; Cardoso, Mário. *O Movimento dos Capitães e o 25 de Abril: 229 Dias Para Derrubar o Fascismo.* Moraes, 1974.
12 Rosa, 2008.
13 Carvalho, 1977.

CHAPTER 3: DISSIDENT CONFETTI

1   The account of Carlos Brito's escape is drawn from Brito, Carlos in *Antologia – O 25 de Abril de 1974: Testemunhas da Luta Pela Democracia.* Edições Colibri, 2020.
2   Rodrigues et al. 1974.
3   Pimentel, 2018.
4   This section on Henrique Galvão is sourced primarily from Castro, Pedro Jorge. *O Inimigo no.1 de Salazar: Henrique Galvão, o líder do assalto ao* Santa Maria *e do sequestro de um avião da TAP.* A Esfera dos Livros, 2010.
5   *Ibid.*
6   Pimentel, 2018.
7   The majority of this account is drawn from: Vaz, Luís. *Palma Inácio e o Desvio do Avião (1961).* Âncora Editora, 2012.
8   Accornero, Guya. *The Revolution Before the Revolution: Late Authoritarianism and Student Protest in Portugal.* Berghahn, 2016.
9   Costa, Jorge in *1962 A Crise Académica* (Os Anos de Salazar vol. 19).
10 Accornero, 2016.

CHAPTER 4: COLONIAL WAR

1   Wakim Moreno, Helena. 'Casa Dos Estudantes Do Império: De associação estudantil do regime às lutas anticoloniais'. https://www.re-mapping.eu/pt/lugares-de-memoria/casa-dos-estudantes-do-imperio.
2   Martins, Helder. *Casa Dos Estudantes Do Império: Subsídios para a História do seu período mais decisivo (1953 a 1961).* Editorial Caminho, 2017.

NOTES

3 Personal information and reflections that focus on Otelo are taken from Carvalho, Otelo Saraiva de. *Alvorada Em Abril*. Publicações Alfa, 1977.
4 Carvalho, 1977.
5 Hipólito Santos, José. *A Revolta de Beja*. Âncora Editora, 2012.
6 Specific references to Salgueiro Maia and his time in the colonial war are primarily taken from Maia, Salgueiro. *Capitão de Abril*. Âncora Editora, 2014.
7 Carneiro, Mariana. '1 de julho de 1970: Início da Operação Nó Górdio'. https://www.esquerda.net/artigo/1-de-julho-de-1970-inicio-da-operacao-no-gordio/75355#footnote-3.
8 Accornero, 2016.
9 Interview with Colonel Vasco Lourenço, May 2023.
10 Marques, Fernando Pereira. *Uma Nova Concepção de Luta: Materiais para a história da LUAR e da resistência armada em Portugal*. Edições Tinta da China 2016.
11 Maia, 2014.

CHAPTER 5: A CONSPIRACY OF CAPTAINS

1 Sections relating to the personal experiences of Eduardo Dinis de Almeida in this chapter are drawn from de Almeida, Dinis. *Origens E Evolução Do Movimento de Capitães*. 1st ed. Edições Sociais, 1977.
2 Carvalho, 1977, p. 131.
3 de Almeida, 1977, p. 114.
4 *Os Homens Sem Sono*, 1975 documentary.
5 Vasco Lourenço, Contemporary History Course Module III, 2014, hosted by April 25 Association https://www.youtube.com/watch?v=GWyf1Z-MEwE.
6 de Almeida, 1977.
7 Pontes, Joana. *A Hora da Liberdade: O 25 de Abril pelos Protagonistas*. Bizâncio, 2012.
8 Lourenço, 2016.
9 Interview with Col. Vasco Lourenço, May 2023.
10 *Ibid.*
11 Carvalho, 1977.
12 Carvalho, 1977.
13 Lourenço, 2016.
14 Carvalho, 1977.

CHAPTER 6: CONFRONTATION

1 Salazar speech, 13 April 1961.
2 Lourenço, 2016.
3 Carvalho, 1977.
4 Lourenço (interview), 2023.
5 Carvalho, 1977.
6 de Almeida, 1977.
7 Lourenço, 2016.
8 *Ibid.*
9 *Ibid.*
10 Lourenço, 2023.
11 Carvalho, 1977.

CHAPTER 7: GENERAL PLAN OF
OPERATIONS (HISTORIC TURN)

1 de Almeida, 1977.
2 Lourenço, 2016.
3 *Ibid.*
4 Rodrigues, Avelino; Borga, Cesário; Cardoso, Mário. *Portugal Depois de Abril.* Intervoz, 1976.
5 Carvalho, 1977.
6 Contreiras, Carlos Almada. *Antologia: O 25 de Abril de 1974: Testemunhas da Luta Pela Democracia.* Edições Colibri, 2020.
7 de Almeida, 1977.
8 Maia, Matos. *Aqui Emissora da Liberdade.* Editorial Caminho, 1999.
9 Contreiras, Carlos Almada. *Operação Viragem Histórica.* Edições Colibri, 2017.
10 Carvalho, 1977.
11 António-Pedro Vasconcelos, Leandro Ferreira. *A Voz E Os Ouvidos Do MFA* (RTP documentary), 2016.

CHAPTER 8: 'IT'S FIVE TO ELEVEN...'

1 Araújo, António. *Matar O Salazar: O Atentado de Julho de 1937.* Tinta da China, 2017.
2 'Salazar. A História E Os Detalhes Do Atentado à Bomba de 1937 de Que O Ditador Escapou', *Observador*, 1 November 2017,

NOTES

https:// observador.pt/especiais/salazar-a-historia-e-os-detalhes-do-atentado-a-bomba-de-1937-de-que-o-ditador-escapou. Accessed 4 February 2023.

3   Fonseca, Ana Sofia. *Capitãs de Abril*. 1st ed. A Esfera dos Livros, 2014.

4   Soares, Marisa. '"Graffiters" Criam Mural Dedicado à Revolução de Abril', *PÚBLICO*, 12 April 2014, www.publico.pt/2014/04/12/culturaipsilon/noticia/graffiters-criam-mural-dedicado-a-revolucao-de-abril-1632047. Accessed 29 March 2023.

5   Carvalho, Otelo Saraiva de. *O Dia Inicial*. 1st ed. Editora Objectiva, 2011.

6   Madeira, João. '"Tudo Depende Da Raiva E Da Alegria": Os Cantores de Intervenção Na Revolução de Abril'. Universidade Nova de Lisboa, 2017.

7   Granular descriptions of troop movements such as these are drawn from Carvalho, 2011.

8   Unless otherwise noted, most of the action tracking Salgueiro Maia is drawn from Maia, 2014.

9   Cunha, Alfredo, and Adelino Gomes. *Os Rapazes Dos Tanques*. Porto Editora, 2014.

10   de Almeida, 1977.

11   Correia, Jorge. 'Joaquim Furtado: Como Se Diz Liberdade?', *Perguntasimples*, 19 April 2022, perguntasimples.com/joaquim-furtado. Accessed 8 February 2023.

12   Carvalho, 2011.

13   'Militar Fez "Bluff" E Conseguiu Sozinho Tomar O Aeroporto', *Diário de Notícias*, 8 March 2010, www.dn.pt/portugal/sul/militar-fez-bluff-e-conseguiu-sozinho-tomar-o-aeroporto-1513717.html. Accessed 29 March 2023.

14   Bravo, Paula. 'Na Secção Memórias: Entrevista Ao Coronel Costa Martins', *Terra Ruiva*, 11 April 2016, www.terraruiva.pt/2016/04/11/entrevista-ao-coronel-costa-martins-o-25-de-abril-para-mim-e-uma-forma-de-estar-na-vida. Accessed 4 February 2023.

15   Contreiras, 2017.

16   *Ibid.*

CHAPTER 9: DAWN IN TERREIRO DO PAÇO

1   Maia, 2014.

2   Carvalho, 2011.

3 Matias, Lucinda Canelas and Jorge Miguel. 'Correspondentes Da Liberdade', *PÚBLICO*, 25 April 1999, www.publico.pt/1999/04/25/jornal/correspondentes-da-liberdade-132654. Accessed 21 December 2022.
4 *Ibid.*
5 Carvalho, 2011.
6 'A Verdadeira História Da Fragata "Gago Coutinho"', *RTP*, 17 November 2022, www.rtp.pt/noticias/25-herois-do-25-de-abril/a-verdadeira-historia-da-fragata-gago-coutinho_n751126. Accessed 6 January 2023.
7 Sottomayor, Fernando. *Contributos para o Estudo do Golpe Militar de 25 de Abril de 1974.* Faculdade de Letras da Universidade do Porto, 2008.
8 *Ibid.*
9 Interview with Fernando Brito e Cunha, 'O Único Civil no 25 de Abril', *RTP*, 24 April 2006, https://arquivos.rtp.pt/conteudos/o-unico-civil-no-25-de-abril.

CHAPTER 10: THE TIME HAS COME

1 Gomes, Adelino et al. *Diário da Revolução pt. 1: O Dia 25 de Abril*, audio documentary, 1994.
2 *Ibid.*
3 Fonseca, 2014.
4 Gomes, 1994.
5 de Almeida, 1977.
6 *Ibid.*

CHAPTER 11: HUNTING FASCISTS AND DISCUSSING THE PRICE OF COD

1 Araújo, António. *Morte à Pide.* Tinta da China, 2019.
2 Rocha, João Manuel. 'O estrebuchar mortífero do regime', *PÚBLICO*, 23 April 1999, https://www.publico.pt/1999/04/23/jornal/o-estrebuchar-mortifero-do-regime-132563.
3 Carvalho, 1977.
4 Lourenço, Vasco, in Contemporary History Module V, hosted by 25 April Association, 2016.

CHAPTER 12: THE DECLINE AND FALL
OF ANTÓNIO DE SPÍNOLA

1   Ramos Pinto, Pedro. *Lisbon Rising*. Manchester University Press, 2015.
2   Rodrigues et al. 1976.
3   Raul Rego, himself a Mason, claims Palma Carlos was appointed through Rego's suggestion and the influence of the Grand Orient of Portugal Masonic Lodge, as reported in *Expresso*, https://expresso.pt/presidenciais2016/2016-01-14-Pressionado-pela-maconaria-Spinola-nomeou-Palma-Carlos-para-primeiro-ministro.
4   Varela, Raquel. *A História do Povo na Revolução Portuguesa*. Bertrand Editora, 2014.
5   Rodrigues et al. 1976.
6   Lourenço, 2016.
7   *Ibid.*
8   Carvalho, Otelo Saraiva de. *Cinco Meses Mudaram Portugal.* Cadernos Portugália, 1975.
9   Rodrigues et al. 1976.
10 *Ibid.*
11 Martins Guerreiro, Contemporary History Lecture Module V.21, 2016.
12 Lourenço, 2016.
13 Varela, 2014.
14 *Ibid.*
15 *Ibid.*
16 Rezola, Maria Inácia. *25 de Abril – Mitos De Uma Revolução*. Esfera dos Livros, 2008.
17 Rodrigues et al. 1976.
18 de Almeida, Dinis. *Ascenção, Apogeu e Queda do MFA* vol. 1, 1978.

CHAPTER 13: CRISIS

1   de Almeida, 1978.
2   'O 11 de Março 40 anos depois: entrevista com Dinis de Almeida', *RTP*, https://www.rtp.pt/noticias/11-de-marco-golpe/o-11-de-marco-40-anos-depois-entrevista-com-dinis-de-almeida_v811121.
3   Lourenço, 2016.
4   These sections are taken from the transcripts of the recorded meeting, in Contreiras, Carlos Almada. *A Noite Que Mudou A Revolução*

de Abril: A Assembleia Militar de 11 de Março de 1975. Edições Colibri, 2019.
5 Rodrigues et al. 1976.
6 Contemporary History Course Module V, 2016 (Vasco Lourenço, seconded by Rosado da Luz).
7 Lourenço, 2016.
8 *Ibid.*
9 Rosado da Luz, 2016.

EPILOGUE

1 Sousa e Castro, Rodrigo. 'RODRIGO SOUSA E CASTRO: "O 25 de NOVEMBRO É UMA DATA QUE NÃO TEM RELEVÂNCIA HISTÓRICA."' *Setenta E Quatro*, 28 April 2022, setentaequatro.pt/entrevista/rodrigo-sousa-e-castro-o-25-de-novembro-e-uma-data-que-nao-tem-relevancia-historica.
2 Cruzeiro in Varela, 2014.

INDEX

INDEX

367

INDEX

INDEX

377